Hymns and Arias

Great Welsh Voices

Hymns
and
Arias
Great Welsh Voices

edited by Trevor Herbert
and Peter Stead

University of Wales Press Cardiff 2001

© The contributors, 2001.

British Library Cataloguing-in-Publication Data
A catalogue record for this book is available from the British Library

ISBN 0–7083–1699–9

Typeset at University of Wales Press, Cardiff
Printed in England at the Bath Press

Contents

Illustrations

Acknowledgements

Our first debt of gratitude is to the contributors to this book. We are also indebted to Dr Helen Barlow and Dr Elizabeth Stead for considerable assistance with this volume. The expert advice and guidance of Elaine Williams, Mark Owen and Liz Veasey of BBC Wales were indispensable and much appreciated, as was Janet Davies's help with the index.

The volume was shaped by the enthusiasm and encouragement of Susan Jenkins at the University of Wales Press where great assistance was provided by Liz Powell, Sue Charles and Sandra McAllister.

Special thanks to Max Boyce for his generosity in allowing us to use 'Hymns and Arias' as the title of this book.

Trevor Herbert and Peter Stead

Contributors

TELERI BEVAN   Former Head of Programmes and Acting Controller BBC Wales

ROBERT BIDELEUX   Reader in Politics, University of Wales Swansea

KENNETH BOWEN   Soloist; former Head of Vocal Studies, Royal Academy of Music

HYWEL TEIFI EDWARDS   Research Professor, University of Wales Swansea

RIAN EVANS   Critic and freelance journalist

PHIL GEORGE   Independent film producer with Green Bay Media

DAI GRIFFITHS   Head of Music, Oxford Brookes University

PATRICK HANNAN   Broadcaster and author

TREVOR HERBERT   Professor of Music at the Open University

GERAINT LEWIS   Director of the Nimbus Foundation

FRANK LINCOLN   Actor and broadcaster

BARRIE MORGAN   Director of External Relations, King's College, University of London

DAI SMITH   Pro-Vice Chancellor, University of Glamorgan

PETER STEAD   External Professor, University of Glamorgan

GARETH WILLIAMS   Professor of History, University of Glamorgan

Prelude

Trevor Herbert

And we were singing hymns and arias,
'Land of My Fathers', 'Ar Hyd y Nos'.

It is hard not to be impressed by the speed and ease with which Max Boyce's refrain became embedded in the repertoire of clichés that populate Welsh popular culture. The chorus of this rugby song quickly achieved folk-song status. It had all the necessary ingredients for such a process to take place: the musical phrase is beguiling, and simple enough to be part of a nursery tune; its tessitura is narrow, and its words are sufficiently meaningful for a popular audience to memorize them in an instant. It was impossible to resist quoting it as the title for this book because the history of singing in Wales – at least in the last two hundred years – has its origins in hymns and arias of one sort or another. Boyce's enormous popularity is well deserved and this is his best line. It is also as good a metaphor as one can summon for the passionate relationship between Wales and singing. It is a metaphor that at once hints at the secular and the sacred origins of that relationship, and one which people within and without Wales seem to have little difficulty in understanding and empathizing with.

Though the phrase 'land of song' is most famously used in the 1949 hit 'We'll keep a welcome in the hillside', the description had common currency by the end of the nineteenth century. And while it is possible to identify an association between Wales and singing as far back as the Middle Ages, popular subscription to the idea almost certainly dates from the 1870s. It was in 1872 and 1873 that Côr Mawr Caradog, or to give it its more formal title, the South Wales Choral Union, won the contest for large choirs at the Crystal Palace. Seen in a cold light, it was not a particularly remarkable achievement: in 1872 no other choir entered the contest, and in 1873 the only opponents were the exotically named 'Paris Prize Choir', a large but insipid group of London choralists under the baton of the tonic sol-fa devotee Joseph Proudman. But such details should not detract from the importance of those heady moments in the summers of 1872 and 1873. The Côr Mawr achievement has enormous

3

significance in the history of Welsh singing. The victories sparked hysterical celebrations in Wales, but they also changed the way that Wales was seen from the outside. It was the first time that there was, by popular and approving consensus, a competitive representation of Wales outside the country. Such achievements were eventually to be paralleled in sporting contests, but the precedent of a Welsh team winning away from home was set by singers.

The conductor of Côr Mawr was the charismatic Griffith Rees Jones – known throughout Wales as Caradog. The choir had been formed by a committee and was drawn from choral societies across south Wales. Their final rehearsals were open to the public, and their journey to London was interrupted by impromptu performances on railway stations where the émigré Welsh paid homage to them as popular ambassadors. When the choir arrived home in 1872, clutching the specially commissioned Thousand Guinea Trophy (now kept at the Museum of Welsh Life in St Fagans near Cardiff), their reception was ecstatic, and if the news that no one had actually competed against them was publicly known, it was kept extremely quiet: it certainly did not mute the celebrations.

The following year the preparations were yet more intensive and the summer air was heavy with expectation. Welsh Americans sent messages of support, as did the Welsh gold-diggers in Australia. News of the victory ignited an orgy of celebration: memorial flags, plaques and cravats were produced; Caradog was carried in an eisteddfodic chair from Ystrad railway station to his home in Treorchy; and epic poems reminiscent of Tennysonian sagas were published in Welsh newspapers ('Waged they the war of song – Ay, the whole world among, . . . Cambria's five hundred'). Pictures of Caradog adorned shop windows in Cardiff. Emblazoned under each of them were the words 'He led them to Victory'.

Within a year, the talented if sycophantic Brinley Richards published his *Songs of Wales*, containing arrangements of Welsh airs and more recent compositions such as his own 'God Bless the Prince of Wales'. The process of defining Wales as 'the land of song' was well under way. The Victorian song industry, one of the most efficient and influential phenomena that the music industry has ever seen, caught the idea and gave it international status. In 1893 an eisteddfod was held at the World's Fair in Chicago, in which Caradog conducted an impromptu performance of 'Hen Wlad fy Nhadau' and the 'Hallelujah Chorus'. The transatlantic traffic of Welsh choirs had already begun.

It was possible for a group of Victorian musical dignitaries to assemble almost five hundred voices to form Côr Mawr because, even by the 1870s, the infrastructure for Welsh music-making was already well established, and found expression both in popular choralism and through the celebrity status of some soloists. The London Welsh community had long promoted the tradition of Welsh singing in the capital, and individuals had been noticed in the most élite circles. One such individual, whose place in the history of Welsh music is unjustifiably obscure, is the brilliant Maria Jane Williams (1795–1873). Her great gift to Welsh music was her *Ancient Airs of Gwent and Morganwg*, published in 1844. This was the first really systematic compilation of Welsh folk-song, and it contributed an important link between the Welsh vernacular and folk tradition and the newer popular music preoccupations that were emerging. In effect, at a key time in the history of Wales, she was a remembrancer of an oral tradition that may have otherwise been lost. But she was also a great singer who became famous on her own terms by singing a Welsh repertoire in an apparently sophisticated but unmannered style. She was known universally as Llinos (the linnet), modestly refusing to acknowledge the more flattering name Eos (the nightingale) that many wanted to give her. As a young girl she moved in London Welsh circles, but she lived most of her adult life in Aberpergwm in the Vale of Neath. When she died *The Times* and *The Athenaeum* carried moving tributes to her, not as a scholar, but as an exponent of the singing art for which the Welsh were so renowned.

By the time of Llinos's death, the bedrock of a singing tradition in Wales was firmly settled in the chapels, the eisteddfodau and the ubiquitous choralism that they spawned. But it would be wrong to ignore more modern developments and see them merely as an offshoot of the undeniable strength of community music in Wales. The mass entertainment industry of the twentieth century took root in Wales with as much potency as it did anywhere else. In the 1930s, 40s

5

and 50s, Welsh popular music was a focus for the nation's entertainment, but perhaps its most brilliant manifestation came at the end of the twentieth century when a group of Welsh rock bands occupied centre-stage of the world music industry. The Stereophonics, the Manic Street Preachers and Catatonia in particular were not just successful in the heady, affluent and transitory world of pop music – they also articulated a distinctively Welsh flavour and, in so doing, gave greatest substance to the term 'Cool Cymru'.

Similarly, new institutions have stimulated and sustained the momentum of Welsh singing. BBC Wales has been one of two seminal influences on the cultural life of Wales. Later in this book under the title 'Singing for All', Teleri Bevan shows how the BBC in Wales became a focus for the performance of popular song and a stage for some of Wales's lyrical singers. But, of course, the influence of the Corporation has been greater and wider than that. By the end of the twentieth century the BBC National Orchestra of Wales had become one of two great, Welsh, professional music institutions to have located the musical life of the country on a global stage. The establishment of the BBC National Chorus of Wales, part of a mission to explore and perform the canonical repertoire and newer or less familiar works, has been one of the main ways through which Welsh singing has sustained its celebrity.

The other great national institution is, of course, the Welsh National Opera. It deserves special mention in a book such as this, not just because its impact has been so great within Wales, but also because it became one of the most remarkable successes of British music in the twentieth century. The WNO should not be seen merely as one of the companies that emerged from the provincialization of British opera in the early 1970s. It benefited from that process, but its ancestry is considerably more substantial than that. It is a phenomenon that must be seen in its own terms. Its origins lie not in some quasi-government initiative, but rather in the raw enthusiasm and endeavour of gifted amateurs in the mid-1940s, whose love of the operatic form was so passionate that it approached obsession.

The WNO success from the 1970s, as it moved incrementally to a fully professional footing with a series of magisterial productions such as those of *Nabucco*, *Madam Butterfly*, *Billy Budd* and *Lulu*, was so spectacular that it compelled the musical world to pay attention. It was also based on a genuinely popular following by ordinary Welsh people who took the company to their hearts. They came in their coaches, caught the sense of theatre, heard the singers and cheered until the roofs of the tiny theatres in which they performed were nearly lifted. As had happened in the *cymanfa ganu* and the eisteddfod, the Welsh recognized and celebrated their musical heroes. As it happened, the WNO also took on the mantle of the major touring company of the English provinces. Audiences from Southampton to Liverpool displayed an empathy with the company that the London companies had never known. The audiences for Welsh Opera performances in those days were spectacular: they were as knowledgeable, open-minded and passionate as they were numerous.

From the time it turned professional, WNO has been led by a succession of brilliant, imaginative and ambitious artistic managers and directors. There was always a balance between the performance of established favourites such as the works of Verdi, Puccini and Mozart with more ambitious, less popular operas, sometimes in radical, often controversial, productions. But, despite occasional controversies, the WNO seems to have done nothing that is seriously wrong. It has satisfied a popular desire for canonical opera, balanced with the need to sustain the type of artistic ambition that assures a place in the global arena.

The company became important to Welsh singing for a number of related reasons. By the late 1970s the WNO had provided the world with a new powerhouse for operatic excellence. It gave a platform from which some of the greatest singers of the later twentieth century were to emerge. Also – and this has been the strategy that lies at the root of its success – while it unambiguously asserted itself by engaging many of the greatest operatic stars of their era (Tito Gobbi, Elisabeth Söderström and Felicity Lott among them), the WNO has never relied, or been built upon, a superstar culture. It has always had great soloists, but primarily it has articulated itself through the strength of its core components and through the quality of its productions.

These core components are the orchestra and chorus. Every production that the WNO has presented has been built on these two assured and impeccably professional constants. The orchestra of the Welsh National Opera is one that most companies in the world would swap a bag of divas for, and the chorus is one of the few operatic choruses in the world that is so celebrated that audiences travel to productions primarily to hear the chorus sing. Their breathtaking brilliance as actors, actresses and singers has proved itself in many diverse areas of the repertoire. Their technique and quality exemplifies the best in opera choralism. It fits effortlessly into the landscape of the productions in which they appear, and the palette of their vocal colours is rich and diverse enough to match any part of the repertoire.

There has been a succession of phenomenally talented chorus masters and repetiteurs: Anthony Hose, Wyn Davies, Julian Smith, Gareth Jones, Derek Clark, Michael Pollock and David Seaman among them. They have honed a chorus that, despite some comings and goings over the years, has retained a loyal core and given a considerable sense of continuity. But the chorus has also been the resource from which a series of soloists has stepped out to take what is euphemistically and misleadingly termed 'small parts' (more properly comprimario). 'Small parts' are the minor solo roles in opera, but many are not so minor. They may include Cherubino in *The Marriage of Figaro*, Papagena in *The Magic Flute* and Ping, Pang and Pong in *Turandot*. Over the years, parts such as these have been graced by chorus singers who have often stolen the show: the names of choristers such as Peter Massocchi, Neville Ackerman, Kenneth Pugh, Margaret Baiton and Yolande Jones are well known to audiences throughout the land. Ieuan Davies as the Emperor in *Turandot* is one of the highlights of the show, and Mary Davies one of the most engaging Papagenas to have taken the part.

The most compellingly interesting feature of the story of Welsh singing is the capacity of the Welsh to produce such a quantity of singers in so many different styles and genres. Even in the 1870s Welsh singing was being seen as ubiquitous, enthusiastic, and also different. *The Times*, commenting on Côr Mawr, said that one voice from the Welsh choir was 'equal to three from the capital city'. Another commentator noted that 'it is unlikely that any but the Welsh . . . could sing like that'. The writers were alluding to what they saw as a distinctiveness in Welsh singing. This distinctiveness has never been adequately defined, but an acceptance of it continues to prevail in writings about Welsh singers: even the respected *Oxford Companion to Popular Music* defines Tom Jones as 'a natural performer in the Welsh tradition'. This is probably true, and it is a descriptor that can be attached to the plethora of popular and art singers that Wales has produced, but what exactly does it mean? Is the 'tradition' defined merely as the practice of singing and the love of singing or is it to do with something more? Are there elements in the manner of Welsh singing that prevail across idioms, and that can be identified in styles as diverse as rock and opera? It is not the purpose of this book to argue such a case, but reading the individual chapters it is sometimes hard to avoid this sense of commonality.

The essays in this book are celebratory and subjective and taken together they provide something of a profile of Welsh singing and singers. It is, of course, neither a comprehensive history nor a compilation of appraisals of *all* great Welsh singers. The individual subjects largely chose themselves. We were anxious to include chapters that acknowledge the various idioms in which Welsh singers have made an emphatic mark. Thus, opera divas rub shoulders with valley choristers, night-club singers and pop stars. A book such as this would be sadly lacking if it did not give space to the likes of Bryn Terfel, Stuart Burrows, Geraint Evans, Gwyneth Jones, Margaret Price, Robert Tear, Dennis O'Neill, Gwynne Howell, Shirley Bassey and Tom Jones. It would also fall short if it contained nothing on Cerys Matthews, James Dean Bradfield and Kelly Jones, singers who have helped define the most important period in the history of Welsh pop music. Other chapters on topics rather than individuals also seemed to choose themselves. The popular Welsh singers who kept millions at home in the radio days, and the solo and choral champions of the eisteddfodau are celebrated here. The agonizing moment came when we had to draw the line. There are others not mentioned here who would have been included by other editors. But this book is a celebration, not an encyclopaedia, and everyone who sings for Wales or relishes the sound worlds that Welsh singers have made for us should be able to identify with what is written in these pages.

Acknowledgements
R. Fawkes, *Welsh National Opera* (London, 1986).
C. Bashford and L. Langley (eds), *Music and British Culture 1785–1914: Essays in Honour of Cyril Ehrlich* (Oxford, 2000).

Robert Rees (Eos Morlais)

Hywel Teifi Edwards

In the course of addressing his audience at the Caernarfon National Eisteddfod in 1877, the Reverend Dr Herber Evans, pre-eminent among the preachers of the day, urged the unsuccessful competitors to persevere and strive to emulate Edith Wynne and Eos Morlais who had made themselves national 'necessities'. Their names were greeted with a prolonged burst of applause as some eight thousand eisteddfod-goers acknowledged the debt owed by the nation to two iconic figures whose voices, unfailingly sympathetic and uplifting, satisfied the intense need of the time for thrilling demonstrations of Welsh *éclat*. Edith Wynne (Eos Cymru, the Welsh Nightingale: 1842–97) was the first London-trained international soprano to emerge from Wales and Eos Morlais (1841–92) was the first in a line of charismatic Welsh tenors to enjoy a special relationship with the people. Born into working-class families – she hailed from Holywell in Flintshire and he from Dowlais in Glamorgan – they were to sing themselves into national prominence and their talents, triumphing over their disadvantaged beginnings, were to anchor them in the people's affections and hold them there long after their passing.

That Herber Evans should name two singers as exemplary 'necessities' is proof of the respect accorded to the emissaries of 'The Land of Song' by 1877. The sunburst of musical fervour in the 1860s, as seen in the spread of the tonic sol-fa movement and hymn-singing festivals, the 'arrival' of Joseph Parry, the coming of the National Eisteddfod in 1861 and consequently the beginning of huge choral competitions, 'the big lung contests', was followed in 1872–3 by the coruscating success of Caradog's great south Wales choir, 'Côr Mawr Caradog', in the Crystal Palace competitions which threatened to leave the nation in a state of permanent euphoria. Fanatic 'choir-following' would predate rumbustious 'rugby-following' by a good twenty heady years, during which time the Welsh would likewise invest their ardour in the rewarding careers of the first generation of professional singers who, after capturing the top awards of the Royal Academy of Music, would set about singing Wales into the world's – essentially England's – good report.

In the struggle to refashion the nation's image after the deep damage inflicted upon it in 1847 by the publication of the infamous Blue Books, the regiment of London-trained and accredited singers, whose nucleus included Edith Wynne, Megan Watts (1842–1907), Mary Davies (1855–1930), Lucas Williams (1852–?), James Sauvage (1848–1922) and Ben Davies (1858–1943), was to be in the vanguard. They were expected to storm the fortresses of England's musical world and do Wales proud. Had the Reverend Eli Jenkins lived in 1877 he would not so much exclaim 'Praise the Lord! We are a musical nation' as 'Praise the Lord! The English think we can sing'. In Victorian Wales 'The Land of Song' took shape as a redemptive 'reality' empowered by a flow of gifted singers and passionate choristers whose excellence, emblematic of the nation's excellence, demanded recognition. Reporting on the St David's Day Concert held in the Royal Albert Hall in 1875, the correspondent for Y *Gerddorfa* (The Orchestra) rejoiced in the superior vocal talents of the Welsh compared with their fellow Celts, ending triumphantly: 'And still they come!' Of those who had already come to be seen by his people as a 'necessary figure', a singer whose song voiced their longings, their aspirations and their spirituality, none counted for more than Eos Morlais.

He was born in Dowlais, 4 April 1841, his parents, Hugh and Margaret Rees, having ventured from Dylife in Montgomeryshire to better their lot in the industrial south. At eight years of age he was orphaned, his father who worked as a 'hitcher' underground struck down in August 1849 by an outbreak of cholera which claimed the mother soon afterwards. It was left to his 15-year-old brother, Hugh, to give the young Eos Morlais what protection he could as he started life as an iron miner. Hugh, and an uncle by the name of William Ellis, would provide him with a home in High Street, Dowlais, until he married Margaret Edwards, a steadfast member of the Methodist congregation at Libanus, in 1867. She died childless, aged forty-five, in 1884 and he was to die on 5 June 1892 and be buried in Aberdulais at the lower end of the Dulais Valley, mourned by thousands who had been enthralled by his song, and by his compeers who 'seemed unable to restrain themselves at the loss of so bright an ornament in the Welsh musical world'.

The talent which was to secure him a nation's admiration was first nurtured by William Ellis who encouraged him to sing and recite in the local 'eisteddfodau' which began to proliferate in the 1840s. He early understood the power of narrative, and shortly before his death he would relate his success as a singer to his realization as a boy eisteddfodwr that an impassioned way with words clearly enunciated struck directly at the heart of his audience. And in the whole of Wales there was no more receptive audience for a talent like his than the pioneering working class of Dowlais. If his voice was heaven-sent, it was Dowlais which fired both him and Megan Watts with a desire to sing that burnt brightly to the end, and it seemed ordained that his last public appearance, a few weeks before his death, should be in Bethania chapel where he conducted a *cymanfa ganu* (hymn-singing festival) that sent him back to Swansea exulting in the beauty of Dowlais voices raised in God's praise. He, too, could have bid his farewell in the words written by Megan Watts as she departed for London to begin her career: 'Farewell Dowlais! I love every stone and every shindry in thy streets. Farewell Dowlais voices, the like of which I may never hear again. Farewell mountains, rivers, the music of the Iron Works and the wild flames.'

He took his bardic name from the river Morlais running through his home-town, and Dowlais was to ensure that he would never have to fake emotion when singing of death, of orphans, of poverty and pain, of brotherhood and community, of love and the joys of home, of yearning for unending summer, of his Saviour and heaven. The boy said to have been born in a miner's cottage directly facing Sir John Guest's Dowlais House, had imprinted on his senses from the beginning an awareness of a grinding industrial order that tested human endurance to the limit. In Dowlais the highs and lows of the human condition were on all sides overpoweringly visible, audible and odorous. And there, too, man's will to surmount the hardships that weighed on body and soul found soaring expression in the song, the hymn, the anthem and the chorus, which turned Dowlais, along with Merthyr, Aberdare and the Swansea Valley, into a powerhouse drawing on the tide of music-making that flooded south Wales in the 1860s and 1870s. One cannot overemphasize the influence that an upbringing in such a thunderous environment had on Eos Morlais.

Dowlais became known as 'Tref y Gân' (The Town of Song) and Eos Morlais, together with Megan Watts who followed Edith Wynne to

London in 1864 and emerged as an impressive mezzo-soprano who enjoyed a brief but acclaimed concert career, were early taken in hand by Abraham Bowen, a one-time blacksmith turned grocer who served his fellow Independents as precentor in Bethania chapel for forty-four years. In his worker's home – known locally as 'The Royal Academy' – was to be found one of only two pianos in the neighbourhood at the time (the other was in Dowlais House!), and Megan Watts remembered 'With what rapture I gazed on it and listened for the first time to the magic tones which came from it.' Abraham's son, David, grew up to be one of the first truly accomplished accompanists in south Wales – he was the accompanist for Caradog's legendary choir – and on his death in 1885 it was reported that ten thousand mourners attended his funeral, a similar number again attending his father's funeral in 1892, some six months before Eos Morlais died. That Abraham Bowen's labour of love was hugely appreciated is a fact beyond dispute, and it is equally beyond dispute that Eos Morlais's talents as choir-master and tenor soloist were beaten into shape in Bethania chapel on the anvil of Abraham's passion for music.

Brought up to master old notation before the onset of tonic sol-fa, by the time he was twenty-two years old he was conducting the second of the Dowlais Temperance choirs, Dowlais (2), a choir of some 200 voices which established his reputation as a skilful, insightful musician in the annual Gwent and Glamorgan Temperance 'Cymanfa' which started in 1854, and in the annual Merthyr eisteddfod launched by the Cymmro-dorion Temperance Society in 1848. A committed teetotaller all his life, Eos Morlais's career serves to highlight the striking contribution made by the temperance movement to music-making in Victorian Wales, especially in places like Dowlais and Merthyr where the sweating thousands in the iron works drank their fill in scores of taverns. It was his Dowlais-bred conviction of music's ameliorative and regenerative power that charged his singing with an intensity that set him apart. Megan Watts was to recall 'a young man, a miner, of exceptional natural talents . . . He was the most promising of all the musical satellites that shone in the neighbourhood at this time. When about the age of twenty he held the baton and conducted that immense [Dowlais (2)] choir like an experienced musician, without Art and next to no theoretical knowledge to aid him.' She saw him prepare a deprived and largely monoglot Welsh proletariat to sing oratorios, anthems, hymns and glees 'with wonderful results so far as their limited use of their gifts allowed them', prompting her to add: 'I felt very proud of every member of that choir.'

By the time he left Dowlais in 1869 to make his home in 16 Henrietta Street in Swansea, where he took up an appointment as precentor in Soar Independent chapel in Walter's Road and later for a short time in the Tabernacle, Morriston, Eos Morlais ranked with the best choir-masters in Wales and before he died he was to add to Swansea's reputation as a progressive music-making town. He conducted the Choral Society in ambitious performances of oratorios in the resplendent Music Hall (later known as the Albert Hall) and the Drill Hall – *St Paul* (Mendelssohn) and *Samson* (Handel) in 1882; *Redemption* (Gounod) in 1883 and 1885; *Eli* (Costa) in 1883 and *Messiah* (Handel) in 1883 and 1885 – all of which were demanding undertakings with a choir of 250 voices accompanied by an orchestra of some fifty instrumentalists which included on more than one occasion members of Charles Hallé's Manchester orchestra. Soloists and instrumentalists with a professional reputation to maintain had no qualms in performing for the stocky former miner whose most significant tutor had been a former blacksmith in Bethania chapel.

His was indeed a remarkable achievement on that score alone and on his death his fellow musicians were loud in their praise of his musicianship, the disciplined vigour of his art as conductor and soloist, and his transparent integrity. Harry Evans (1873–1914), yet another Bethania product who as a precocious boy often acted as accompanist for Eos Morlais before blossoming into a brilliant choir-master whose work with the Liverpool Welsh Choral Union was highly regarded by Sir Edward Elgar, wrote with much warmth in 1911 about 'the old minstrel's' dedication to his craft, his great generosity of spirit and his gift of inspired interpretation, which allied to a rare tenor voice, gave him 'Y PETH cyfriniol hwnnw nad oes diffinio arno'n dragywydd' (that mystical SOMETHING which can never be defined). As choir-master, singer, eisteddfod adjudicator and incomparable conductor of hymn-singing festivals, his was a palpable loss to a small nation aching for achievement on a large stage.

But above all else it was the stilling of the irresistible tenor voice that had resonated throughout Wales for almost a quarter of a century that saddened the people most. In the National Eisteddfod held at Carmarthen in 1867, Eos Morlais won the tenor competition, singing Handel's 'Thou shalt break them' with resounding conviction. The adjudicator, W. H. Cummings, a professional London artiste hired for the evening concerts, foolishly acceded to a request that he should show the Welsh amateurs how to sing the aria, only to be quickly told by his audience that he was vocally ill equipped to teach Eos Morlais anything. The Dowlais tenor had truly made his national mark, and from then on he would captivate audiences wherever he went and acquit himself just as triumphantly in England and America. In Wales he was to resemble the great English tenor, Sims Reeves, in the adulation his singing earned him and had he in 1877, after his performance in the Caernarfon National Eisteddfod, allowed himself to be persuaded by John Hullah, Madame Patey and Signor Foli, the outstanding bass voice of the day, to embark on a London-based career, his financial gain would have been considerable. It was his total rapport with his Welsh audiences and his lifelong commitment to chapel culture, more so than his imperfect command of English, that wedded him to Wales. He was never happier than when singing for 'ordinary' people and he would have loudly applauded the superlative John McCormack's rebuttal of the critics who resented the inclusion of 'common' songs in his programme: 'The world is full of men and women with humble thoughts and simple sentiments, and who shall despise them – for are they not men and women?'

Starting as a boy alto with the Dowlais (1) Temperance Choir – Dowlais supported two temperance choirs of some 200 voices each! – he was to develop into a glorious tenor who in his early twenties sang in performances of Haydn's *Creation* and his 'Twelfth Mass' (misattributed to Mozart) without inhibition. Megan Watts recalled 'a miner of exceptional natural talents. He possessed the genius of a musician and all the artistic instincts of an educated singer. A voice that was silvery in quality, solid, firm, crisp, notes produced as naturally as breathing.' Professor David Jenkins and Harry Evans marvelled at the compass of a voice that soared to A and B flat and struck top C like a bell. And in 1879, following his appearance with the redoubtable Signor Foli in a performance of Handel's *Samson*, the Swansea *Cambrian*'s report enthused about the way he had thrown 'into his interpretation the virile vigour for which his voice is remarkable. In the various recitatives, in the pathetic lament, "Total Eclipse", but especially in the declamatory duet with Harapha, "Go baffled coward", the Eos rose to the level of his subject, and finally warranted the name he bears all over the country. He is undoubtedly "the great Welsh tenor".' It was to further assert after his death: 'As a tenor vocalist, it is not too much to say that, in many respects, "Eos Morlais" has seldom been equalled and hardly ever been surpassed . . . Gifted with vigorous common sense, coupled with deep religious feeling on the one side, and a real sense of true humour on the other side, his repertoire was a very wide and varied one . . . He never failed to catch, to hold, to impress, and to delight, his audience.'

Supreme in oratorio and sacred cantata, he also carried all before him as a singer of Victorian ballads, traditional Welsh songs and especially the freshly minted Welsh solos and scenas composed by the likes of Joseph Parry (1841–1903), D. Emlyn Evans, (1843–1913), R. S. Hughes (1855–93), John Henry (1859–1914) and William Davies (1859–1907), which were to be taken up by a host of eisteddfod competitors and concert singers from the 1870s onwards, studding the repertoire of the major Welsh performers down to our own time when an artist of world renown like Bryn Terfel sings and records them with manifest pleasure. The vogue of the distinctive Welsh solo started in 1873 when D. Emlyn Evans won the prize at the Mold National Eisteddfod for composing a tenor solo. It was the first of many such Victorian patriotic pieces entitled 'Bedd Llewelyn' (Llewelyn's Grave) which Eos Morlais sent ringing the length and breadth of Wales – even as Sims Reeves conquered England with John Braham's 'The Death of Nelson' – the first such solo composition to bear on its cover the proud boast, 'As sung by Eos Morlais'. Others were to follow and not to have heard him sing 'Arafa Don' (R. S. Hughes), 'Baner ein Gwlad' (Joseph Parry) and 'O! na fyddai'n haf o hyd' (William Davies) was to have missed an experience that crystallized the emotivity that marked the flowering of 'The Land of Song'. His was truly the 'necessary' voice of that pulsating period in the social history of Wales, and as late as 1930 Sir Thomas Hughes, who heard him singing 'Gwlad y Delyn' (John Henry) at the Wrexham National Eisteddfod in 1888, paid tribute to 'the purest tenor I ever heard or hope to hear . . . What a consummate artist he was. One had but to shut one's eyes to be wafted over the border into Paradise.'

From 1872 until 1891 when he conducted the National Eisteddfod choir in a performance of Gounod's *Redemption* at Swansea, no 'National' was complete without him. He lived to see Ben Davies from Pontardawe, for whom he acted as mentor with the same generosity that marked his support for Megan Watts, come out from the Royal Academy to make his name as the first fully-fledged professional Welsh tenor who was to sing with great distinction at home and abroad. But as fine a singer as Ben Davies was, there was no removing Eos Morlais from centre stage in Wales. When the Welsh Liberals celebrated their election victory in 1880 with a grand banquet and concert at the Crystal Palace, Eos Morlais took his place among the young, nation-boosting professionals – Ben Davies, James Sauvage, Mary Davies, Marion Williams, Martha Harries, Lizzie Evans and Lucas Williams – and set the standard for the evening. Had 'The Land of Song' ever marched in an Olympiad of music during the Victorian heyday its flag-bearer would have been the irreplaceable Dowlais tenor, and no torch would have been required to light a fire, it would have been enough simply to ask Eos Morlais to sing Handel's 'Sound an alarm' which I like to think no other Welsh tenor, with the possible exception of the magnificent Rhondda tenor, Tudor Davies, has ever sung with such inspirational power.

Piety, pity and patriotism – Eos Morlais had the voice and the feel for words which made audiences wherever he sang very responsive to him. His was a potent, affective talent in an age receptive of art intended to appeal to the nobler instincts and finer sentiments. When he sang Joseph Parry's 'Y Gardotes Fach' (The Little Beggar Maid) and 'Yr Eneth Ddall' (The Blind Girl) or John Henry's 'Bwthyn yr Amddifad' (The Orphan's Cottage), Eos Morlais was tapping into a very deep pool of present pity. In an industrial society where death was an untiring reaper and depression a widespread sclerosis it was no small thing to be moved by songs that seemed to be the very distillation of human sympathy and goodness. To mock them as merely 'sentimental' is simply to indicate that our 'sophistication' has dulled our humanity. It is, of course, mere ignorance that makes us dismissive of the historical context of Eos Morlais's art. In the industrial murk of south Wales the tears flowed when he sang R. S. Hughes's 'Bwthyn bach melyn fy nhad' (My father's little yellow cottage) or Alaw Ddu's 'Y Bwthyn yng nghanol y wlad' (The cottage in the country). What is there to sneer at in such songs composed in a century which ached with the heartbreak of a myriad farewells? If only Eos Morlais had lived another ten years to record them for us.

By the time he died his legend was such that it was said he sang the lovely Welsh song, 'Y Deryn Pur', on his deathbed. There were even claims that he sang 'Sound an alarm' almost at the very end! It is true he told a friend that could he live his life over again he would sing more in praise of his Saviour, and his words were included by Myfyr Emlyn in the verses for D. Pughe Evans's famous tenor solo, 'Yr Hen Gerddor' (The Old Minstrel), composed in tribute to Eos Morlais and the composer who gave him so many splendid songs to sing, R. S. Hughes. They will both live in memory as long as Welsh tenors celebrate 'Yr Hen Gerddor'.

He was to enjoy many a triumph during a career that saw him sing in London's famous Ballad Concerts, in St James's Hall, St George's Hall, Hanover Square and Covent Garden. He took the tenor role in Joseph Parry's all-conquering opera, *Blodwen*, and with Lizzie Williams made the duet, 'Hywel a Blodwen', an instant and enduring 'hit' with the nation. In 1879 he undertook a three-month tour of Vermont, New York, Pennsylvania and Ohio, singing in thirty-six concerts, invariably getting 'the most uproarious applause' and moving the Scranton *Republican* to say of him: 'He is not only a very effective singer, but is highly cultivated, and a great artist. There is nobody that can compare with him in New York.' And it was he who sang 'Hen Wlad fy Nhadau' on the stage of the Royal Albert Hall in 1887 when the prince of Wales and his family deigned to visit the National Eisteddfod for the first time. The prince got to his feet as Eos Morlais burst into song and the status of 'Hen Wlad fy Nhadau' as the undisputed national anthem of Wales was royally confirmed!

It is best now to leave him – the iconic tenor who sang his way into the heart of a nation – on the heights of that intoxicating victory in July 1873 when Caradog's choir of 450 voices defeated Sir Joseph Proudman's London Tonic Sol-Fa Choir in the Crystal Palace competition. It was to him, the tenor who had sung Wallace's 'Yes, let me like a soldier fall' before twenty thousand supporters within the walls of Caerphilly Castle during an open-air fund-raising rehearsal and who had subsequently sung Handel's 'Sound an alarm' with equally stunning effect before a huge audience in the Colston Hall in Bristol, that Caradog turned when Welsh ecstasy hardly knew how to express itself.

At his leader's behest he stood before the exultant thousands in the Crystal Palace and sang J. R. Thomas's simple song of love for homeland, 'Annwyl yw Gwalia fy Ngwlad'. The Reverend J. A. Thomas (Ioan Arma) relived the moment in 1892, and his account, highly charged with emotion, is worthy of a Victorian 'Mabinogion' in which a Dowlais tenor performs a feat of wondrous promotion for his people:

> Had the Queen herself arrived she could not have received a bigger ovation. Surrounded as the singer was by applauding thousands, representing several nations, and all grades of social standing, he stood there the very embodiment of courage, self-possession and true manliness. But hush the Nightingale sings! What is it? 'Annwyl yw Gwalia fy Ngwlad' and he renders it with a passion that is sublime, he carries us to the highest flights of musical inspirations. Higher and higher, tenderer and stronger. Now he gives us the crescendo, bursting into a loud forte, rending the sky, and awakening the echo. Now his voice is like a sweet silver bell, and then in the majesty of his imperial voice, he rushes to the golden stairs of music and strikes C above the staff. The song king is controlling and accumulative in force and inspiration as he advances brilliantly through the stanzas, until the effect at the close is simply wonderful.

'Viva' Eos Morlais! Remember him whenever the drowned sailor asks Captain Cat, 'How's the tenors in Dowlais?'

Bibliography
Hywel Teifi Edwards, 'Y Gân a ganai Morlais', in *Codi'r Hen Wlad yn ei Hôl* (Llandysul, 1989).

A Gift to the World – The Tenors of Wales

Kenneth Bowen

For more than a century Wales has produced fine solo singers, but in the early years it was the tenors who were pre-eminent and the Welsh tenor was a well-recognized species both in the British Isles and in the United States. The roll call is impressively lengthy and pleasure can be drawn from tracing a tradition in which farm workers, miners and steelworkers became acclaimed professional performers. The pioneers of this tradition were born in the 1850s: Dyfed Lewys from Llan-crwys in Carmarthenshire, Maldwyn Humphreys from Machynlleth and Hirwen Jones from Cwm Coed, Cardigan, were all trained in London at the Royal Academy of Music and all developed fine careers. Jones often sang with Adelina Patti, and his recordings made between 1906 and 1908 reveal a charming, light lyric voice with soft high notes reminiscent of John McCormack.

In 1858 the most famous Welsh singer of this generation was born in Pontardawe. Benjamin Grey Davies entered the Academy at the age of twenty and studied with Fiori and Alberto Randegger. On leaving he joined the Carl Rosa company and made his stage début at Birmingham in Balfe's *Bohemian Girl* in 1881. In 1887 he started a two-year run in Cellier's *Dorothy* at the Gaiety and Prince of Wales theatres, and in 1891 he created the title-role in Sir Arthur Sullivan's *Ivanhoe* at the new English Opera House (now the Palace Theatre) in Cambridge Circus. A year later, he made his Covent Garden début in Gounod's *Faust* before embarking on extensive tours in Europe, throughout the British Empire and in the United States where he sang at the World's Fair in Chicago. He retired from opera midway through the 1890s and soon became one of the finest concert singers of his day. Ben Davies was a great favourite of Queen Victoria and Princess Alexandra and he gave many command performances at Windsor Castle. He made many recordings but, sadly, some of these were when he was past his prime and well into his seventies. In the second edition of Grove's *Dictionary* Fuller Maitland wrote, 'Davies' artistic way of singing, his fine voice, and the geniality of his disposition, which is entirely free from the effeminacies and affectations to which many tenors are prone have made him a universal favourite.' Sir Thomas Beecham was equally complimentary, 'His was a voice of uncommon beauty, round, full and expansive', while Dame Nellie Melba called him affectionately 'Caro mio ben' after the eighteenth-century song by Giordani. In 1925 he became the first male singer to be awarded the degree of D.Mus (*honoris causa*) by the University of Wales. Remarkably he continued to sing in public until 1937.

Within ten years of Ben Davies's birth there were born two Welsh tenors who went on to make big reputations in the United States: Dan Beddoe (1863–1937) and Evan Williams (1867–1918). Both made many gramophone records, now much sought after by collectors. Dan Beddoe was born in Aberaman near Aberdare and was briefly a schoolteacher in the Rhondda Valley. After a tour of the US with the Welsh Prize Singers he was drawn to the American way of life and settled with his young wife in Pittsburgh and Cleveland. His solo career was slow to take off, but in 1903 he reached a turning-point after singing Wagnerian excerpts under Walter Damrosch. Later, under the same conductor, he sang in the Berlioz Requiem during the New York celebrations of the composer's centenary as well as the title-role in a concert version of *Parsifal*. Twenty extremely busy years followed on the concert platform, including a performance of Beethoven's ninth symphony conducted by Gustav Mahler. Later Beddoe became a leading exponent of Mahler's 'Das Lied von der Erde'. In 1919 he accepted a teaching appointment at the Cincinnati Conservatory, but he continued to fulfil important engagements on both sides of the Atlantic until 1925 and went on singing until 1934. Caruso made it a rule never to attend the recitals of other tenors; he only broke it to go to hear and admire Dan Beddoe.

(Harry) Evan Williams was born of Welsh immigrant parents in Mineral Ridge, Ohio. A fluent Welsh speaker throughout his life, he was brought up in the eisteddfod tradition and won important prizes in his late teens. He worked as a coal-miner and in a steel mill before studying in Cleveland and New York where, it is said, Ben Davies was one of his teachers. Evan Williams went on to enjoy a long and distinguished career in the United States and in Britain, appearing in over a thousand concerts. He made records on both sides of the Atlantic – nearly 300 of them – and only Caruso and McCormack earned more in royalties from the Victor Company. In purely musical terms his recorded legacy was uneven, but it was always impressive vocally and technically as evidenced by his ringing tone and clear coloratura in 'Sound an alarm' from Handel's *Judas Maccabaeus*.

Meanwhile, back in Wales talented singers were making a considerable impact. The career details are fascinating. John Roberts may not have started his professional career until he was thirty-five but he came to be highly regarded, with one critic describing him as the Welsh Sims Reeves: high praise indeed. Roberts was born in Llansamlet in 1873, and after a period of study in London he began a successful career and appeared in small parts at Covent Garden. He was a favourite of Madame Patti and often sang at Castell Craig-y-nos. The records he made in 1909–10 were of good quality, displaying a graceful, lyrical voice, but those made in 1914 were less good. Edward Davies who hailed from nearby Morriston was born in the same year as John Roberts. He studied in Cardiff, London and Milan before joining the Carl Rosa company in 1907 and going on to sing in the English seasons at Covent Garden between 1907 and 1909. Between 1921 and 1925 he sang at the Teatro Dal Verme in Milan, and after one performance as Cavaradossi in *Tosca* he was congratulated by Caruso. Edward Davies retired in his early fifties and became a successful teacher in Cardiff. His recordings included a duet from Benedict's *Lily of Killarney* with Peter Dawson.

Gwynne Davies was another tenor of the same generation. He came from a farming family in Ferryside, Carmarthenshire, and worked as a schoolmaster before beginning his studies at the Royal College of Music under Emil Kreuz. Later he sang for the Carl Rosa and British National Opera companies and appeared at Covent Garden. Sir Henry Wood thought highly of him and employed him often. Eventually he became a professor at the Royal College of Music. He left some recordings made between 1912 and 1916. Very few biographical details are available about Rhymney-born Gwilym Wigley who, in 1905 and 1907, sang as Signor Michele Wigley at Covent Garden. His singing was vocally robust and impassioned and can be heard on a number of records in English, Welsh and Italian recorded between 1911 and 1922. Furness Williams, who was born in Ruthin in 1880, studied with Sir Charles Santley and is remembered for being the first British tenor to sing in German at Covent Garden (in *Der fliegende Holländer*). He also sang in Australia, the USA and at the Teatro Colon in Buenos Aires. After retiring as a performer he started his own Academy of Music in Liverpool.

Cynlais Gibbs was born in Ystradgynlais in 1884. He spent his early career as a reporter on the local paper before moving to London as a foreign correspondent. He took some private lessons as a baritone before entering the Royal Academy of Music in 1906 where he studied with Edgardo Levi and Signor Moretti. He won many prizes as a student and became a successful oratorio singer, performing under distinguished conductors like Hans Richter. Around 1912 he joined Joseph O'Mara's opera company and became a respected interpreter of Wagner roles. When O'Mara retired in 1926 Gibbs became director of the company.

George Hughes Macklin from Tal-y-sarn near Caernarfon was a near contemporary of Cynlais Gibbs. Hughes Macklin worked briefly as a schoolteacher and in a slate quarry before moving to London in 1905. A year later he was awarded a scholarship to the Royal College of Music where he studied under Gustave Garcia. In 1912 he joined the Carl Rosa company and sang at Covent Garden under Arthur Nikisch in Wagner's *Ring*. After the First World War he toured in Europe and was a special favourite in Italy, where he was known as Ugo Macklin. He had a firm, strong voice and was well equipped to take on taxing roles like Canio, Lohengrin and Radames. In March 1936 he sang the lead role in a BBC broadcast from the Queen's Hall of Shostakovich's *Lady Macbeth of the Mtsensk District* conducted by Albert Coates – a considerable achievement. Three months later he was dead, found drowned in the River Tyne near Newcastle. He had been staying with his sister in Whitley Bay and never returned from a stroll. He left a number of recordings of ballads, operatic arias and English and Welsh songs.

The Walters brothers were brought up on the family farm in Dunvant. Ivor was born in 1886 and as a young man he worked in the Ben Evans department store in Swansea, before going on to study at the Royal College of Music and in Berlin, Paris and Milan. During the First World War he served with the Welsh Borderers. Later he resumed his career as a singer of opera and oratorio and became a producer of operettas and musicals. He is best remembered for giving the first performance of Alan Murray's 'I'll walk beside you' at a National Sunday League Concert. He also sang with his wife Marion Browne at the reopening of the BBC Television Service from Alexandra Palace in 1946. His brother Thomas Glyn Walters changed his name to Walter Glynne and enjoyed a very prosperous career as a recording artist. He entered the Royal College in 1911 (a year after his brother) and studied under William Sewell. He was then spotted by Sir Ronald Landon, the musical adviser to HMV, and made many appealing records. Walter Glynne had a charming, lyrical voice and impeccable diction and tuning. His recordings of excerpts from Joseph Parry's *Blodwen* are a particular treasure. Like his brother he served in the Great War and afterwards resumed a busy concert career appearing frequently at the Boosey, Chappell and Cramer Ballad Concerts. He also ventured into opera, albeit briefly, with the Carl Rosa and D'Oyly Carte companies. His voice was never robust and he once said that he preferred to leave heavy singing to heavy voices 'and make quality not quantity'. He retired in 1943 and returned three years later to a farm on the Gower.

Dan Jones was born in Pontardawe in 1889. His first employment was in a tin-plate works. In 1911 he won the tenor solo competition at the Carmarthen National Eisteddfod, and shortly afterwards he was invited by the Duke of Connaught to sing at the Royal Command of King George V and Queen Mary on board the royal yacht in Cardiff. Two years later he became a student of Gustave Garcia at the Royal College of Music. After war service he became an extremely busy concert singer and a prolific recording artist; between 1915 and 1930 he recorded more than 300 titles, many under names other than his own. His most interesting and important contribution was in the title-role in *The Dream of Gerontius* under Joseph Batten (the bass-baritone part was sung by the Llanelli-born David Brazell). Dan Jones was excellent and delighted Elgar, but it is a great shame that the recording was not complete. After working in films and with the D'Oyly Carte company he retired to Llansteffan.

Parry Jones, one of the best-known British tenors between the wars, was born in Blaina, Monmouthshire in 1891. He studied singing at the Royal College of Music with Albert Visetti and composition with Sir Charles Stanford. In 1915 he toured the USA with a group that visited all forty-eight states, Canada and Alaska. On their return in May of that year their ship, *Lusitania*, was sunk by a torpedo; Parry Jones was one of 500 survivors. He resumed his studies, first at the College, then in Weimar and Milan, and he also received lessons from the great English tenor John Coates. Later he became a principal tenor with the Beecham, Carl Rosa and British National Opera companies, and he sang in the international seasons at Covent Garden during the 1920s and 1930s. During this period he sang many heavy roles including Lohengrin, Walther and Parsifal. From 1947 he appeared frequently in comprimario roles with the new Covent Garden Company. He sang in many British premières including works by Busoni, Schoenberg, Berg and Hindemith. Moreover, he was a sought-after oratorio singer and sang in twenty-six consecutive Promenade Concert seasons. In an obituary article in *Opera* Sir David Webster (general administrator at Covent Garden) wrote of him: 'To be a singer is not an unusual gift for a Welshman but to be a singer and a musician at the same time is unusual and for a Welshman almost remarkable. It was this combination that put Parry Jones into a special category.' He was renowned for his wicked sense of humour, heavily tinged with sarcasm, and this can be heard on an extraordinary record on the *Art and Teaching of Singing*. The record was introduced by Sir John Barbirolli with these thought-provoking words: 'Parry Jones is at once both a most Welsh of Welshmen and a most un-Welsh. The intense Welshness of him is found in his eloquence and love of singing: the un-Welshness lies in his capacity for hard, concentrated thought and study in relation to his art – a gift that is unfortunately denied to many of that gifted and mercurial race.' Parry Jones made many records, but not all of them are appealing. Indeed, Sir David Webster's comment that 'his voice was more remarkable for his incisiveness rather than for sheer sensuousness' is a fair description.

He was at his best in his full-throated account of 'O na fyddai'n haf o hyd'. He became a professor at the Guildhall and died in 1963, a leading figure in the musical establishment.

Ifor Owain Thomas was a highly promising tenor whose career ended prematurely through ill health. He was born on a farm near Benllech in Anglesey in April 1892 and during his childhood suffered from chronic asthma. In 1913 Sir Walford Davies heard him at the Abergavenny National Eisteddfod and recommended that he should study in London. Just a year later he entered the Royal College of Music and, unfit for military service, he studied there throughout the war years. In 1919 he was coached by the great Polish tenor Jean de Reszke, and he also worked briefly with Gigli in Milan. He sang at the Proms in 1925 and made his opera début in Milan in 1926 as Dmitry in *Boris Godunov* with Chaliapin in the title-role. Later he sang in Nice, Monte Carlo and Paris before going to America where he sang with the Philadelphia Opera. In America he was very highly regarded by the Welsh community as the successor to Evan Williams. Indeed, he was all set to work at the Metropolitan Opera in 1929 when his asthma worsened and he was forced to begin a withdrawal from the singing scene. A man of many talents, he soon became an extremely fashionable photographer for *Collier's* magazine, photographing President Roosevelt, Winston Churchill and many film stars. He retired in 1948 and took up painting in oils and water colours. A fervent Welshman he founded the Cymric Society of New York in 1945. His last visit to Anglesey was in 1955, not long before he died in New York in 1956.

One of the finest voices ever to come out of Wales was that of Tudor Davies, born at Cymmer, Porth in November 1892 and one of twelve children. After working in the colliery as a fitter his outstanding potential prompted a collection to enable him to take up a scholarship at the Royal College of Music where he studied with Gustave Garcia. His studies were interrupted by war service in the Royal Navy, and after demobilization he studied at the University College in Cardiff. In 1921 he was engaged by Lilian Baylis to sing Tamino at the Old Vic before going on tour to the USA, Canada and Australia. On his return in 1922 he began a distinguished operatic career with the British National Opera Company with whom he made his Covent Garden début as Rodolfo to the Mimì of Nellie Melba in *La bohème*. His roles for British National Opera included Faust, Don José, Cavaradossi, Pinkerton and the tenor leads in the world premières of Holst's *At the Boar's Head* and Ethel Smyth's *Fête galante*. On 14 July 1924 he sang the title-role in the first professional performance of *Hugh the Drover* by Vaughan Williams. He had a voice that was strong, virile and dramatic, he acted with great intensity, and he had the advantage of striking good looks. In the words of J. B. Steane, 'He was as passionate as any Italian.' His account (on record) of 'Sound an alarm' is superb, and he sings Tamino's arias from *The Magic Flute* (in English) with 'unusually full-blooded relish'. Tudor Davies made many magnificent records, including excerpts from a live performance of *The Dream of Gerontius* at the Three Choirs Festival in Hereford in 1927 conducted by Elgar himself. He also recorded a complete *Madam Butterfly* (in English) conducted by Eugène Goossens, as well as splendid Wagnerian excerpts from the *Ring* and *Tristan und Isolde*. He was married to the dramatic soprano Ruth Packer, and in his last years taught in Cardiff. There is no doubt that Tudor Davies was one of those genuinely great Welsh singers. He would surely have enjoyed a huge international career had he been born thirty years later.

Ben Williams was born in Llansamlet in 1894. He studied in Padua, Turin, Milan, Paris and with the great French baritone Dinh Gilly. Later, he sang with the Fuller Opera Company in Melbourne and Sydney and with the Carl Rosa and British National Opera companies and, for a while in the 1930s, he was prominent on the London musical stage. He also made a number of appearances at Covent Garden, and in 1933 he became a member of the Sadler's Wells Company. Francis Russell was another tenor blessed with a strong voice. He was born in Tonyrefail in 1895 and worked as a coal-miner for twelve years. Later he joined the Carl Rosa company for a brief period before going to Milan where he studied for three years with Ernesto Coronna. He was also taught by Ben Davies. During the 1920s and 1930s he became an extremely busy concert singer and performed at all the major festivals. In 1929 he sang at Covent Garden under Bruno Walter in *Der Rosenkavalier*. He taught at the University College in Cardiff between 1938 and 1941, and from 1947 in South Africa where he died in 1982. Francis Russell left some fine recordings; especially good are an urgent, stentorian Prize Song and a fearless 'Sound an alarm'. John Myrddin (Jones) was born in Briton Ferry in April 1901. He worked in a steelworks before winning a scholarship to the Royal College of Music. He joined the Carl Rosa company as a principal tenor and toured the United Kingdom and South Africa. Between 1950 and 1952 he sang the heavy roles of Hoffmann, Manrico and Don José for Welsh National Opera and in the late 1960s he took several comprimario roles for the company.

Another singer born in 1901 was Trefor Jones from Cymer near Port Talbot. He worked for some years as a coal-miner before winning a scholarship to the Royal College of Music in 1922. His studentship was most distinguished for during it he sang the title-role in a performance of *Parsifal* under Sir Adrian Boult, created the title-role in Vaughan Williams's *Hugh the Drover* (on 4 July 1924, just ten days before Tudor Davies's professional première) and sang in *Messiah* at the Three Choirs Festival in Hereford. After leaving the College he toured in Europe, and sang at Covent Garden, Sadler's Wells and in many West End musicals. Between 1927 and 1939 he sang at most of the Three Choirs Festivals, and from 1930 to 1935 he sang the title-role in the popular performances of Coleridge-Taylor's *Hiawatha* at the Albert Hall. Unfit for military service he worked for ENSA and CEMA during the Second World War. He also appeared in a number of films including *The Great Mr Handel* and *The Queen's Affair* with Anna Neagle, and he was a regular broadcaster early in the Marconi House days of the BBC. Amongst his recordings Novello's 'Shine through my dreams' is much the best. In it his voice is generous and warm-toned, and he sings with ardour.

Morgan Jones was born at Pontrhydfendigaid in 1903, but his family moved to the Merthyr area when he was a small boy. After studying at the University College in Cardiff he won a scholarship to the Royal College of Music where he studied under Dan Price for six years, before embarking on a busy career as an oratorio singer. In the opening season at Glyndebourne in 1934 he sang Curzio in *Figaro*.

His association with Sadler's Wells began in 1932, and in June 1945 he created the role of Bob Boles in the world première of Britten's *Peter Grimes*. (The Welsh baritone Roderick Jones was also in the historic cast as Captain Balstrode.) Dan Morgan Jones, as he was known, became a popular choral conductor, conducting *cymanfa-oedd canu* throughout Wales and amateur opera in London. He was the founder conductor of the Hammersmith Welsh Male Voice Choir in 1938, retaining the post for some thirty years.

David Tree was born in Treherbert in 1905. He studied at the Royal Academy of Music and worked with the Carl Rosa, Glynde-bourne and Sadler's Wells companies and at Covent Garden where he gave innumerable performances of character roles in the late 1940s and 1950s. Between 1951 and 1962 he sang for Welsh National Opera. Dai Tree, as his colleagues affectionately called him, was essentially the archetypal Welsh comprimario tenor: shortish and stocky with an incisive voice, excellent diction and an easy, lovely stage presence. During the Second World War he was entertain-ments manager at a Royal Ordnance Factory. He was married to the Sadler's Wells mezzo-soprano Olwen Price.

The legendary and much-loved David Lloyd was born in Trelogan, Flintshire in April 1912. He left school at the age of fourteen and was apprenticed as a carpenter. Many eisteddfod successes in his late teens prompted the people of Flintshire to start a fund which would enable him to study for a professional career. In 1933 he won a scholarship to the Guildhall School of Music, where he studied with Walter Hyde and won the Gold Medal in 1937. A year later he made his Glyndebourne début as Macduff in Verdi's *Macbeth*, and he sang there as Don Ottavio in the 1939 season. Shortly afterwards he appeared in Mozart at Sadler's Wells and sang in Belgium, Denmark and Sweden. His career was set to take off into the stratosphere and apparently there were plans for him to appear at La Scala and at the Metropolitan Opera in New York, but these plans had to be abandoned after the outbreak of war and he joined the Welsh Guards. During the Second World War he gave many concerts and continued to broadcast. He was a fine-looking man and cut a very handsome figure on the platform in his uniform. His voice was of exceptional quality – warm, round and smooth and probably the most beautiful of the Welsh tenor voices. Allied to his vocal and musical gifts was a generous and outgoing personality and he became enormously popular, especially in Wales where his fondness for singing Welsh hymns generated a deeply emotional response and made him a national hero. Sadly, in 1954 he suffered a serious accident on stage and he never really recovered. For many years his health was very poor and by the time he died in 1969 he had become a forlorn figure. But his great days were never forgotten as witnessed by a generous national testimonial made to him in 1961. David Lloyd made nearly eighty recordings: songs in Welsh and English, folk-songs, Welsh hymns, ballads, songs by Rachmaninov and some operatic items. Occasionally a hint of sentimentality crept in, but his best work on record was characterized by glorious tone, a secure technique, impeccable intonation, clear diction and great charm. His Mozart arias, sung mellifluously with marvellous breath control and elegant phrasing, are very highly regarded.

Another important tenor born in 1912 was Edgar Evans, the youngest of thirteen children from Cwrtnewydd in Cardiganshire. He was articled to an architect before leaving for London to study with Dawson Freer. Later he studied with the famous Scottish tenor Joseph Hislop and with Luigi Ricci in Rome. He was deemed unfit for military service and joined the Police War Reserve during which time he sang in more than 500 concerts for ENSA and CEMA. Edgar Evans was a founder member of the newly established resident company at Covent Garden and he sang in their opening performance of Purcell's *The Fairy-Queen*. His major début was in March 1947 as the Chevalier des Grieux in Massenet's *Manon*. He went on to sing fifty-four roles at Covent Garden: everything from the comprimario to the colossal. For Welsh National Opera he sang Gwyn in a revival of Arwel Hughes's *Menna* in 1955. At the Rome Opera he sang in *Das Rheingold* under Erich Kleiber. On record he sang Melot in Furtwängler's *Tristan und Isolde* and the mayor in Britten's *Albert Herring* conducted by the composer. When his singing days were over he was appointed to the professorial staff of the Royal College of Music. As I write, in 2001, he is alive and well and approaching ninety years old.

The career of Richard Lewis was highly distinguished. Born in Manchester in 1914 he always described himself as English in the

Glyndebourne programmes (with one exception at the Edinburgh Festival in 1948 when he was listed as Welsh), but apart from his lack of the Welsh language he was as Welsh as David Lloyd George, who was also born in Manchester of Welsh parents. Lewis's parents came from Llansanffraid-ym-Mechain near Llanymynech in Powys. His real name was Thomas Thomas, and he did not take his stage name until he was over thirty. His paternal grandfather's name was Richard and his mother's maiden name was Lewis, although another reason for the choice of Richard was Lewis's great admiration for Richard Tauber. Richard Lewis was an exceptionally fine boy soprano winning many prizes in eisteddfodau. After gaining his School Certificate he worked for nine years as a clerk in a calico printing firm. In 1938 he won the Gold Medal of the Associated Board of the Royal Schools of Music and a year later he entered the Royal Manchester College of Music to study with Norman Allin. Before his call-up in 1940 he was able to make his opera début for the Carl Rosa company. During the war he served with the Royal Corps of Signals and the Guards Armoured Division. He sang frequently and undertook major concert engagements including performances of Britten's *Serenade* for tenor, horn and strings and *Les illuminations*. After demobilization his Manchester scholarship was transferred to London where Norman Allin was teaching at the Royal Academy of Music.

Engagements began to pour in and he was soon recognized as the outstanding British tenor of his time. He was a particular favourite at Glyndebourne, appearing there more than 300 times between 1950 and 1979. His début for the Covent Garden company was as Peter Grimes in November 1947. He created the role of Troilus in Walton's *Troilus and Cressida* in 1954, Mark in Tippett's *The Midsummer Marriage* in 1955 and Achilles in Tippett's *King Priam* in 1962. He also sang Aron in the famous Covent Garden production of Schoenberg's *Moses und Aron* in 1965. The Tippett roles of Troilus and Aaron were among his finest creations. For Welsh National Opera he created the role of Gwyn in Arwel Hughes's *Menna* in 1953, and for the Handel Opera Society he sang the title-roles in *Jephtha* and *Richard I*. He appeared in Berlin, Buenos Aires, Vienna and often in the United States, especially in San Francisco where he sang many roles. On the concert platform he was especially re-nowned for his Gerontius which he recorded with Sargeant and Barbirolli. In the 1960s Lewis lived in Bermuda for five years during which time he taught at the Curtis Institute in Philadelphia. In 1963 he was appointed CBE and received honorary doctorates in music from St Andrews in 1984 and Manchester in 1986. After some years in poor health he died in November 1990 aged seventy-six. He pos-sessed an attractive, pleasing lyric voice which was really beautiful in the first half of his career. It lost a little of its bloom later as he undertook roles which were arguably too heavy for him. Nevertheless, the voice never lost its individuality and it was always instantly recognizable. He was an excellent musician and much admired for the prodigious speed of his study. Tall, well-built and always impeccably attired, he had great style and presence. Some thought him aloof, but in reality he was a very private, rather shy person.

Gerald Davies was born in 1914 at Maerdy in the Rhondda Valley. He worked in a coal-mine before winning a scholarship at the age of eighteen to the Webber-Douglas School of Singing and Dramatic Art in London. In 1936 he made his Covent Garden début in the British Music Drama Season as the Simpleton in *Boris Godunov*. His military service in the Pioneer Co. lasted seven years. After the war he sang for the South African Opera Company in Johannesburg before returning in 1948 to become a principal at Sadler's Wells. It was at this time that Sadler's Wells was popularly known as Sadler's Welsh! In the 1954–5 season, for example, four of the six principal tenors were Welsh: Gerald Davies, Rowland Jones, Gwent Lewis and Robert Thomas. For Welsh National Opera, Gerald Davies sang five roles: Jenik, the Duke, Alfredo, Faust and Pinkerton. His silvery voice was most appealing and his technique totally secure. Even-tually he became an extremely sought-after singing teacher in south Wales. He taught at the Welsh College of Music and Drama for many years and was very highly regarded there. His approach to voice production was analytical and thorough and he often lectured on vocal technique. As I write he is approaching his eighty-seventh birthday, living in Gwent and still teaching.

Rowland Jones was a champion euphonium player before he took up singing. He was born at Gwauncaegurwen near Ammanford in

1918 and became a proficient player at the age of twelve in the local silver band. He was later invited to join the Black Dyke Mills Band and afterwards the Bickershaw Colliery Band. His serious vocal training began under Tom Burke in 1939, and after the war he sang a formidable list of roles at Covent Garden and Sadler's Wells. For Welsh National Opera he created the roles of Clitandre in Arwel Hughes's *Serch yw'r Doctor* in 1960 and Randall in Alun Hoddinott's *The Beach of Falesá* in 1974. He was a frequent broadcaster and a fine concert singer. When his performing career was over he retired to the Vale of Clwyd, teaching at Bangor Normal College and Cartrefle College Wrexham. Rowland Jones had a delightful personality with a charming, cheerful disposition: a real gentleman of the operatic stage. These qualities were reflected in his warm, generous voice which can be heard on a record of *The World's Best Loved Songs*. He died in 1978.

Brychan Powell was born at Halfway near Llangadog in 1922. He studied at the Guildhall School of Music and then sang for Touring Opera, Carl Rosa, Welsh National Opera, and at Sadler's Wells and Covent Garden. He had a virile Italianate voice which was well-suited to the bel canto repertoire. His high notes were ringing and fearless and may be heard on a fine record he made of operatic arias conducted by Vilem Tausky. The excerpts from Giordano's *Andrea Chenier* are especially exciting. Interesting too is a disc he made of Welsh songs and folk-songs with orchestral arrangements by Osian Ellis conducted by David Ffrancgon Thomas.

One of the finest comprimarios of his time was Edward Byles who was born at Cwm near Ebbw Vale in 1924 and studied at the Royal College of Music where he won the coveted Queen's Prize in 1953. He sang with the English Opera Group at Aldeburgh in Poulenc's *Les Mamelles de Tirésias*, for Touring Opera 1958, for the Carl Rosa Company and for the New Opera Company in Werner Egk's *The Government Inspector*. He worked with the Sadler's Wells Company from 1959, Welsh National Opera from 1960 and he joined the English National Opera in 1974. He created the roles of Papa in Grace Williams's *The Parlour* (1966) and Father Galuchet in Hoddinott's *The Beach of Falesá* (1974). Edward Byles was unrivalled as a character tenor and in this capacity sang upwards of thirty roles. He was renowned for his impeccable diction: in the vastness of the London Coliseum his every word was clearly heard.

Wales was a troubled country between the wars, but it continued to give birth to fine tenors and if space allowed I would have reflected on the careers of Ronald Hill, Clifford Bumford, Gwent Lewis, John Stoddart, Robert Thomas, David Galliver and many others. I was also particularly interested in the singing of both that talented entertainer Harry Secombe and the Birmingham Welshman David Hughes who very successfully bridged the gap between light entertainment and classical opera: he topped the bill at the London Palladium and was a television regular as well as appearing for Welsh National Opera and at Sadler's Wells and Covent Garden. Hughes died in 1972 after collapsing on stage at the Coliseum. Records convey the expansive, intense passion of his full-throated delivery: a fine singer cut down in his prime. Sadly Keith Erwin was another tenor who died in his forties. Born in north Wales in 1942 but brought up in County Durham, he sang all the leading tenor roles for Welsh National Opera between 1967 and 1973.

Finally tribute must be paid to the very high standard of amateur and semi-professional singing in Wales: the soloists in so many concerts, oratorios and local musical productions. In my lifetime one tenor stood out in this respect, for Richie Thomas (1906–88) turned down an offer to join Sadler's Wells in 1946. By day he worked at the woollen mill at Penmachno, but meanwhile he achieved a national reputation as a concert and oratorio singer. He had a silvery, high, lyric voice: occasionally, such as in the recordings of 'O Paradiso' and 'Sound an alarm', his fearless high notes rang out confidently.

It has been a great pleasure to write about this fine array of Welsh tenors from the past. The tradition continues, for there are a number of splendid Welsh tenors working today in many parts of the world. Let us salute them for their achievements and wish them well for the future.

Acknowledgements
Kenneth Bowen is a distinguished tenor, teacher and conductor whose career places him very much at the centre of the story he has to tell. This essay is a considerably

shortened and edited version of a lecture given by him at the University of Wales, Swansea during which recordings of many of the singers were played.

In compiling this essay the author relied heavily on a variety of musical dictionaries and sleeve notes, as well as opera histories and the back numbers of *Welsh Music*. He is grateful for information received from John L. Davies, Elizabeth Forbes and Eric Rees. Amongst many books consulted were:

Frederic Griffith, *Notable Welsh Musicians of Today* (London, 1896).
J. Sutcliffe Smith, *Impressions of Music in Wales* (1948).
Donald Brook, *Singers of Today* (London, 1949).
Gladys Davidson, *Opera Biographies* (London, 1955).
J. B. Steane, *The Grand Tradition* (London, 1974).

Geraint Evans

Patrick Hannan

In October 1958, Geraint Evans went to Ireland to take part in a production of *Don Giovanni* being put on by the Dublin Grand Opera Society. It was not an obvious engagement for him to accept, for during the previous decade he had already established himself as a considerable figure in the British operatic world and become a fixture at Covent Garden. As long ago as 1949 he had sung Figaro there – a character who would figure among his most famous and familiar roles and one which he would perform more than five hundred times in the course of a long professional life. He was also, it was to turn out, on the brink of the kind of international career which was entirely unprecedented for a British singer. There seemed to be no great necessity to go to Dublin. And yet there was a particular purpose behind the expedition. Evans had already sung the role of Leporello, Don Giovanni's devious and cowardly servant, many times. He was particularly brilliant at it, always at ease with the opportunities for comedy it provided and always at home in Mozart. Now, David Webster, the general administrator of Covent Garden Opera, had suggested he might take the title-role. The Dublin production was thus a convenient opportunity for a try-out.

Don Giovanni is one of the great baritone parts in opera. By turns he is cruel and tender, violent and charming, cunning and defiant. From his seduction of Zerlina in one of the most famous of all Mozart duets, 'La ci darem la mano', to the hectic drive of the 'Champagne aria', he is a compelling figure. Leporello may get the laughs but the Don is the one they are watching. It soon becomes clear why, at the age of thirty-six, it might have seemed a logical step forward for Evans and those who were watching his career develop. Later, he was to write that he thought that he had given a pretty good performance. Nevertheless, doubts over whether he should take it on at Covent Garden persisted in his mind, and he delayed making a commitment. Eventually he went to see Rudolf Kempe, the German musician who was due to conduct the new production. He explained why he was dubious. The reasons were not musical.

'I think,' he said, 'I have duck's disease.'

'What is that?'

'My bottom is too near the ground.'

That is to say, he thought he was too short to make a convincing Don.

In the world of opera that seems an extraordinary story. What singers looked like, particularly forty years ago, was not of particular relevance. In general they were there for the sound they made, rather than for any sense of realism they brought to their roles, either by their appearance or their ability to act. 'It ain't over till the fat lady sings,' became a popular saying because people could recognize in a single phrase the way in which opera and real life are so often kept apart. After all, as late as the 1930s a prima donna might send her maid to rehearsals to indicate where her mistress intended to stand for particular arias during the performance itself. Even today, when there are so many good-looking singers bounding athletically around the stages of the world, you can still see a short, portly tenor declare his undying passion for a mountainous soprano. People might notice it a bit more than they once did, but it does not spoil their evening.

His decision not to sing the part of Don Giovanni is one indication of how immersed Evans was in the idea of opera as a complete theatrical experience. He was unhappy if he could not find his way physically into a part. He was not simply a singer going through the planned moves, but an actor too, always in search of the materials for a performance. 'He was a stage creature,' says the critic Rodney Milnes. 'He had an extraordinary relationship with the audience. He had them in the palm of his hand and he would not let them go.'

In a television programme made in the last year of his life, Evans explained graphically how he set about creating character from observed physical characteristics. In this instance it was Falstaff – perhaps, if such arguments can ever be resolved, his greatest role. 'I look around at people. There was a man in my village we used to call Fatty Osborne. He was twenty-six stone or something. He could hardly walk. I remember going round to watch how he walked and how he leant against the windowsill if he was sitting outside.' This attention to detail illuminated his performance. According to

Rodney Milnes: 'He was one of the greatest comic singers I've seen. His Falstaff was complete magic.'

The same approach was to serve him particularly well when he took on the title-role in *Wozzeck* in San Francisco in 1960. There could hardly have been a greater contrast between Verdi and Falstaff and Berg and Wozzeck but one of those fortunate accidents gave Evans the key he needed.

> Trying to build up the character during rehearsal, I needed a pair of jackboots to give the effect of a soldier's plodding, trudging walk. The wardrobe master had no boots in my size, only in a couple of sizes bigger and he thought they would be too uncomfortable for me to use. But I said I would try them anyway and, after I'd been in them for a few minutes, I realised that the bigness gave me just the effect I wanted, the monotonous trudge, trudge, trudge from one place to another. After that I always asked for boots two sizes too big for me in *Wozzeck*, just as I demanded very tight shoes for Beckmesser [in *Die Meistersinger*] making me feel all the more irritable because the shoes were pinching. All my characters have been built from the feet up.

The effect of this kind of intensely individualistic approach was described in the *Financial Times* in August 1971 by Elizabeth Forbes in a review of Evans's performance in *Wozzeck* at the Salzburg festival.

> Words, music and gesture are all used to express what Wozzeck in his inarticulateness can never directly express, his own thoughts and feelings. His shambling gait, half walk, half run, as he crosses the huge width of the stage, the way he rolls his tunic and aligns his boots before lying on the Doctor's couch, the desperate stillness with which he watches Marie and the Drum Major dancing in the tavern garden, all speak for him much more clearly than words.

What these stories tell you about Evans's character and his approach to opera make his decision not to play Don Giovanni the one you might consequently expect. If he could not *be* the Don in a physical sense he could not sing him with conviction. Perhaps Rudolf Kempe understood it when he heard Evans's final decision. 'I know you could sing the Don, and a good Don,' he said, 'but why not be the best Leporello?'

These stories also explain in part an idea over which it is still possible to have an argument, even years after Geraint Evans's death. 'Ah well,' some people say, 'old Geraint had a pretty good voice but it was the whole package that really mattered, his brilliance on stage, his qualities as an actor.' The implication is that Evans was not actually quite at the top of the first division as a singer, but whatever minor lack of quality there might have been was more than made up for by his dramatic authority. Evans himself was understandably touchy about the suggestion: with good reason, since an account of his career suggests the opposite.

That there was a career at all is something that has its remarkable aspects. It has its romance, too – the tale of a working-class boy, born in south Wales at a time of acute economic depression, deprived of much of an education, but who nevertheless was carried by his remarkable talent to fame, honours, wealth and international acclaim. He was born in Cilfynydd, near Pontypridd, on 16 February 1922. His father, William John Evans, was a miner. When Geraint was eighteen months old, his mother, Charlotte May, died in childbirth. She was just twenty-two. The young child stayed with his grandparents in the house where he was born, while his father went back to live with his own parents at the other end of the village. It was not until he was ten years old and his father had remarried that the family were united in Hopkinstown, another mining village a few miles away.

Cilfynydd was at the very southern edge of a coalfield which, in 1922, employed almost a quarter of a million men. It was a period of bitter dispute between miners and the owners, at the centre of which was to be the General Strike of 1926 and the long lock-out that followed in south Wales. Jobs were uncertain and wages under constant pressure as Britain struggled through the Depression and the mass unemployment that went with it. It was not to end until an even greater threat, a world war, changed the picture. This was not a time or a place much filled with hope.

One way out was through education, but the young Geraint failed 'the scholarship', as it was known; the examination that decided who would go to the grammar school and who would be effectively excluded for good from academic progress. A single day's tests often mapped out the rest of a child's life. The result in this case was that Geraint Evans left school at fourteen. He got a job as an errand boy, that now forgotten breed, in Taff Street, Pontypridd, working for a branch of that once famous but long extinct chain, the Maypole Dairies. Before he began work there, though, he accepted a job across the street with a Mr Theophilus whose shop sign announced that he specialized in 'High Class Ladies' Fashions'. Evans was eventually to become a window-dresser, an occupation which gave him ideas of perhaps going on to become a fashion designer. It wasn't at all bad. Seven-and-six a week (37.5p today) as well as being safe and clean, perhaps even offering modest *prospects* and, above all, not down the pit, so fulfilling the devout wish of every collier father. It might have been the foundation for a long and comfortable life, with Evans one day even having his own shop, something he was indeed eventually to be offered by Mr Theophilus.

But there was one other aspect of life in south Wales in those days which was to change his whole life. Music. Today, the idea of Wales being a place in which many communities are characterized in part by a shared musical experience is largely the recourse of visiting television producers who have little imagination and not enough energy to investigate for themselves. Industrial Wales, chapel Wales, Welsh-speaking Wales, have all changed beyond measure, but when Geraint Evans was growing up in the 1920s and 1930s music was a vital spark. His father was a keen amateur musician who took a correspondence course with one of the London colleges. Evans himself began competing in local eisteddfodau at the age of four, and from then on there seem to have been almost unlimited opportunities to experience a whole range of music. He played the violin in the local youth orchestra; he sang in a local production of *Lilac Time*; he became a member of a famous glee party, the Lyrian Singers, which broadcast regularly. When he was persuaded to take part in the Pontypridd Operatic Society's Christmas pantomime, *Ali Baba*, his performance of 'On the Road to Mandalay' was so impressive that two people who knew what they were talking about, one of them, Bert Gregory Evans, a former opera singer, told him that he should have his voice trained. His father borrowed money so that he could take some lessons from a teacher in Cardiff.

Soon Geraint Evans's reputation spread and he was invited to take part in *Welsh Rarebit*, one of the most famous radio programmes ever produced in Wales, in the section 'Youth Takes a Bow.'

In an interview in the *Guardian* in March 1971 he told Christopher Ford: 'I played the piano, I was a bit of a child prodigy, yet like all kids I wouldn't practise.' Prodigy seems to be right. He told Ford that at the age of twelve he was a chorus bass in Elgar's *The Dream of Gerontius*, conducted by Sir Henry Wood in Mountain Ash, a small town half a dozen miles north of Cilfynydd. It seems extraordinary, but at the age of sixteen, at most seventeen, Geraint Evans was singing Elijah in a performance of Mendelssohn's oratorio, put on by Bethel Chapel, Cilfynydd. It was in costume, and he was hooked. That was the magic ingredient, he was to say later. To take the wig and the beard and the flowing robes and become someone else. 'That was the first time I had made up, felt the greasepaint. There was a marvellous atmosphere about it all. That's what I think started to change the whole thing because before that my intention was to become a fashion designer.'

The striking thing about this chronicle of amateur boyhood performance is the sheer amount and variety of music and performance that was part of everyday life. It was a chance to learn and, even more important perhaps, to get noticed. You wonder whether such a talent would necessarily get its opportunity in the greatly changed world of the twenty-first century. Maybe. After all, because of his performances at eisteddfodau another great Welsh baritone, Bryn Terfel, had a huge following in Wales as a teenager, long before he went to the Guildhall School of Music and Drama. However, there was another avenue of progress which is no longer available to poor but talented young people. When the war came, Evans joined the RAF. A talent contest organized by the British Forces Network got him noticed and he became a regular broadcaster with the BFN chorus. Later he transferred full time to BFN's music department where, by chance, he was heard by the Austrian bass, Theo Hermann, who was living in Hamburg. Hermann offered to give him singing lessons and Evans went to him three times a week until, in 1947, it was time to go home to be demobbed.

It is the sort of story that was repeated many times in Evans's career. His abilities were so immediately apparent that they persuaded influential and knowledgeable people that they should not be wasted.

Forces broadcasting was the cradle of many a substantial career. The war gave a lot of people the chance to explore what they might be and, perhaps, the nerve to pursue that goal. Evans left Germany with some firm advice. 'A colleague there said I would be a fool if I didn't take up singing as a career.' And, at the age of twenty-five, that is what he did, despite the blandishments of Mr Theophilus who said wistfully: 'I had made up my mind that one day one of the stores would be yours.'

Geraint Evans's own account of his life and career, *A Knight at the Opera*, makes his subsequent progress seem easy, although that impression may be due in great part to the traditionally unchallenging nature of performers' autobiographies. Even when he clearly takes a dim view of someone you have to dig between the lines for it. In 1950, for example, he auditioned for Sir Thomas Beecham at Glyndebourne. He sang from *Ariadne auf Naxos* in German. Beecham demanded: 'What's this? The *Messiah* in Welsh?' Evidently there were days when even Beecham did not live up to his reputation as a great wit.

In general, though, from the moment he decided to make his career in music subsequent events justified it. By 1948 he was making his debut at Covent Garden. The following year the young Peter Brook, who was to become one of the most brilliant of British directors, picked him to sing Figaro for the first time. In the same year at Covent Garden he also sang Escamillo in *Carmen*, one of the great glamour parts of the operatic stage. And on it went. What was at the heart of this talent which was so swiftly recognized? A kind of magic, some people say, or, in the more robust words of Sir John Tooley, a former general director of the Royal Opera House: 'He was a rattling good actor with a splendid voice and he was a great professional. He made a big impression very early and amongst the men he was one of the greatest of his generation in the world.'

His friend, the composer Alun Hoddinott, formerly professor of music at Cardiff University, says that one of Evans's great strengths was his apparent ability to interpret exactly what the creator of an opera thought of the roles. 'Opera's a very fancy business and sometimes when you sit in the audience it all seems so unreal. Geraint made it real. He made the Mozart operas real and I am sure he did so in the way in which Mozart thought.' As for those arguments about the voice, perhaps they arise in part from the fact that it was so particularly suited to opera. 'It was a rich voice, a dark voice,' Hoddinott says, 'but it was not a concert voice.' Not beautiful, others say, in the sense that you might sit down to listen to it for an evening's relaxation, but instead one that belonged to drama, unsettling often, rather than soothing.

Evans had one other advantage for someone making a career in opera. He was a strikingly handsome man with big, dark eyes and a strong nose, features particularly designed to draw an audience's attention to the stage. There was something slightly exotic about him and he sometimes attributed his popularity in Italy to the fact that opera-goers there assumed that he must be at least part Italian. Perhaps, though, it was the result of the blood which a great grandfather was reputed to have brought into the family by marrying a gypsy. Whatever the reason, if you passed him in the street you would not have had much difficulty in guessing his profession.

This combination of talents kept Evans busy throughout the 1950s and would certainly have sustained him in a substantial career until the time eventually came for him to retire. But it would have been a *British* career, because British singers were not much sought after by opera houses around the world. Evans's pioneering role in changing that tradition not only gives his achievement a special importance in the musical history of the United Kingdom, but it also underlines his outstanding quality as a performer. Early in 1960 he was asked to sing the familiar role of Figaro once more. But this time, almost unbelievably, to do so at La Scala, Milan, arguably the greatest of the world's opera houses. Not only that, but the opera was to be conducted by Herbert von Karajan, one of the most important conductors of the twentieth century. It certainly surprised the Italians who clearly had a pretty low opinion of British singers. Evans was the first to sing a leading role at La Scala since Dame Eva Turner in *Turandot* thirty-five years earlier, and he records that at the theatre people were saying in astonishment to each other: 'Un Inglese cantare Figaro alla Scala'. Less of the 'Inglese', he might well have remarked, but they were to understand that soon enough.

There was similar consternation in Vienna where he made his début less than a year later. 'Who's this English?' they asked, hearing him sing roles that until that time had been almost entirely the preserve of Austrians or Germans. Such was his success there, though, that von

Karajan asked him to become a permanent member of the Vienna State Opera, an offer he eventually declined. A year later he was invited to sing Figaro at the Salzburg Festival. As he said himself: 'It was the peak of achievement for any Mozart singer.' He was now embarked on a glittering international career that was to continue for another twenty years.

In the words of Sir John Tooley, 'He was among the first British singers to be accepted abroad. He was blazing the trail for others.' As those others of later generations made their names in opera houses around the world (not just Welsh singers, although there were plenty of those too) it was perhaps easy to forget how much of a pioneer Evans had been. And in its turn that worked its way into the operatic world in Britain. 'He demonstrated the strengths and talents of British singers,' John Tooley says, and his presence added to the reputation of Covent Garden in particular both at home and abroad.

Geraint Evans's fame lay largely in those great comic roles like Figaro and Papageno and Falstaff, and he was well aware of what suited him. Even so, he sometimes took on the unexpected, the darkly evil Claggart in *Billy Budd,* for example, although he had withdrawn from the opportunity, in 1951, to take the name part in the first performance of the opera, feeling that his voice was not right for the part. And there was *Wozzeck* too, another modern opera, which he sang first in San Francisco in 1960, although he said himself: 'I never thought of *Wozzeck* as an opera. To me it was a tragic play to which the music brought a feeling of emotion that spread within you as the character came to life.' He also said of it: 'It was like banging your head against a wall. I'd play Wozzeck once a year – six performances, then I'd try to sing Mozart afterwards.' To people like Rodney Milnes these parts never seemed entirely in harmony with Evans's own stage character. 'He was such an ebullient personality that internalising, as you have to do with Claggart and Wozzeck – two screwed-up people – was not really in his nature.'

In 1982, at the age of sixty, Evans decided to retire. He might well have meant it, even if musical retirements are famously temporary. Farewell performances were arranged but at one of them, a televised concert at the National Eisteddfod in Swansea that summer, he was taken ill on stage. In his dressing room he was instantly diagnosed as suffering from diabetes. It was an illness severe enough to insist on a major change in the way he lived.

During his time as one of the world's leading singers the whole business of opera was changed, in particular by the rapid expansion of international air travel. You could sing different roles in different continents in the same week. The best singers could command enormous fees and some of them chose exile under more tax-friendly regimes in order to hang on to as much of the cash as possible. Evans, however, had always preferred Wales and, despite his fame, he chose a modest lifestyle in the distinctly unglamorous surroundings of Orpington in Kent and Aberaeron in Cardiganshire, where he finally settled. A profile published in the *New Statesman* in 1973 drew attention to the contrast between his two worlds. 'Perhaps opera singers should be more absurd than Sir Geraint, should not live in Orpington, should not, if they have a small yacht, keep it in Cardigan Bay but at St Tropez, and if they have a Mercedes not one that's six years old and not have been married for 25 years to a clever, pretty woman from their small, coal village.'

Although that article was anonymous, it was almost certainly written by the late John Morgan who, among many other things, had at one time been assistant editor of the *New Statesman*. Morgan was the man who organized the consortium which was, as Harlech Television, to win the commercial television franchise for Wales and the West of England. His friend Geraint Evans became a director of the company. He was to show little interest in the mechanics of business, but he spent a lot of time with the staff, dashing in and out of cutting rooms and enthusing about programmes. It was much appreciated by the workers, although rather less so by the management of the company and the rest of the board who did not think that non-executive directors should actually go round talking to people.

He did other non-musical things too, including charity work and, at the end of his life, he became high sheriff of Cardiganshire, a ceremonial role performed in old-fashioned costume, lace and breeches and buckles and all that sort of thing. It might have seemed a little odd except, as a friend pointed out, it was perhaps of a piece with his career. 'You see,' he said, 'he just loved dressing up. Geraint could never quite get away from the stage.'

Acknowledgements
In writing this article I have made extensive use, particularly for the chronology of Geraint Evans's life and career, of his autobiography, *A Knight at the Opera*, published by Futura in 1984. A number of people have generously made time to talk to me, not all of whom are acknowledged in the text. I must, however, offer particular thanks to Professor Alun Hoddinott and Nicola Heywood-Thomas.

Gwyneth Jones

Robert Bideleux

Dame Gwyneth Jones has been at the top of the operatic profession since the mid-1960s – a remarkably long time. For this she was awarded the CBE in 1976, became a *Kammersängerin* of the Vienna State Opera in 1977, was made a Dame of the British Empire in 1986, and received a German Cross of Merit. However, the highest point of her career came in the summer of 1976, when she achieved one of the greatest distinctions ever to be achieved by a Welsh – or, indeed, British – opera singer. She had been chosen to take the lead role of Brünnhilde in the centenary production of Richard Wagner's monumental tetralogy *Der Ring des Nibelungen* at that year's Bayreuth Festival. Not only is this the biggest and most taxing soprano role in the entire operatic repertoire, but this particular venture came to be recognized as a major landmark in the history of opera production. Aided by an exceptionally strong team of singing actors, the visually challenging sets of Richard Peduzzi, and the drama, passion and beauty which the French conductor Pierre Boulez drew out of the orchestral score (particularly in *Die Walküre*), the French theatre director Patrice Chéreau succeeded in pioneering a new style of operatic production that placed the main emphasis on finding and revealing anew the inner meaning of the drama. The mindless catcalls and booing which greeted the production (though not the singers) on its first showing in 1976 were replaced by a chorus of acclaim for the revivals and further refinement of the production and design concepts in 1977, 1978, 1979 and 1980. To her credit, Gwyneth Jones staunchly defended and praised the producer from the outset. She has nearly always thrown her heart and soul into fulfilling the producer's wishes. It is thus no accident that she remained a great favourite with bold and innovative opera producers such as Chéreau and Götz Friedrich, and with conductors such as Leonard Bernstein, Karl Böhm, Pierre Boulez and Carlos Kleiber.

The 1980 television recording of the Chéreau/Boulez *Ring*, which was broadcast in a number of countries to mark the centenary of Wagner's death in 1983 and was issued by Phillips on video as well as on LP, audiocassette and CD, was ultimately seen by several million people and conclusively established Gwyneth Jones as *the* Brünnhilde of her time. The total dramatic conviction, femininity and striking stage persona and looks which she brought to this role contributed immeasurably to the success of the production, in which she was superbly partnered by the great New Zealand bass-baritone Sir Donald McIntyre as her father Wotan, the ardent and very personable tenor Peter Hofmann as her half-brother Siegmund, and the attractive soprano Jeannine Altmeyer as her half-sister Sieglinde and as her rival-in-love Gutrune. There was also truly outstanding singing-acting from Heinz Zednik as the mercurial demi-god Loge, from Hanna Schwartz as Wotan's beautiful but shrewish wife Fricka, from Matti Salminen as a wonderfully black-souled and black-voiced Hunding and Hagen, and from Hermann Becht as the eponymous Nibelung, to round off this exceptionally strong cast. *Die Walküre*, in which the only scene that did not come off brilliantly was the Ride of the Valkyries, must have had one of the most committed, best-directed, best-looking and most completely convincing casts ever to have graced this most human of Wagner operas. Especially in the Chéreau production, Gwyneth Jones has brought out more fully than anyone else I have seen or heard the special tenderness, intensity and ambiguity in Brünnhilde's relationship with Wotan, although in this respect Anne Evans (the other great Welsh Wagnerian soprano of the late twentieth century) has been her nearest rival. Is their special warmth, tenderness and femininity specifically Welsh? I like to think so. Gwyneth Jones and Anne Evans have also shared the ability to cut through and rise above Wagner's great waves of orchestral splendour, without resorting to 'can belto'.

Nevertheless, the role of Brünnhilde in the Chéreau-Boulez *Ring* was merely the culmination of a meteoric ascent. In an affectionate essay written in 1970, the critic Kenneth Loveland attributed both Gwyneth Jones's 'fighting spirit' and her 'passionate urge to sing' to her roots in Monmouthshire's eastern valley. She was born in Pontnewynydd in 1937. Her mother sang in several choirs and her father, a tin-plate worker, was an accomplished pianist. After Twmpath Secondary Modern and a secretarial course, Gwyneth started an office job at Pontypool foundry and was soon combining her post as the manager's secretary with a full diary of choral and solo singing. With characteristic good fortune, Loveland first heard her when she appeared as a soloist with the Abersychan and Pontypool Co-op Choir. By the time that she was nineteen she had won a hundred eisteddfod prizes and four silver cups. Against the advice of her friends and a boss who warned that a professional music career was 'no bed of roses', she set her heart on full-time training. A Monmouthshire County Scholarship took her to the Royal College of Music where, singing as a mezzo, she was from the outset a regular prize-winner.

From the Royal College of Music she went on to study voice at the Chigiana Academy in Siena and later in Zurich, a city which was closely associated with Wagner (who started composing *Tristan und Isolde* while living in a house beside its famous lake). She made her professional début as a mezzo-soprano in 1962 in Zurich, which also provided her first break in a major soprano role (Amelia in Verdi's *Un ballo in maschera*), and she joined the Zurich Opera Company in 1964. Zurich eventually became her home after her marriage to the Swiss businessman, Till Haberfeld, who was her agent until their divorce in the late 1990s. From 1963 to 1968 she was also a member of the Royal Opera House, Covent Garden, where she achieved over-night celebrity in 1964 by successfully standing in at short notice for an indisposed Leontyne Price in Verdi's *Il trovatore* (of which there is a recording conducted by Carlo Maria Giulini, dating from that same year, on the Legendary label). This blazed the trail for other Verdi roles at Covent Garden, on the Continent and in the United States. The most notable were: Desdemona in *Otello* (which she recorded for EMI under Sir John Barbirolli in 1970); the title-role in *Aida*, of which 'live' audio and TV recordings were made under Sir Edward Downes at Covent Garden in 1968, opposite the Radames of Jon Vickers and Charles Craig, respectively (the former was issued on CD by Melodram); Elisabeth de Valois in *Don Carlos* (recorded in Vienna under Berislav Klobucar in 1967, and issued on CD by Melodram); the soprano part in the Verdi *Requiem* (recorded in 1967 under Zubin Mehta, with Franco Corelli and Grace Bumbry, and issued on CD by LRC); and Lady Macbeth in *Macbeth* (recorded much later under Gustav Kuhn in Tokyo in 1992, and issued on CD by Sine Qua Non). She also made a fine commercial recording of arias from Verdi operas under Edward Downes for Decca in 1968.

Gwyneth Jones has been a great singing actress in Verdi's dramatic soprano roles, and their tessitura has seemed to suit her voice very well. Even though (as a Wagnerite and Straussian) I admire the total dramatic conviction that Gwyneth Jones has always brought to her Wagner and Strauss and can readily comprehend her overriding desire to sing the great Wagner and Strauss soprano and mezzo-soprano roles, I cannot help feeling that her singing of Verdi and Beethoven has on the whole been even better than her Wagner and Strauss. She has always seemed to sing her Verdi and Beethoven roles without any hint of vocal strain or discomfort, and Verdi has offered her more abundant opportunities to capitalize on her exceptional ability to float soft, gentle musical phrases to great expressive effect. When she has sung Wagner, it has often been apparent that her voice was being put under extreme pressure and pushed to (and sometimes beyond) its natural limits, with results that are not wholly pleasing to all ears. In my view, however, the occasionally obtrusive vibrato and shrillness when her voice is under such pressure are more than compensated by the power of her vocal acting, as was also the case with Maria Callas. One becomes too completely caught up in the power of the performance as a whole to be much bothered by such technical imperfections, which sometimes heighten her vocal and dramatic expressiveness.

While the 1960s were dominated by her Verdi roles, Gwyneth Jones was also branching out into other repertoire, including Puccini. Her impressive allure and stage presence made her a particularly convincing Tosca at Covent Garden and elsewhere (there have been several unofficial audio recordings and a German television broadcast of her in that role over the years), and she was also successful in the role of Madam Butterfly (a Zurich perform-ance was taped in 1979). Since 1984 she has also given numerous performances of the title-role in Puccini's *Turandot*, including a performance that was televised from Covent Garden in 1987. However, even though she has received acclaim for her distinctive interpretation of this role, for which she received coaching from Dame Eva Turner (its most famous exponent), I wonder whether it really shows off her special qualities to best advantage. Her other major Puccini role has been that of Minnie in *La fanciulla del West*. She also recorded the role of Poppea in Monteverdi's *L'incoronazione di Poppea* in 1978. However, she did not take on any Italian *bel canto* roles until her début in the title-role of Bellini's *Norma* in 1996, at the age of fifty-nine.

More significant were her first sallies into the German repertoire, aided by many hours of individual preparation and coaching from the late Sir Reginald Goodall in his eyrie (nicknamed 'Valhalla') at Covent Garden. Shortly after her first Covent Garden Leonora in *Il trovatore*, she stepped in at short notice to sing Leonore in Beethoven's *Fidelio*. She made her Vienna State Opera début in this role in 1966 and recorded the part opposite James King's Florestan under Karl Böhm for Deutsche Grammophon in Dresden in 1969, but Jones and King made a much greater impact in the famous Vienna State Opera performances conducted by Leonard Bernstein in 1970, one of which was happily recorded by Austrian Radio. This 'live' recording is much more moving and inspirational than either Böhm's Dresden recording or the Vienna-based studio recording which Bernstein made for the same company with different lead singers (Gundula Janowitz and René Kollo), and must rank among the best ever. Gwyneth Jones also made exciting recordings of the soprano part in Beethoven's Ninth Symphony in the studio under Karl Böhm in 1970 and 'live' under Bernstein in 1979, both on Deutsche Grammophon.

Soon after her first *Fidelios*, Gwyneth Jones began her long and splendid association with the operas of Richard Strauss. She took the role of Octavian in celebrated performances of Richard Strauss's *Der Rosenkavalier* at the Vienna State Opera opposite Christa Ludwig's Feldmarschallin and Lucia Popp's Sophie under Leonard Bernstein in 1966. Her original training as a mezzo paid dividends in this role, which is given to mezzos more often than to sopranos. A sumptuous studio recording was made for CBS (now Sony) between performances of a revival of this production in 1971, but one suspects either that by then the production had lost some of its original spontaneity, spark and *élan*, or that something was lost in translation to the recording studio. In 1977, opposite Brigitte Fassbaender's ardent Octavian and Lucia Popp's exquisitely sung Sophie, Gwyneth Jones performed the role of the Feldmarschallin with great dignity, serenity and allure in a Bavarian State Opera production suavely conducted by Carlos Kleiber. A revival of this production with the same trio of female lead singers was televised in Germany and the UK in 1979 and subsequently issued on video by Deutsche Grammophon. This remains very impressive, but it is not quite as engaging, heart-warming or uplifting as the rival performance on video from Covent Garden, with Kiri Te Kanawa, Anne Howells and Barbara Bonney under Sir Georg Solti.

Gwyneth Jones made a highly successful 'live' recording of the title-role in *Salome* under Karl Böhm at the Hamburg Opera in 1970 for Deutsche Grammophon, with Richard Cassilly as Herod and Dietrich Fischer-Dieskau as John the Baptist. She did not display the phenomenal vocal security, precision and power of a Birgit Nilsson, nor did she sound quite as thrillingly erotic and ecstatic as Ljuba Welitsch under either Fritz Reiner or Lovro von Matačić. Hildegard Behrens under Karajan, or Cheryl Studer under Giuseppe Sinopoli, but she sounds convincingly youthful and seductive, and the recording successfully captures (with remarkably few distracting noises) what must have been a hugely exciting evening in the theatre. She was videotaped in the same role at Marseilles as late as 1994, when she was fifty-seven.

I greatly regret never having heard Gwyneth Jones in one of her many renditions of the title-role in *Elektra*, but was partially compensated by hearing her give a radiant and larger than life performance as Elektra's sister Chrysothemis at Covent Garden in 1977. This was an 'electrifying' performance all round, with the great Birgit Nilsson (nearing the end of her career) as Elektra and Sir Donald McIntyre as Orestes, stunningly conducted by Carlos Kleiber.

Dame Gwyneth has been a renowned interpreter of the Dyer's Wife and the Empress in *Die Frau ohne Schatten*. She famously saved a performance of *Die Frau* in Zurich in 1985 by singing both of the female lead roles on the same night – a truly astonishing feat, considering the strenuous vocal demands made by both roles, and further testimony to her dedication, resilience and remarkable stamina. There exist live tapes of her in this and several other productions of this opera, including one that was televised from Marseilles in 1995. Gwyneth Jones also made a speciality of the role of Helena in *Die aegyptische Helena*. She headed the cast in a sumptuous studio recording of this opera for Decca under Antal Dorati in 1979, and there are also numerous 'live' recordings of her in that role (including a televised performance at the Bavarian State Opera in 1990). We cannot leave Strauss without also mentioning her radiant recording of his *Four Last Songs* (on CD, Koch, 1991), and her recording of twenty Strauss lieder accompanied by Geoffrey Parsons (on CD, Capriccio, 1988).

Finally, we come back to Wagner. Gwyneth Jones has been the only British singer ever to have sung a wide range of major Wagner soprano roles at Bayreuth, having been invited back year after year for some fifteen years. Indeed, she has been one of the few sopranos of any nationality to have been honoured in this way since 1951 – only Astrid Varnay, Martha Mödl, Birgit Nilsson and Waltraud Meier have achieved comparable feats. After singing Senta in *Die fliegende Holländer* and Sieglinde in *Die Walküre* to great acclaim at Covent Garden in 1965, Gwyneth Jones made her Bayreuth début as Sieglinde in 1966 in the two *Ring* cycles conducted by Otmar Suitner. The Bayreuth *aficionado* Penelope Turing reported in her account of that year's festival in her *New Bayreuth*: 'Gwyneth Jones created one of the chief sensations of the season with her Sieglinde. Lovely to look at, radiantly feminine, with a big and thrilling voice, she gave an outstanding performance. Her Sieglinde, already famous in London, took Bayreuth by storm.' However, the famous Wieland Wagner *Ring* production in which she took part in Bayreuth that year was recorded under Karl Böhm instead of Suitner, and with Leonie Rysanek as Sieglinde. Consequently, we have been left without a commercial recording of Gwyneth Jones in one of the Wagner roles to which she was best suited in terms of voice, personality and appearance. However, she repeated this role in Bayreuth in 1972 and an unofficial 'off the air' recording of this exists, as does one made at Covent Garden in 1965.

At the 1968 Bayreuth Festival she sang Eva in a Wolfgang Wagner production of *Die Meistersinger von Nürnberg*. However, this role did not suit her vocally and was not repeated. According to Penelope Turing, she looked the part, but 'her voice proved too large' and she had trouble adjusting to the role's lyric requirements. 'At times there was too much sheer sound.' This is presumably the main reason why she has also sung so little Mozart, although she did sing Donna Anna quite successfully in a production of *Don Giovanni* at Covent Garden conducted by Sir Colin Davis in 1967 and repeated that role at the Vienna State Opera in the 1970s (a performance of which was recorded by Austrian Radio in 1974). Her voice was simply too big and unwieldy for most of the Mozart soprano roles. With regard to its size and power, it was best suited to the dramatic soprano parts provided by Verdi and Beethoven, and to roles such as Senta, Sieglinde, Chrysothemis and the Dyer's Wife, rather than to either the lyric or the 'Amazon' soprano roles. She has sung several of the latter to great acclaim, but (as mentioned above) such roles have sometimes appeared to push her voice to or even beyond its natural limits.

She returned to Bayreuth in 1969 and 1970 to sing the role of Kundry in the celebrated Wieland Wagner production of *Parsifal*, under Horst Stein and Pierre Boulez, respectively. Writing about the 1970 festival, Penelope Turing noted that Gwyneth Jones's Kundry aroused 'considerable anxiety on behalf of this singer. Potentially, this was, and still can be, one of the most beautiful dramatic soprano voices on the operatic stage today. But her 1970 performances at Bayreuth and elsewhere have all too often given evidence of over-singing. Her soft singing can be exquisite, but the full voice spreads sadly.' We are in a position to judge for ourselves, however, since the 'live' recording which Deutsche Grammophon compiled from the 1970 performances is still widely available. The misgivings have been somewhat exaggerated, even if they were not altogether unfounded. Her performance is sometimes squally or shrill, but actually that is quite in keeping with Kundry's character, and Gwyneth Jones sings the part with great passion and dramatic cogency. Moreover, instead of bowing to suggestions that she was over-taxing her voice, Gwyneth Jones went on to confound her critics by successfully specializing in heavy duty roles, primarily in the Wagner and Strauss operas, from the 1970s onward. Although the occasional vocal shrillness and unsteadiness were never completely eliminated, she increasingly took even the heaviest roles completely in her stride. Far from wrecking her voice, she became renowned for her resilience and stamina.

At the 1970 and 1971 Bayreuth Festivals, she also very successfully sang the role of Senta in *Der fliegende Holländer*, which was recorded under Karl Böhm by Deutsche Grammophon and was still being chosen as the best currently available recording of the work for BBC Radio 3's 'Building a Library' in 2000. Ever since I first acquired it on LP in 1972, I have regarded this 'live' Bayreuth recording as the best-conducted *Flying Dutchman* ever, and was delighted when it was successfully transferred to CD. Its main strengths, apart from Böhm's exceptionally lithe and dramatic conducting (never has the score sounded so consistently inspired and so coherent), are the thrilling choral singing and the ability of Gwyneth Jones to encompass the extreme dynamic range of her role, vocally as well as dramatically. For once, even Senta's Ballad is beautiful, hypnotic and mysterious, rather than embarrassingly and excruciatingly tedious (even to a Wagner addict!). Her soft singing is exquisite, hauntingly beautiful and otherworldly, and her passion for the Dutchman is deeply heart-felt, palpable and affecting. Unfortunately, the male lead singers do not rise to the same heights. So it is primarily for the truly 'elemental' contributions of the conductor, orchestra, chorus and Gwyneth Jones that this performance demands to be widely known and cherished.

In 1972 Gwyneth Jones pulled off the rare feat of singing both of the female lead roles (Venus and Elisabeth) in Götz Friedrich's Bayreuth production of *Tannhäuser*, this time not in order to save the show by covering for an indisposed colleague, but as an integral part of the production concept. She successfully repeated this vocally taxing double-act at subsequent festivals, and in 1978 the production was video-taped (it is still available from Phillips). She looks bizarre (on account of the ridiculous costume she was made to wear) and sounds strained as Venus. However, she is warm, radiant, personable and in excellent voice as Elisabeth, a role to which she seems almost perfectly suited. She succeeds in making Elisabeth far less prissy and goody-goody than usual, and hence much more appealing than she often is.

During the 1980s and 1990s Gwyneth Jones sang many successful performances of the role of Isolde in *Tristan und Isolde*, in Britain, in the US and on the Continent, though not to my knowledge at Bayreuth. Perhaps her greatest triumph in this role took place at Covent Garden on 13 May 1982. In the words of Harold Rosenthal's review in *Opera*, Colin Davis, Jon Vickers and Gwyneth Jones succeeded in 'casting a Wagnerian spell over a Prom audience', not least because 'she was the Isolde of one's dreams, and vocally in far better form than for a very long time. She displayed few of those ugly top notes that have troubled us in the past, and seems to have conquered that wobble that afflicted her Wagner performances both here and at Bayreuth in recent years.' It is almost scandalous that neither the BBC nor Britain's record companies saw fit to record or videotape the Jones-Vickers partnership for posterity. This is the biggest gap in her official discography, though fortunately perform-ances by her as Isolde were televised in Germany, France and Belgium (and thus presumably survive on video), and there also exist unofficial 'off the air' audio tapes of her as Isolde in San Francisco (1980) and Toulouse (1994). But why no recordings or broadcasts of her British performances?

The only major Wagner soprano role which Gwyneth Jones has not sung on stage is Elsa in *Lohengrin*, perhaps as a result of her inauspicious experience as Eva in *Die Meistersinger*. She has, however, sung the demanding mezzo-soprano role of Ortrud in *Lohengrin*, both in a Bavarian studio recording under Raphael Kubelik for Deutsche Grammophon in 1971 (for which she was not in best voice) and on stage at Covent Garden in 1996. Gwyneth Jones has also performed and recorded rare repertoire, such as Cherubini's *Medea* (for Decca, 1967), Poulenc's *La voix humaine* (Paris, 1989, film), and the role of Esmeralda in an acclaimed recording of Franz Schmidt's *Notre Dame* (for Capriccio, 1989).

Although Dame Gwyneth Jones is hailed as a great *Welsh* soprano, one widely held regret must be that she has made so few appearances with the Welsh National Opera company. She performed Lady Macbeth in Verdi's *Macbeth* for WNO in 1963, and she returned to sing Leonore in Beeethoven's *Fidelio* in 1964, both under Brian Balkwill, but that was all. Perhaps there is still time for some amends to be made by engaging her to sing 'character' roles such as the Kostelnicka in Janáček's *Jenůfa* and the Mother in Engelbert Humperdinck's *Hänsel und Gretel*, both of which are in her repertoire and that of WNO. It is also a pity that her dream of turning Craig-y-nos, Dame Adelina Patti's mansion and theatre between Swansea and Brecon, into a Welsh Glyndebourne came to nought. Nevertheless, she will continue to be remembered as a great Welsh soprano with tremendous staying-power, powerful stage-presence, rare acting ability, and a strong and radiant voice, successfully deployed across a wide range of roles – above all those of Verdi, Beethoven, Wagner and Richard Strauss.

Acknowledgements
Penelope Turing, *New Bayreuth* (London, 1969).
Harold Rosenthal, *Opera* (July, 1982).

Margaret Price

Rian Evans

Margaret Price's singing has consistently been described with superlatives. The *Penguin Guide* verdict on her role as Amelia in Sir Georg Solti's recording of Verdi's opera *Un ballo in maschera* is typical. 'Shining out from the cast of Solti's set of *Ballo* is the gloriously sung Amelia of Margaret Price in one of her richest and most commanding performances on record, ravishingly beautiful, flawlessly controlled and full of unforced emotion.' This voice – pure and clear as a bell in the early years, velvet and even more expressive of a variety of vocal colours with maturity – has always been thrilling, with a technical assurance that makes the listener forget entirely the way in which such sounds are achieved and focus instead on the sheer beauty and dramatic power of the music. Margaret Price has achieved the highest acclaim in the realm of opera, on the concert platform, in the recording studio and as a consummate lieder singer. But if there is a single way of describing her, it is that she is regarded as one of the supreme Mozart singers of her time. To sing Mozart requires nothing short of perfection, and to be recognized as a supreme Mozart singer is quite simply the greatest accolade of all.

Margaret Price's professional career spanned over thirty-five years, during which she graced the stages of the world's most prestigious opera houses. As a lyric soprano, she excelled not only in Mozartean roles but in Verdi too and her repertoire included many of the great operatic figures, among them Norma, Ariadne and Adriana Lecouvreur. Her vocal artistry and musicianship were sought by some of the great conductors of the twentieth century, including Sir Georg Solti, Wolfgang Sawallisch and Carlos Kleiber and, happily for her admirers and for posterity, she made recordings with them. This major international career culminated in her being awarded a damehood in 1993, joining a very select band of singers. And yet, even among those who have sung her praises loudest and most consistently, there is a note of regret – a feeling that she may not have reached the highest possible peak of her potential. For some there is the regret that she was never contracted by Covent

Garden, an honour boasted instead by the Bavarian State Opera House in Munich. It is recognized that she herself may have contributed to such a state of affairs, by being her own sternest critic, sometimes withdrawing from roles, or simply not entertaining the idea in the first place. For a singer, erring on the side of caution is preferable to taking untoward risks, but in later years Margaret Price might understandably have grown to wish that she had ventured more. Nevertheless, it is the singer possessed of acute sensibilities, one who can empathize with the whole gamut of human experience, who is the most successful in reaching the emotional heart of music. Margaret Price is certainly one of these and, while the last quarter of a century has on the whole been an age of tenor adulation, to the cognoscenti she ranks with the all-time legends. If she has not become a household name, it is perhaps because alongside the perfect sound of heart-rending beauty there is a slightly enigmatic quality which also colours the work and the personality. It is partly this which makes her such a fascinating singer.

She was born in Blackwood in 1941, well before any Manic Street preaching. Music seems to have been part of her destiny: she was named Margaret Berenice, an operatic name if ever there was one (Berenice is the eponymous heroine of an opera by Handel and a character in Mozart's *La Clemenza di Tito*). Her parents were musical – both played the piano – her father, Glyn, a teacher who went on to become principal of Pontypool College of Further Education. Paternal pride in the intelligence and musical talent of the young Margaret was understandable, and all the more poignant in view of the fact that her brother John had what would now be termed very severe learning difficulties, then described more matter of factly as a mental handicap. Margaret was always deeply devoted to her brother but, for all that it was a warm and in many ways typically Welsh background, family life can hardly have been easy.

Singing was encouraged at her grammar school in Pontllanfraith as well as at home, but occasionally it became the subject of heated discussion. Her mother wanted her to compete in local eisteddfodau, but her father was against competitions. The upshot was that she did not compete, although Glyn Price seems to have relented in the case of one school eisteddfod when his daughter was in the fourth form. It was just as well since the adjudicator, Max Davies, was so impressed that he asked Margaret (who until then had intended teaching science) if she had thought of taking up singing seriously. His observation to her parents was that this was 'a voice in a million'. At Davies's instigation, Margaret went up to Trinity College of Music in London where she sang for Charles Kennedy Scott. Scott said that she should come and study with him immediately, apparently concerned lest such a highly promising voice be damaged through misguided advice. He saw to it that she was awarded an open scholarship to Trinity. She was just fifteen years of age.

Since her speaking voice was relatively low-pitched and, unusually for someone still only in her teens, had to it a dark quality, she was assumed at that stage to be a mezzo-soprano. Thus it was mezzo repertoire that was given to her, and she shone in it. By the end of only her second year at Trinity, she had won the coveted Elisabeth Schumann prize. At home during vacation time, the budding professional frequently sang in concerts. The late Kenneth Loveland, critic and journalist, remembered hearing Margaret Price at this time and realizing that here was a rare talent. In view of the singer's later propensity for self-criticism, it is perhaps not insignificant that Loveland also noted 'parental critics' in the audience, evidently unhappy at her choice of an ambitious encore, but unable to stop her. Back in London, more honours came her way. Trinity College's Ricordi Prize for Opera which she won in July 1961 was an augury for the future, though at that time an operatic career was still not what Margaret herself envisaged.

Although prizes brought kudos, performances brought only the bare minimum of expenses, and Margaret still needed to earn a living. While at Trinity, she began to sing for the semi-professional chorus, the Ambrosian Singers, and did so until 1962. But it was not enough. Glyn Price thought she ought to be doing more and took it upon himself to introduce his daughter to various opera houses. The first company to offer her an audition was the Welsh National Opera Company and Margaret was cast as the page Cherubino in Mozart's *Marriage of Figaro*. The production opened at the Grand

Theatre in Swansea on 7 March 1962. This would be the first step in an illustrious career, and she was still one month short of her twenty-first birthday.

Successful as that début performance was, it was as nothing compared with an extraordinary night just over a year later at the Royal Opera House, Covent Garden. This was the stuff of fairy tales. Auditioned first by Parry Jones, an outstanding Welsh tenor of an earlier generation, and then by the Royal Opera House's music director Georg Solti, Margaret Price was engaged as an understudy to the mezzo-soprano Teresa Berganza, again as Cherubino, in the production with Geraint Evans and Tito Gobbi. On Whit Monday of June 1963, the Spanish star fell ill shortly before the curtain was due up. When the announcement of her indisposition was made the audience groaned. By the end of the night they were cheering the hitherto unknown Welsh girl for a famous début.

Fêted in a blaze of press coverage, great predictions were made for Margaret Price's future. In the wake of the publicity, she even stood in for Shirley Bassey at the Sunday Night at the London Palladium. Singing Cherubino's aria 'Voi, che sapete', she was accompanied on a white piano by bandleader Jack Parnell. But the fuss soon subsided and while there were a couple of important engagements – first at Aldeburgh with Benjamin Britten's English Opera Group and then singing the part of Tatiana in a BBC television production of *Eugene Onegin* – there was none of the expected clamour for her services. However, as a result of her Covent Garden success, what was arguably the most formative relationship of her career began to develop. At her initial audition, she had been accompanied by James Lockhart, then pianist and repetiteur at the Royal Opera House. Scottish-born Lockhart, ten years Margaret Price's senior, became her coach and mentor and worked with her constantly for a period of twelve or so years. With Kennedy Scott at Trinity, Price had no voice training as such. He was more concerned with working through repertoire and nurturing the voice gently through a vulnerable stage. Under Lockhart's guidance, however, she developed a more sophisticated and conscious vocal technique. Her voice also gradually went up and she began to tackle soprano repertoire with growing confidence. Operatic work came in fits and starts – the role of Zerlina with Scottish Opera in 1964 and then a nun in Covent Garden's production of Puccini's *Suor Angelica* – but patience was rewarded when she won the prestigious Kathleen Ferrier Memorial Scholarship also in 1965.

In 1966 she made an impression as the angel in Handel's *Jephtha* at Glyndebourne, but she had to wait two years before what is counted as her main début there. Singing Konstanze in Mozart's *Die Entführung aus dem Serail*, a highly demanding role more usually taken by a coloratura, Margaret Price was brilliant. It marked an important turning point. Offers now began to arrive, among them one from Covent Garden to sing Pamina in their 1969 revival of Mozart's *Die Zauberflöte*. Most heartening was the invitation from Otto Klemperer to sing Marzelline in Beethoven's *Fidelio* at Covent Garden and to record with him the Mozart roles of Barbarina and Fiordiligi. Klemperer's support was a major factor in the progress of Price's career at this stage and crucial in strengthening her own self-belief. But she had also gained another advocate closer to home.

Geraint Evans was by now a firmly established international star and keen to do what he could to support other Welsh singers. It was his suggestion to Kurt Adler, general director at San Francisco Opera, that Adler take Margaret Price as Pamina in their *Zauberflöte*. That performance in October 1969 marked her American début; enthusiastic critic Arthur Bloomfield said in *Opera* that he was put in mind of Elisabeth Schumann, one of the most admired singers of her day. Given that Price had won the prize bearing Schumann's name at Trinity College thirteen years before, the remark must have pleased her. Later that autumn, it was at Geraint Evans's invitation that she returned to Wales and Welsh National Opera to sing the role of Nannetta in Verdi's *Falstaff*. Evans himself sang the title-role, also directing the production which brought some of Wales's most celebrated voices together to celebrate the investiture of the prince of Wales.

Margaret Price's career really took off in 1971 when the French producer Jean-Pierre Ponelle, who had been impressed by her in San Francisco, cast her as Donna Anna in his production of Mozart's *Don Giovanni* at Cologne. The critics raved. She was hailed as one of the sopranos of the century and her performance deemed 'a perfect sensation' in the German press. Following this with further success in Munich in the role of Amelia in Verdi's *Un ballo in maschera*, she was contracted to both houses, an irony never lost on those who would have liked to see her contracted to Covent Garden. From this point on, not only did her career take on a distinctly European perspective, but her personal life did too. She abandoned her base in London to live on the Continent, returning to Wales at regular intervals to visit her family and occasionally to perform.

Recital work had long since assumed as important a part of her career as opera. She and James Lockhart had become firmly established as a recital team, giving hundreds of performances over the years. Undoubtedly, the particular quality of her voice suited the intimacy of the medium, but Price's affinity for lieder had first been nurtured at home with her father when she was in her early teens. From the beginning of the partnership with Lockhart, her own instinctive musicianship and the efficiency of his coaching allowed her to embrace an ever widening range of music and styles with comparative ease. In performance, the understanding that existed between singer and pianist was implicitly reflected in interpretations of incredible sensitivity.

Price had several major attributes as a recitalist. Prime among these was an innate capacity to give colour and expression to words already crystal clear. Her considerable linguistic facility also meant that her recitals might feature any one or indeed all of five languages: German, French, Italian, Spanish and Russian, as well as English and Welsh. Thus recital programmes might include Mozart, Tchaikovsky, Debussy, de Falla and Schoenberg, with Britten arrangements as well as the more predictable German Romantic repertoire. The second Viennese school featured as often as the first and Berg's *Seven Early Songs* were particular favourites.

In 1968 Lockhart became musical director of Welsh National Opera and, over and above their recital work, he conducted many performances in which Price sang. His subsequent acceptance of the musical directorship of Germany's Kassel Opera in 1972 necessarily changed the pattern of their long-standing partnership. Lockhart's role as a mentor is one which Price has acknowledged generously. However, the idea, often mooted, of his role as a Svengali figure, enabling her to do things of which she would otherwise not have been capable, is surely mistaken. Whatever regrets there may have been, her career continued to blossom long after his influence had waned. Indeed far from receding in her priorities, lieder took on an increased importance.

Having made Munich her home, Margaret Price's distinction as a lieder singer was appreciated in Germany as never before and, in the person of Wolfgang Sawallisch, musical director and later intendant of the Bavarian State Opera, she found a musician whose integrity and innate pianism brought a polished warmth to their performances and recordings. Sawallisch was to be a vital influence during the Munich years and under his guidance Price was to undertake many new leading roles, notably in operas by Richard Strauss.

In 1976 she was engaged by the Paris Opera for her first Verdi part under Sir Georg Solti. She was to sing the role of Desdemona in *Otello* with Placido Domingo singing the title-role. The company engaged Royal Shakespeare Company director Terry Hands as producer; he was then associated primarily with highly acclaimed productions for the Comédie Française in Paris. Hands, presently director of Clwyd Theatr Cymru, remembers that before rehearsals for *Otello* began, he had been warned that Margaret Price could be difficult, but he found her to be 'absolutely lovely'. For both Price and Domingo it was essentially their first foray into such highly dramatic roles, and while this initially made for an element of vulnerability, Hands found working with them an immensely rewarding process. Unfortunately, what emerged as a stupendous partnership was denied the public at large on disc. Contractual obligations meant that Domingo was the only member of the cast absent from what is still classed as the definitive recording by Decca, but a live recording made at the Paris Opera issued on a French label, Forlane, is still talked about with bated breath by collectors.

Price and Domingo came together again for Covent Garden's *Otello* under the baton of Carlos Kleiber in 1980. It was a production that has assumed the status of legend and its opening night has been deemed to be one of the great nights in the opera house. Price was accorded the welcome of a returning heroine, and it must count as one of the landmarks of her career. Harold Rosenthal, the highly respected editor of *Opera* magazine, praised her beautifully burnished tones and described Price as holding the house in her thrall in the 'Salce' and Ave Maria. In thinly veiled criticism of Covent Garden management he declared it almost a scandal that she was not a regular visitor, while the rest of the British press 'discovered' her once more and wondered why she had been neglected. Why indeed? Together with Donna Anna and Maria Boccanegra, Desdemona is unquestionably one of Price's greatest roles and she was further acclaimed with Domingo in her début at the Metropolitan in New York in 1985. But what is particularly interesting about the Covent Garden production is that it convinced Carlos Kleiber that he had found the voice he needed to record Wagner's *Tristan und Isolde*. Although this was a role she desperately wanted to sing, Price knew she did not have the vocal stamina required to perform it on stage without damaging her voice. So her first reaction to Kleiber's request was that he must be mad. But Kleiber insisted that he did not want a German 'wobbler' for the young, innocent purity of Isolde. Price protested her unsuitability for several months, but eventually agreed to try the role. In due course, on the understanding she would never be persuaded to do it on stage, the recording was done in takes of sixteen to seventeen minutes over a period of weeks.

Price came to regard Kleiber as a genius and he elicited from her what is thought of as one of the most beautifully sung and subtle interpretations of the role. It was a huge achievement and Price said that when it was over she had felt that were she to drop dead the next day, she would at least die knowing she had done what she had most wanted. It was a golden time. In the same year as recording Isolde, she had been awarded a CBE, adding that to the honour accorded her in 1981 by the Bavarian State, who made her a Kammersängerin. In 1983, the University of Wales awarded her an honorary doctorate and around the same time, she sang in an unforgettable Verdi Requiem at the newly opened St David's Hall, a role which became almost a trademark.

So the kind of career of which a singer dreams was now effectively hers. Yet one cannot but suspect that Margaret Price was never as comfortable with life as she might have been. While the 1970s and

1980s had several high points, there must also have been anguish. For one thing, it could not have been easy to try and maintain a high-profile career at a time when producers and public were dictating that lithe, lissom sopranos made opera plots more believable. While she was philosphical about roles like Violetta in the early days – 'Who ever heard of a consumptive with my frame?' she is quoted as saying – it would not always have felt like a laughing matter. More damaging within the profession was a growing tendency to be bracketed with the great Italian pianist Arturo Benedetti Michelangeli, known for cancelling performances. Price clearly felt the need to husband her vocal resources with the utmost caution, but in an interview for BBC Radio 3 in 1999 she admitted that, while her aim had always been to keep her voice for as long as possible, her highly exacting approach might have cost her a better career.

In that same interview, Price discussed Covent Garden's 1987 *Norma*, a production created for her in recognition of the twenty-fifth anniversary of her début there. With a self-deprecation verging on self-sabotage she pronounced it 'a disaster from the word "go" '. Sir John Tooley, general director of the Royal Opera House wanted her to choose any opera she liked and she opted for *Norma*, having already sung the role with Zurich Opera in 1979 and in 1985 at the Munich Festival. It is understandable that the memory of 1987 was in retrospect painful: she suffered bronchitis and by the third performance had to withdraw. But her suggestion that the role was 'a big mistake' for her is hardly borne out by the review of Rodney Milnes, not a man given to hyperbole. Although he suggested that the staging was best forgotten, he thought her singing truly glorious. It is worth quoting him further, since his words are a forceful reminder of what made this one of the great Welsh voices. They also illustrate something of the complex nature of Price's career and the occasional disparity between her own perception and that of others.

She is no Sarah Bernhardt, but she has a natural dignity and eloquence of gesture all the more telling for its spare economy. Add to this her profound understanding of Bellini's idiom – i.e. an abundant musicianship that is creative not just instinctive – and the pungency of her diction and you have a Norma to be reckoned with. Time and again the sheer beauty of her voice (so rich, so creamy, so even from top to bottom) and her phrasing make one hold one's breath lest one miss an extra refinement of shading, a supple piece of portamento, a minutely calculated change of vocal colour – and all this not just in the set numbers but throughout the recitative as well. This was singing of the very highest order in which the burden of the drama was for the most part conveyed through the use of the voice and that I suppose is what bel canto is all about. A musical performance of great distinction, if only the visual side had come anywhere near it.

That hardly bespeaks 'all-round disaster' but perhaps it is inevitable that, even twelve years on, it should still have felt that like to Margaret Price. The successes of subsequent years were to be considerable – paramount among them recordings of Schubert and Schumann lieder with pianist Graham Johnson – but they were somehow not enough to obliterate that *Norma*. A perfectionist feels responsibility and disappointment acutely.

In the quick-flick annals of music history that are musical dictionaries, it is interesting to observe that Price, Margaret (after Leontyne in alphabetical order) is only a couple of entries away from that for prima donna. Yet for all that she has been strong-willed and outspoken, she has not generally subscribed to *grande dame hauteur*, or prima donna behaviour in the pejorative sense. As divas go, Margaret Price has demonstrably been a goddess with feet of clay – drinking, swearing, even smoking, and eating trifle. Yet part of a diva's role is to give us glimpses of a heaven and, in this instance, one that is not Valhalla.

After her retirement in 1999, Price returned to Wales to live in relative seclusion. She undertakes occasional masterclass teaching, where she sticks to her exacting principles and shows singers of a new generation how to strive for the perfection which she herself so often achieved. Early in 2001, she gave a masterclass for students at the Welsh College of Music and Drama, where I was present for a few brief minutes. Among the students was a young soprano singing the 'Et incarnatus est' from Mozart's C minor Mass. Her voice was pure and clear, her intonation good, and she appeared unafraid of heights. Margaret Price encouraged her to consider a way of breathing which would allow her to create a sound which underlined the transcendent beauty of what she suggested was Mozart's most heavenly music. One could not but feel a momentary pang of nostalgia and regret the passing of time.

Some weeks later I mentioned to a friend that I was writing this piece. 'Ah! Margaret Price!' she sighed. 'I shall never forget hearing her sing in a performance of Mozart's C minor Mass at Worcester Cathedral. It was the most beautiful sound I have ever heard. By the end of her aria there were several of us with tears in our eyes. It was just out of this world.'

Acknowledgements
Opera has been indispensable. See especially: A. Blyth, 'Margaret Price', *Opera* xxxvi (1985).
Ivan March, *Penguin Guide to Compact Discs and Cassettes* (1999).

Stuart Burrows

Phil George

When I was young and observing the adults in the Rhondda, I noticed a key accolade – 'he knows how it goes'. At its worst it is a phrase that suggests conformity, a fitting in with people's prejudices. At its best, it praises intuitive understanding, good judgement, an awareness of the people around you. There is no doubt that this positive sense applies perfectly to Stuart Burrows as a man and as a singer. From the moment he started singing as a boy, he knew how it went. In a professional career spanning forty years, he avoided vocal coaching and stayed with what came naturally.

At least, that was true of the sound. It was always full and pure, without any sense of the voice being forced. Across the whole range, he got on to phrases cleanly and without strain. But in a Mozart aria like 'Il mio tesoro' or in the extraordinary high pianissimo of the Sanctus from the Berlioz Requiem, descriptions like 'clean' or 'pure' carry no connotations of vocal blandness. Stuart Burrows has a warmth and tenderness that match his ease of delivery. No wonder that he led the revival of ballads and sentimental songs in hugely successful television series and recordings. In back kitchens throughout Wales, older citizens play a Stuart Burrows tape to cheer a grey day with emotion.

But 'doing what comes naturally' is clearly inadequate as an account of a major, sophisticated vocal career. How did he develop his remarkable refinement of taste and an aptitude for fine phrasing? How did he know what to avoid, what would not work for him? When I visited him in his spacious, memento-filled house in St Fagans, I wanted to press him on how he learned to be a singer and to discover whether there were any regrets at repertoire not pursued – for example, as a prominent international recitalist, he had never taken on a Schubert song-cycle.

Stuart Burrows is a fascinating mixture of warm generosity and shrewd judgment. His friendliness to strangers and to fans is well known. He told me lovely stories: of a chance meeting on a plane with a Jewish archaeologist who showed him the skull of a Hebrew slave from the time of Nabucco; of the gift-giving generosity of a rich Japanese fan reduced to tears by his Lensky in *Eugene Onegin*. But the shrewdness is always evident. Solti had once pressed him to sing Wagner, saying 'a good Mozart singer can sing anything within reason'. Yet even the iron-willed maestro could not persuade Burrows to take on Wagner's orchestration. 'Too thick, too heavy for my voice to carry.' He lasted forty years at the top because he knew how to take care of himself.

This canny quality is the key to how he learned. If style in singing came naturally, it was because he was instinctively shrewd and observant. It is in the same way that we talk of great rugby players as intuitive, meaning something more than the possession of physical gifts and spatial awareness. We also mean that, from day one, they had the ability to watch and learn. So it was with Stuart Burrows, who happened to be a very good rugby player. In fact when he was still a schoolteacher on £9 a week, he was offered a lucrative contract with Leeds Rugby League Club. He went as far as Cardiff Station, meeting the scout with the train tickets to 'go north', and then, very politely, changed his mind. The career that soon began to shape, winning the Blue Riband at the 1959 National Eisteddfod and making his debut with Welsh National Opera in 1963, was the prize for his spontaneous decision.

However, Stuart Burrows had done his key watching and learning well before this time, in and around the bustling town of Pontypridd. Famously born in the same Cilfynydd street as Geraint Evans (who was to help him in his early professional career), his mother sent the boy with the wonderful voice to a singer and teacher called Bert Gregory Evans. Burrows remembers the wise teacher saying, 'he knows how to sing'. Evans decided that he would not mess with the voice, but he would teach him phrasing and show him around the repertoire. For a couple of years from the age of ten, Stuart Burrows sang about three concerts a week around south Wales, working his way through the Schubert and Handel in the old *Novello Song Book*.

At the age of nineteen he discovered his tenor voice and started to build a huge repertoire in oratorio. He remembers key figures like the remarkable Pontypridd choral director, Gwyneth Pearce, and a music-making German family with whom he used to practise. 'One Sunday we tried "Comfort ye" and "Ev'ry valley" from *Messiah* and I couldn't manage the breathing on the long runs in the aria. My German friend said that I was young and didn't yet have the technique. I told him I'd have it by the next weekend. And I did.' It was simply a matter of harnessing his natural lung-power, a capacity that sustained wonderfully long phrases throughout his career, perhaps most notably in the aria 'Fuor del mar' from *Idomeneo*. The key point in Burrows's anecdote is the combination of a 'can do' self-belief with a performing outcome of beauty and poise. Fashions in Baroque performances may have changed, but his *Messiah* recordings with Davis and Richter are still noble and eloquent. And he was doing it as he had always done it.

The story of Stuart Burrows's international career as a lyric tenor began with a happy case of talent spotting. Working for the BBC in television studio opera, he was seen by Stravinsky who whisked him off to Athens to sing in his *Oedipus Rex*. That was in 1965, and two years later he began an association with the Royal Opera House which lasted twenty-five seasons. In houses across the world, notably in Vienna, San Francisco and the Metropolitan Opera, New York, he starred in Donizetti, Massenet, the Berlioz *Faust*, *Onegin*, and as Alfredo in *La traviata*. It is probably fair to say that he was not characteristically a Verdian: there was plenty of voice, but it did not have what is usually meant by 'an Italianate ring'. But wherever a role required refinement of tone and line, he was first choice across the world, particularly in Donizetti, the French repertoire and in Mozart.

In Mozart opera, Stuart Burrows reigned supreme. It is extraordinary that in Margaret Price and Burrows, Wales produced two of the greatest Mozartians of the twentieth century. Any stereotyping of Welsh singing that fixes it only in the glories of Verdi's rousing and burnished intensity needs to remember the elegance of these two singers. Burrows was the natural successor to Fritz Wunderlich and surpassed the stylish German as a Mozartian tenor. From early in his career he had a love affair with Don Ottavio's aria 'Il mio tesoro' from *Don Giovanni* and no one sings Ferrando's 'Un' aura amorosa' from *Così fan tutte* more beautifully, particularly in the gentle way he returns to the opening phrase of the tune. He loved singing Tamino in *The Magic Flute*, which was his major début role at both Covent Garden and Vienna. 'It needs body in the voice as well as a lovely, easy sound', he says. And the earthiness of Stuart Burrows is apparent when he relishes the clean-cut, portamento-free Mozartian arias as 'like eating a slice of the best bread and butter'.

Some of Burrows's best and worst moments have been in Mozart on the operatic stage. He remembers with pride when he was singing

Ottavio with Karajan in Salzburg. He was front-stage and saw the exacting maestro put his baton down and let him sing. But he remembers in one producer-driven European house having to sing 'Fuor del mar' while climbing up a step-ladder. In the end he refused: it made the piece unsingable. You can tell that he tolerated producers' ideas as long as they never got in the way of the music. You sense he was never excited by concept-productions. He preferred Vienna where they did it straight, 'no messing', although he took against Viennese high-handedness when he had to do a two-and-a-half-hour rehearsal of *Faust* on the morning of the performance, having been available all the previous week.

However, his relationships with great conductors were full of empathy and delight and they reflect the range of his repertoire beyond Mozart and Italian *bel canto*. He enjoyed singing French music – Berlioz, Massenet, Fauré songs – and had a real affinity with the line and the colours of that repertoire. He felt particularly at ease with Berlioz orchestration and would regularly fly all over the world just to sing the six or seven minutes of the Sanctus in the Requiem. He recorded it with Leonard Bernstein, and in a great performance at Les Invalides in Paris they agreed to divide the piece in half, splitting it between high pianissimo and full voice. 'It suited me down to the ground', he says with pleasure. The thrilling recording is notable for taste and accuracy as much as for ease in voice production.

Stuart Burrows's working relationship with Solti was one of the most significant of his musical partnerships – he does a very good Solti imitation, an example of his excellent ear for languages. In fact, he learned Lensky from *Eugene Onegin* in Russian, parrot-fashion, with the help of a Cardiff University Russian specialist. Telling the story, he is pleased that he could learn the Russian from his Welsh base, even though in the six weeks it took him to master the words he was jetting to performances far and wide. The pleasure he takes in this Welsh launch-pad and his demystifying sense of himself as a working singer are totally characteristic and without affectation.

It is important to note that he had sung Lensky previously in English and really understood the role. Listening to the Solti recording, particularly the gorgeous singing of the Second Act aria, you are reminded of his detailed attention to the musical unfolding of feeling and character. Superficial criticism has sometimes suggested that he was concerned to achieve mere beauty of sound. In this aria, the emotional storyline is beautifully sustained with a refinement of tone that was more than an end in itself. It is another sign of that musical discrimination – of knowing how it goes – that Burrows has always shown in his work.

It is typical that he never resented Solti the taskmaster. It was important to get things right, otherwise why bother. And though he never capitulated to Solti's pressure for him to sing Wagner, he would go a long way to meet the maestro's demands. He was once singing Alfredo in *La traviata* with Beverley Sills in Boston (I should say that my reservation above about the great tenor's Verdi style needs to take on board his huge success in this role, particularly at the New York Met in the mid-1970s). Boston performances finished late and he still had not 'come down' from the show at three in the morning. Suddenly there was a phone call from Chicago. Solti was put through to him saying 'Stuart, I want you to record Beethoven Ninth with me here tomorrow.' Limousines, flights had all been fixed. In a final local flight to the recording venue in the Mid West, Solti would go over the score with him: 'Stuart, you *must* come. You need to leave in a couple of hours.' Burrows did the trip, made the well-known recording in two takes and flew back to sing another *Traviata* in Boston.

The story reflects his huge respect for Solti, because he was always well known as a singer who looked after himself. Sing the wrong role, take on excessive physical challenges and you could do serious damage. To last forty years in an international singing career, you had to know how it goes. Jet lag and air travel can cause major voice trouble and at the very least dry out the voice for a performance. Stuart Burrows was blessed with a flexible, natural instrument – 'I'd wake up at 6 in the morning and sing without any big warm-up' – but even he had to take care and he knew how to do it. A notable exception was when he was doing *Maria Stuarda* with Joan Sutherland and went on despite having tracheitis. He did it because the public had come to see the great coloratura. She and they should not be let down. But he is still appalled at the recklessness of it. You have to look after yourself.

However, Stuart Burrows is most widely remembered for looking after his audience. He took to television, as to recording, like a mellifluous duck to water. *Stuart Burrows Sings* was a huge hit for eight years on BBC network television in the late 1970s and 1980s, reaching up to eighteen million viewers for a programme. The audience loved the way he mixed his repertoire, championing operetta and sentimental ballads in a way that produced audible sniffs from critics who admired him in opera and oratorio – and audible sighs and cries of 'Bravo' from the general audience. As one critic wrote of his *Songs for You* disc, 'Like his illustrious predecessor the great John McCormack, Stuart Burrows is not only a distinguished lyric tenor, but also a popular entertainer who can by his artistry give great pleasure to countless people with simple, unsophisticated musical tastes.' Yes.

Burrows was totally confident and unapologetic in this aspect of his career. As a deeply-rooted performer, he knew and respected both audience and material. The same good judgement and warmth mixed with refinement were brought to the lighter repertoire as to Mozart. 'In Vienna they sing Lehar as seriously as any great Viennese Classic,' he says. And he is totally opposed to the notion of 'sentiment' as meaning weak-minded slush. Releasing his record *Songs of Love and Sentiment*, he believed that if you wanted to say 'I love you' to the great love of your life, you could say it with 'Love, could I only tell thee' and feel it was just right, rather than shameful indulgence. The important thing was not to parody Victorian ballads as some singers did in the revival of the repertoire that Burrows began.

Not the least intriguing and bold feature of his engagement with such material is that he took it on to the recital stage all over the world. Accompanied by John Constable, Stuart Burrows had a busy and widely praised international career as a recitalist in New York, Tanglewood, Salzburg, and Vienna. Before coming to his use of ballads in this context, it is worth reflecting on the classical core of his solo performances. He was once described as 'jolly and confident', enjoying himself on the stage. Yet both his range and his exclusions are more thought-provoking than that description suggests. There is a revealing paragraph in a *Music and Musicians* review of a Wigmore Hall recital in 1978, a performance before an audience which included fellow singing stars like Janet Baker.

As recitals go it was a pretty popular programme with old favourites by Beethoven, Strauss and Fauré sung with splendid tone, telling sensitivity and perfect control, notably in Beethoven's *Resignation*. It would be good to hear Burrows getting his teeth into meatier stuff, even a *Winterreise*, and there are not so many singers that one would wish that on. Not that there was anything pallid here, chestnuts like Strauss' *Zueignung* were given the full works with John Constable splendid in the thick textured accompaniments. A Fauré group was perhaps a shade on the heavy side, but again beautifully phrased with good sound.

This is revealing in two ways. Firstly, that Stuart Burrows had 'telling sensitivity' and a gift for depth of sound in darker pieces. Secondly, that there was some regret that he had not taken on 'meatier stuff'. In fact, I asked him if he had ever been tempted to interpret a Schubert song-cycle. He said that he preferred variety and that anyway, you did not go for this repertoire when Fischer-Dieskau was at the 'height of his powers'. Some of his admirers may wish he had shown less caution in such choices.

However that may be, Burrows had remarkable success in introducing so-called lighter material to the mix of his concert programmes. The Wigmore Hall reviewer went on to describe how he moved through some of Britten's most popular folk-song settings to 'a gaggle of Welsh folksongs'. The broadly positive and friendly reviewer showed his distance from this kind of music when he noted that Burrows ushered in his encores with '*The Mountains of my home*, which, for those of us in the audience who do not hail from the land of the leek, he sang in English.'

London provincialism was put in its place by a much more heartfelt embrace of Stuart Burrows's taste for English and Welsh ballads at one of Europe's most prestigious venues. He was an extremely popular recitalist at the Brahmssaal in Vienna and, on one occasion, they would not let him go at the end. He winked at John Constable at the piano and launched into some of his songs of love and sentiment to respond to the demand for encores. They brought the house down. So much so that the director of the Brahmssaal asked him back to give a complete recital of this largely Victorian repertoire in English and Welsh. He had another resounding success. The audience treated the songs with respect because they had no league-table mentality or discourse of deprecating the sentimental. They came to the unfamiliar material totally fresh.

In the English ballads, Stuart Burrows emphasized the importance of singing them correctly, without irony or inverted commas. Above all, he was passionate about good enunciation. These songs had lapsed from memory and the diction on recordings was crucial to their revival. Whether it is 'Until', 'I'll sing thee songs of Araby', or 'I'll walk beside you', 'the listener should be able to learn the words of the song from the disc'. We may not all share Burrows's taste or seriousness about some of these songs but, with many of them, he releases a really affecting charm that moves and surprises.

Perhaps more importantly, he championed the fine Welsh-language song repertoire that he believes can rival some of the best German lieder. The extended form and storytelling dramas of these songs are qualities he was determined to bring to an international audience. Particular favourites were Bradwen Jones's 'Paradwys y Bardd', Morfydd Owen's 'Gweddi y Pechadur', and Morgan Nicholas's 'Y Dieithryn'. The fact that this tradition of song has lived at Carnegie Hall or in the record collections of English-speaking Welsh people, and not just on the eisteddfod stage, is down to the commitment of Stuart Burrows. He sings them with the subtlety, refinement and attention to detail he brings to Schubert's 'Du bist die Ruh' or to Fauré's 'Sylvie'.

Burrows is fascinating when talking about the challenge and the psychology of the solo recital. As with his television presentation, he projected an inviting, pleasure-taking persona, a stage reflection of his own delight in singing. But the challenge is remembered and relished with the young rugby-player's 'go for it' attitude. The piano accompaniment may give the voice more scope to be heard in its vocal gymnastics but 'You're there on your own in the end, naked – it's you and your voice.' You can tell that he loved it. Yet the great artist also reflects on the opportunity to 'get inside' each composer in a recital. Once again, as with his extraordinary singing of Lensky on the operatic stage, he was always drawn to a detailed unfolding of the emotional experience. It was all there in the music, to which you owed ultimate respect. Those early teachers in south Wales taught him that respect.

Stuart Burrows has taken to retirement with grace. A period of illness after an operation seemed to act as a watershed. He does not miss singing now. Nevertheless, he participates fully in the musical world in the way that great retired singers are expected to do. In recent years he has been in demand as an adjudicator at some of the world's leading vocal competitions, including the Sommerakadamie Mozarteum in Salzburg, the Queen Elizabeth International Music Competition of Belgium, and Cardiff Singer of the World. He has given international masterclasses in London and was invited by the Kodály Institute to give masterclasses at the Chetham's School of Music in Manchester. He enjoys teaching immensely.

When I told friends and colleagues that I was going to interview Stuart Burrows and write this essay, there was a general murmur of affection for the great tenor. A leading Welsh singer simply said 'lovely man, great Mozart singer'. Our friend and childminder recalled him coming to a shop where she worked – 'real gent', she said. In fact, there is a sense in which the full range of his achievement became almost invisible in Wales because he belonged so completely to the public. His popularity on television, his unaffected personality and his deep rootedness in Welsh life made him 'ours'. But the shrewd judge and fine artist also belongs to a wider world – the Met and Carnegie, San Francisco and Santa Fe, Tanglewood and Paris, Brahmssaal and Vienna Opera, Karajan and Solti. And ultimately he belongs to himself, with that sure sense of 'doing what comes naturally' and of his own gift that he has always shown.

I left him in St Fagans to prepare for an evening of memories and anecdotes that he was giving in the Valleys. He does it often, usually in the context of charity fundraising. He'll do it with plenty of sentiment but without a moment of falseness. Always there will be the sharp observation to match the warmth of feeling. Walking to the door, we were still talking about the ballads for which he cares so much. 'I tell you what', he said, 'I have a lot of fun using some equipment to turn old tapes into CD compilations for friends and people who are interested. Would you like one?' Two days later, it came in the post.

Acknowledgements
With warm thanks to Stuart Burrows for a frank, vivid and wide-ranging interview.

Gwynne Howell

Barrie Morgan

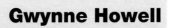

Those of us who were fortunate enough to see Gwynne Howell's portrayal of Hans Sachs in English National Opera's 1984 production of *The Mastersingers of Nuremberg* witnessed an outstanding artist realizing his full musical and dramatic potential. The poet cobbler is a monumental role that demands both great vocal and artistic maturity. It has been likened to climbing Everest and then jumping off the top. A bass in particular has to conserve his vocal power in the first two acts to handle the high baritonal tessitura of Act Three. Harold Rosenthal commented in his review of the first night in *Opera* that Howell sang 'Sachs with a richness and beauty of tone which was unbelievable' in the last act. However, earlier in the evening where I was sitting in the upper circle, his voice had been at times swamped by a less than translucent orchestra. Four weeks later Howell had gained sufficient experience to pace his performance to perfection, with the same critic noting that he 'was in glorious voice right from the first entrance'.

These performances were the culmination of a full year's preparation. His coach, Alastair Dawes, who had recently returned from South Africa and was in need of a London address, moved in with the Howell family for the first three months. He and Howell worked together for two hours every morning and afternoon, with Howell singing longer and longer sections of the opera as he learned it to build up his vocal stamina. It was after a performance in his second series of performances in 1989 (Reginald Goodall had forced him to withdraw from a series of performances in 1986 to prepare his first Gurnemanz in *Parsifal*) that Howell for the first time had the satisfaction at curtain-call of feeling fresh enough to sing the part again: having reached the summit and jumped off, he was ready for another ascent. 'I went home and said to Mary, my wife, that if I never sang again I would feel fulfilled as an opera singer.'

Howell was born in Gorseinon in June 1938, but lived for the first seven years of his life in Tonpentre in the Rhondda Valley. He grew up bilingual from speaking Welsh to his mother and her parents, and at a Welsh Sunday school. This stood him in good stead when his parents moved to Gwauncaegurwen, which he estimates was then 80 per cent

Welsh-speaking. Howell's mother was musical and he was no stranger to strains of melodies from light operetta and musicals in the home. His first formal introduction to music was piano lessons, but he preferred to practise snooker. The arrival of the eleven-year-old Howell at Pontardawe Grammar School coincided with the appointment of a new music teacher, Caryl Williams, who was instructed by the headmaster to start a choir. This is where it all began: for the first time, as a boy soprano and then boy alto, Howell started to enjoy making music as a founder member of that choir.

Unusually his voice did not break in the sense that he was unable to sing for a period. It changed gradually in tone rather than pitch, and he continued to sing both as a boy mezzo and a very light baritone. The first piece of advice he received about his voice came during this period from the local doctor. Dr Thomas was visiting his mother and heard Gwynne singing upstairs, whereupon he shouted in Welsh 'Hey, Mario Lanza, shut up and give your voice a chance to develop'. Mario Lanza, the tenor lead in various films of musicals, was almost a cult figure in south Wales in the mid-1950s. I recall participating in a heated discussion in Barry Grammar School about the relative merits of Mario Lanza and Jussi Björling, during which the music master threw a record on to my front desk saying, 'Let's listen to this new recording.' I recoiled, expecting it to shatter, but it was my first introduction to the new 33rpm vinyl records. In this digital age, it is easy to forget the large gulf between the excitement and joy of experiencing live music and listening to recorded music in the 1950s.

Gwauncaegurwen enjoyed a very rich musical life for a town of its size. Howell recognizes that this, along with being immersed in the musical lilt of the Welsh language, gave him two significant advantages in 'mining' the raw material of a beautiful voice. The local cinema converted to a 1,000-seat concert hall in which as a young grammar-school boy he saw the Cwmgorse and Gwauncaegurwen Operatic Society mount productions of such old favourites as *The Arcadians* and *Desert Song*. On another occasion he recalls the tenor Rowland Jones and the baritone Roderick Jones, principals at Sadler's Wells Opera (the forerunner of ENO), giving a celebrity concert. His first 'professional' performance was in the hall in a concert with the London Philharmonic Orchestra conducted by Norman Del Mar. 'The only way the organisers could get an audience was for the choir to be made up of boys from the local grammar schools so that their parents would buy a couple of tickets.'

Howell received his first individual singing lesson when he was in the sixth form from Phil Adams of Neath, a member of the Glynneath Operatic Society in the evenings and a shunter on the railway during the day. The 'lessons' largely comprised Phil, a thunderous high baritone, and Howell singing the same part at the top of their voices to the consternation of the neighbours. He still had no aspirations of entering the profession and in 1958 went up to University College Swansea to read geography and play rugby. But he continued with his singing lessons in the first and third years, this time with Redvers Llewellyn. Like many geographers before and after him who became town-planners (I must have taught more than a hundred and married one), Howell on graduation obtained a job as a planning assistant with Kent County Council. Cut off from his Welsh roots, he rather lost heart for singing as a member of the local choir rehearsing for a performance of *Messiah* in Dover. The conductor, 'a toffee-nosed young Cambridge graduate', was only satisfied that the eight basses were blending together when Howell stopped singing and mouthed his words.

To qualify as a chartered town planner, it was necessary to attend a postgraduate diploma course. It was a happy coincidence that the University of Manchester offered one of the best courses in the country and that Redvers Llewellyn had recommended studying singing at the Royal Manchester College of Music. Once he had settled in the city, Howell approached Frederick Cox, the principal of RMCM, to enquire if it would be possible to have some singing lessons. Although he made it clear that he had no ambition to be a professional singer, Cox asked Howell to sing and, recognizing the potential in his voice, asked Gwilym Jones to work with him. Jones was from north Wales, and teacher and pupil soon enjoyed a natural affinity. He was instrumental in making Howell the star he was to become, both developing his voice and giving to it the technical security that is one of its hallmarks. It is one of Gwynne Howell's abiding regrets that during his first year as a professional singer Gwilym Jones died, so that he never enjoyed the full fruits of the seeds he had nurtured.

The newly qualified town planner stayed on for three years in Manchester working for the city corporation. He sang in concert performances of *Otello* and *The Trojans* with Barbirolli and the Hallé Orchestra, and appeared in various student productions. Just as *The Mastersingers* was later to represent the climax of Howell's career, it was also its launching pad. Tom Hammond of Sadler's Wells Opera heard him sing Pogner at a student performance at RMCM and invited him to audition for the company. The audition, auspiciously, took place on St David's Day, 1 March 1968: Howell felt predestined not to fail. He was offered a contract to start within a month, but true to himself insisted on giving his employers adequate notice.

Howell, who had just turned thirty with eleven stage performances under his belt and no repertoire to speak of, drove from Manchester to London on 31 July and reported for work the following morning at Sadler's Wells Theatre. The change in his lifestyle was equally abrupt. Within two years he had made 280 stage performances in a wide range of minor roles, including the Night-Watchman in the second series of *Mastersingers* performances which established Reginald Goodall late in his career as a great Wagnerian. His new singing teacher, Otakar Kraus, guided him through these important years, giving him advice on interpretation and how to develop a professional career. Howell was invited to audition for the Royal Opera House, and made his Covent Garden debut as the First Nazarene in *Salome* under Georg Solti, its musical director, in June 1970.

It was in oratorio, however, that Gwynne Howell initially captured the limelight. Within four years of turning professional, he was singing the Verdi Requiem with Solti and the Chicago Symphony Orchestra in Chicago and at the Carnegie Hall. By this time he had sung two performances of the Missa solemnis, which has a 'dreadfully difficult bass part'. The first was in a broadcast concert at the Proms with Colin Davis. 'There was I in nappies singing alongside three icons of oratorio – Heather Harper, Josephine Veazey and Richard Lewis.' The second was with Carlo Maria Giulini in a televised concert in St Paul's Cathedral to celebrate Britain's entry to Europe, during which Howell became so mesmerized by Giulini's direction that he forgot to breathe during a three-beat pause in the Agnus Dei. 'It was as though, after a kick-around at Gwauncaegurwen park, my first real game was at Cardiff Arms Park and my second at Wembley.'

Howell pays particular tribute to three conductors in his

development: Georg Solti, Reginald Goodall and Colin Davis. Solti was very supportive and inspirational over a ten-year period. 'In many ways he nurtured me, but you never get too long a time with these maestros. I remember going home after a performance of the B-Minor Mass saying "that's it, I feel I won't work with Solti again" and I didn't. My voice had not been quite as agile and flexible because I had been singing bigger and more demanding roles.' Howell looks on Reginald Goodall both as mentor and guru. 'Reggie would elate, frustrate, praise and destroy you all at the same time, but on reflection it was something very special.' He remains especially appreciative of Goodall's capacity 'to get inside music' and, as a singer, of his unconventional, and not always clear, beat which meant the orchestra was careful and lacked the confidence to play Wagner too loudly.

While he also learnt a great deal from Colin Davis, their relationship was different in the sense that in one way they were embarking on a journey of discovery together. Although previously musical director of Sadler's Wells Opera, Davis could still be described primarily as an orchestral conductor who conducted opera when he assumed the musical directorship of the Royal Opera in 1971. Davis's overall mastery of interpretation bringing orchestra and voices together, and Howell's diction and mastery of singing long, legato phrases, were learnt with the House's Italian coach, Ubaldo Gardini. The impact was immediate. While his wife used to complain that she could not hear any of his English words, when he returned to ENO as Raleigh in *Gloriana* she understood every word.

Recording sessions with Benjamin Britten stand out in Howell's memory from his early years. He was asked to go to the Kingsway Hall to do a test recording as Christus in the *St Matthew Passion*. Twenty minutes into an hour-long session the pianist had still not turned up, at which point Britten, who unbeknown to the rookie Howell was one of the world's greatest accompanists, said rather diffidently 'I hope you don't mind, I think I will have to play for you'. Christus is largely recitative and rather than just put a chord down for Howell to pitch the phrase he played the vocal melody, as though wanting him to succeed. After missing the original recording with a cold, Howell recorded his part in the intimate setting of Aldeburgh with only Britten, Pears and Stuart Bedford, the harpsichordist.

'Touching music' with great conductors, creating music in 'fine lace' by one-to-one contact over a piano is something from which Howell has gained immense pleasure, although he fears that demands on conductors' time make it less and less common. 'Getting a feeling of what the conductor wants from his hands and from his face; taking every word to be sung, whether it is too soon, too heavy, too light, to paint a colour picture of a person with the voice.' Ricardo Muti likes to prepare this way, and Howell did it with Antonio Pappano, the new musical director of the Royal Opera House, in rehearsing the thirty-four notes the Jailer sings in *Tosca* in his most recent recording.

Howell took tremendous inspiration as a young singer from hearing Boris Christoff sing the title-role in *Boris Godunov*. 'I was always fascinated how in the death scene he managed to get into his tone a sound that seemed to come from his body but filtered through his vocal chords.' However, not only did Christoff not speak to him in the eighteen performances they did together but he actively tried to undermine him. Renowned for his loathing of fellow basses, he met his match in the unassertive Welshman. On the first night Christoff, sitting on the throne near to death, started making a gurgling sound as Pimen began his tale of the shepherd, so loudly that Howell was put off his singing. He banged his stick on the stage and looked straight at Christoff which caused the audience to look at him, making him stop.

Their next encounter came in *Don Carlos*. At the dress rehearsal, Christoff as Philip II stepped between him and the conductor at the tempo change at the start of the confrontation scene with the Grand Inquisitor. At least this time he had given his adversary a chance to prepare his reaction. When he tried to do it again on the first night, Howell had taken an extra half-step forward and thrust the Inquisitor's five-foot stick parallel to the stage at chest height to stop him moving. As they strode off, Howell ten yards in his wake, Christoff remaining in character stopped outside his adversary's dressing room and half inclined his head, as if to concede. While it was never directly articulated, the respect extended to Howell's singing. A dresser told him some years later that on one occasion when he was on stage as Pimen, Christoff turned up the volume on the internal speakers he had asked to be installed in his dressing room and told him how good Howell's voice was.

The other singer who made Howell realize how much more he had to develop if he were to reach the pinnacle of his profession was Joan Sutherland when he sang Raimondo with her in the title-role of *Lucia di Lammermoor*. In the Act II duet in the dress rehearsal, he entered after her and sang till he ran out of breath, only to find she was still in full flight. 'She could still have been singing when she got back to the dressing room!' She told Howell to squeeze her arm so that they could 'come off' together. Later in the mad scene, for the first time in his career, he felt his ears ringing with the vibration of a soprano's voice, it was so powerful and focused.

Great nights at the opera, of course, are not altogether predictable. Some ten years later I saw Sutherland for the first time when she was nearing the end of her career in *Esclarmonde*, with Howell as Emperor Phorcas, an evening Peter Stead, the coeditor of this volume, and I had been greatly anticipating. While much of her singing was exciting and beautiful, her voice was not under such secure command and phrases which previously she would have caressed were being clipped. And then there was a bomb scare! Having evacuated the theatre, any remaining magic was lost in watching the cast crossing Floral Street in single file in the rain. The performance restarted, but my memories of Sutherland, unlike those of Howell, must be from records rather than from the thrill of live performance.

Throughout his career Gwynne Howell has been an outstanding interpreter of basso cantabile parts, to which he brings purity of utterance and musical line. Seldom do a voice and personality meld so perfectly as to make a singer so suited for a particular type of part. He has a beautiful voice: it is pure, rich-toned, mellifluous and sonorous. He develops lines with a pure, Italianate legato. His characterizations have been variously and consistently described as: dignified, benevolent, sympathetic, compassionate, noble, gentle, human, mellow, paternal, touching, warm. Most of these characteristics are readily discernible in his personality. This mix has made him one of the foremost interpreters of Sachs, Gurnemanz, Pimen, Pogner, King Mark (*Tristan and Isolde*), Fiesco (*Simon Boccanegra*), Bluebeard (*Duke Bluebeard's Castle*), Gremin (*Eugene Onegin*) and Dosifey (*Khovanshchina*). Surprisingly, given his well-developed sense of humour, Howell is not noted for his portrayal of comic characters, although he has had plenty of experience of playing Basilio (*Il barbiere di Siviglia*), Bartolo (*Le nozze di Figaro*) and the Cook (*The Love for Three Oranges*).

Howell's performances display fine musicianship. He tells a story of Carlos Kleiber just making swinging gestures at rehearsal when he was conducting him as Colline in the 'Coat' aria of *La bohème* at the Met. When asked if everything was all right, Kleiber replied 'I don't need to conduct when you sing.' Invariably vocally secure because of his sound technique, Howell has maintained a very high standard of performance over the thirty years of his career. I must have read at least 150 reviews of his performances in *Opera* while preparing to write this article, and I would only describe five as negative. Many allude to his consistency and reliability.

It is also noticeable how often Howell, perhaps building on his bilingualism, has been complimented for his pronunciation of foreign languages, from French to Russian. Building on his training at Covent Garden with Gardini and the German coach, Hilda Beal, he is arguably the best exponent amongst present-day singers of English diction, a most unmusical language. For example, Andrew Porter wrote about his performance as Pimen with Welsh National Opera in 1998: 'his beautiful voice making sense at once of the music and the words, for Howell knows how to sing in English, how to give English phrases the clarity, colour and stresses that bring them to life'. He is now passing on his experience to young singers as a coach in ENO's Jerwood Young Singers Programme.

And yet, Gwynne Howell has not achieved the fame of many of his fellow countrymen featured in this book. This is probably in part because powerful and dark voices that thrill the audience are currently in fashion; Howell's vocal characterizations are moving rather than thrilling. If one moment caught the essence of Howell's artistry it was as King Mark singing softly and tenderly about his love for his wife while sitting on the prompt box to engage directly the audience at the Coliseum. However, operatic fame also tends to reflect the number of stamps in your passport rather than the number of roles in your repertoire which are delivered at an international level of distinction. Howell has largely chosen to follow a different type of career to the jet-setting star, because he has been driven more by the pleasure he and audiences take from his performances than by self-aggrandizement.

These choices need partly to be understood in the context of the personality of an unassuming man who has an unusually strong belief in predestination ('you have the career you are meant to have') and perhaps lacks a little self-belief.

Howell turned down two roles in particular which a more ruthlessly ambitious singer might have accepted because they might open doors. It was planned that he sing Pogner and Fasolt in the Solti *Ring* at Bayreuth. He did not take up the offer when he was only offered Fasolt because rehearsals clashed and it would have meant three months' rehearsals for three performances. In 1990 he was offered the opportunity to sing Sachs in the last two performances of a series of *Die Meistersinger* at the Royal Opera House under Dohnányi. He declined because he did not feel he could do the role justice by jumping in for two performances without adequate rehearsal. Artistic reasons also led him to reject the opportunity to sing Wotan in an entire *Ring* cycle under Goodall at ENO. Howell had sung the Wanderer, a much more congenial character with more of a cantabile singing role, in *Siegfried* to critical acclaim, but he did not feel he was right for the role of Wotan either vocally or dramatically.

Howell feels that his best work has been achieved when working with sympathetic colleagues in a team environment. His choice of overseas venues has been very influenced by this. He has tended to spend one period abroad most years, and has enjoyed working in San Francisco, Chicago, Cologne and Santa Fe. He did not enjoy the musical climate at the Met or the physical climate of New York, but he has sung more performances there than in Cardiff. The lack of opportunity to satisfy his *hiraeth* of singing at home with Welsh National Opera has been a disappointment, particularly as he was the only international Welsh bass of his generation.

Much of his best work in the United Kingdom has been achieved at English National Opera with its very well-developed sense of company. The only other regrets he expresses about his career are not to have sung Sachs and Boris (which he has sung in Toronto) at Covent Garden. While the management of the Royal Opera superbly nurtured home-grown talent, it too often seems to have opted for foreign stars in a close casting call. It would not be in Howell's make-up to pressure or scheme his way into a role. The nearest he came to singing Sachs at Covent

Garden was during a performance in May 1983, when Hans Sotin's voice ran out and he was forced to whisper his way through the last act. He asked Howell, who was playing Pogner, to sing the last monologue. 'I would have sung it in English if I could have done, although I don't know what Colin (Davis) would have thought, but I was still learning it.'

Whereas a bass who spends most of his time on the international circuit will sing a large number of performances of Boris and Philip II in different places, a London-based peer has to be versatile enough to sing a lot of roles in two houses. This means Howell has had far more opportunity to accept new challenges and to explore himself as an artist; to try to ensure that his voice has a different colour and shines differently according to the demands of various roles. I have heard Howell sing twenty-one roles written by eleven composers, and this is probably less than half of his repertoire. Now in his early sixties he confines himself to smaller parts, but he is still accepting new challenges and remains in excellent voice. As Alan Blyth commented in an *Opera* profile ten years ago 'his continual nourishment of the basic soil of operatic life is in no doubt'.

In 2000 he sang in *The Silver Tassie* at ENO, a new opera by Mark Anthony Turnage. Hugh Canning wrote in *Opera*: 'To have the great Gwynne Howell for the Croucher's brief monologue was a luxury beyond anyone's reasonable expectations'. This luxury was not some chance occurrence; it was a beneficial outcome of the career Gwynne Howell has chosen to follow. There is more than one way to earn the adjective 'great'.

Acknowledgements
Alan Blyth, 'Gwynne Howell', *Opera* 42 (1991), 1018–25.

Robert Tear

Peter Stead

In March 2001 Welsh National Opera brought its new production of *Le nozze di Figaro* to Swansea's Grand Theatre, that cosy and welcoming palace of the people, where over the years I have been introduced to the whole repertoire of grand opera. On this occasion I took my seat in the stalls with some apprehension, for Neil Armfield's production of this most deeply satisfying of operas had received wildly conflicting reviews. In particular, it had been denounced in *The Times* for an emphasis on broad comedy that had subsumed much of Mozart's romantic sensitivity and musical sophistication. Once the action was under way, however, the sense of relief in the audience was palpable: clearly this was going to be a memorable evening. Certainly one missed the more usual sexual melancholy, but that could be forgiven since not only was the show extremely funny, it was being sung magnificently. Nuccia Focile was the most natural and fluent of Susannas and, as the Count, Gidon Saks huffed and puffed, appropriately embodying *droit de seigneur*. And there, too, was Robert Tear doubling up as Don Basilio and Don Curzio, singing beautifully whilst outrageously acting everybody else off the stage and thereby establishing the over-ripe craziness of what the singer himself has described as 'this ghastly household'.

I was still cherishing memories of that evening when a week or two later I listened to BBC Radio 3's *CD Review*. In the 'Building a Library' feature Graeme Kay discussed the available recordings of Vaughan Williams's 'On Wenlock Edge'. Apart from the instant dismissal of Peter Pears, Kay gave little away as he proceeded through the eight versions to hand. He kept the best till last, suddenly announcing that the most fully satisfying version was that recorded by Robert Tear with Vernon Handley and the City of Birmingham Symphony Orchestra in 1980. At the time, critics had commented on the way in which Tear had brought out the 'dramatic quality' of Housman's words, and in his summing up Kay described the tenor as a 'master story-teller'. The extract played from 'Bredon Hill' amply proved the point, for the words were sung clearly and boldly, the voice was unaffected, less operatic than other versions, certainly very maturely and satisfyingly English.

It was pleasing to have this double confirmation of Robert Tear's standing. The tenor, who was now in his sixties, was not only vocally and dramatically stealing scenes in the opera house but could rest content that his reputation as a recording artist, especially of English music, was secure. I reflected on the range and stamina of an artist I had first heard sing professionally at the Festival Hall in 1965 as his 'Comfort ye, comfort ye my people' opened a performance of Handel's *Messiah*. At that early stage I associated him entirely with oratorios and church music; only later did I catch up with his vital role in the development of English singing and his increasingly challenging range of operatic roles. For a while in the 1970s and 1980s he was ubiquitous, and the tenor, who could later boast of having made more than 250 recordings, loomed larger in the review pages of the music magazines than any other British artist. All of this was of great interest to me for, in the traditional way of Welsh music lovers, I was 'rooting' for one of my favourite singers. As it happened I had known Bob Tear long before 1965, for we had grown up near to each other in the Bristol Channel seaport of Barry. At Barry Grammar School I had particularly associated him with the very good cricket team, and even now the image of him that comes to mind is one in which he stands with arms folded in the 1956 First XI photograph; his whites are immaculate, his hair is neatly parted and, of course, his broad face is clean-shaven. Years later I was delighted to hear him tell a radio interviewer that there was nothing to beat the elation on those days when everything about the voice is right; 'it's like in cricket', he added, 'when you're seeing the ball and playing shots off the middle of the bat'.

The Barry of the end of the twentieth century was a sad town and clearly Robert Tear did not enjoy the visits he made in the 1990s to visit his hospitalized mother. He described it as 'a town of boarded depression' and as being his 'emotional sphincter'. But at other times he has fully acknowledged his musical indebtedness to the town. In the 1950s we had both lived at the highest point of the town in council houses that gave access to spectacular views of Exmoor, the Channel and the docks where his family had found employment. The greatest influence on his career was a grandfather who was 'a thinker manqué' and who gave up a possible footballing career with Arsenal to stay in Barry. He worked as a blacksmith on the docks, whilst earning such a reputation as a singer that praise came from the great Ben Davies. Bob likes to think that the payment which his grandfather received for singing at local cinemas during the change of films made him a professional; certainly it was from him that the youngster derived his love of Victorian songs. His own public career began with his roles as mascot and treble soloist for the Barry Ladies Choir. This was but one ensemble in a town which had forged a reputation for its choral singing. Leslie Tusler, a distinguished local conductor in his own right, has explained how the young town, that had mushroomed into existence at the end of the nineteenth century, was led by representatives who were determined to give it distinction. Brilliant and energetic teachers were lured to Barry by higher than average wages, and in education, sport, music and in the churches standards of excellence were achieved by undoubted pioneers, well aware that in 'a lively rumbustious town' they were 'creating institutions from scratch'. To Barry in the 1900s came two particular teachers, D. J. Thomas, the founder of the Barry Male Voice Choir, and W. M. Williams, from north Wales, who launched the international prize-winning Romilly Boys' Choir. W.M.'s daughter, Grace, the accompanist of the choir, went on to become one of Wales's great composers. Grace Williams was later to speak of how she had been 'brought up with choirs' and of how her career was inspired by the National Eisteddfod in Barry in 1920 where she heard the music of Stravinsky and that of one of the adjudicators, Vaughan Williams, with whom within a few years she was to study.

It was the quality and intensity of musical life in the Barry of the first half of the twentieth century that made possible the careers of Grace Williams and Robert Tear. In the case of the singer, the crucial agencies were first the grammar school, and the inspired, if unorthodox, class-room methods of A. S. Brinn, and then the Church in Wales (referred to by Nonconformists like myself as the Anglican Church). The main Anglican churches in Barry were impressive and unmistakeable structures, albeit ones which I rarely entered and which I generally regarded with some suspicion. St Mary's, where Bob first sang in the choir, left me unmoved but St Paul's, to which he later transferred, was altogether darker and more atmospheric, and I was quite prepared to believe that worshippers there were on to something. What that congregation had access to was, of course, the glorious music of the Anglican liturgy.

'The choirs in which I sang', Bob once explained, 'would not have been seen dead nibbling on *Bread of Heaven* or cooking fried eggs in *Sospan Fach*.'

Only years later, at a time when Nonconformity was in spectacular decline, did I begin to realize how much spiritual and aesthetic pleasure I was taking in the relatively successful survival of Anglicanism. As I tuned into the BBC's *Choral Evensong*, visited all the great English cathedrals and always on my travels looked out for Sung Eucharist, I came to regret the years in which I had ignored the Church and became increasingly envious of the ready access which Robert Tear had been given to a pattern of music that constituted one of this country's greatest treasures.

The grammar schools of Wales had been established to give talented children professional careers and, in our droves, we had become academics, teachers, scientists, engineers, surgeons and musicians. What Bob Tear had become was a singer. From Barry Grammar School he went to King's College Cambridge, where the boy who had grown up 'in a house without books' read English. More crucially, the choral scholar sang in the great King's College Choir under the direction of David Willcocks. The composer Howard Goodall has recently asked us to consider just how remarkable is the uninterrupted 800-year-old tradition of choral singing in the great churches of England, particularly as Catholic Europe has willingly defaulted in that respect. Singing in a choir in a Cambridge chapel, both dating back to the 1440s, Robert Tear was aware that amidst the flickering candle light and blue-grey smoke 'an almost tangible awareness of mystery seemed to seep out of the chapel walls'. Perhaps those walls 'stored the voices of the others who had sung in the building since the reign of Henry VI'. 'Did I once', he wondered, 'see Orlando Gibbons point his index finger at the roof and say "I think the major 3rd's a trifle flat, Mr Tear".'

Robert Tear went up to King's in 1957, the year in which David Willcocks took up his appointment, and under his direction he was to enjoy an ever-expanding repertoire including the works of Gibbons, Byrd, Tomkins (a Welsh pupil of Byrd), Bach and, above all perhaps, Handel. It was the conjunction of Willcocks and Handel which really launched Tear's post-scholarship career, for the director arranged for him to sing in a *Messiah* in Cambridge in which Gwyneth Jones was the alto and for which he was paid £5. (Recently he has estimated that he sung in more than 300 *Messiahs*.) In the years after university the legacy of King's paid off for he was in constant demand to perform as a soloist in all the great works of the Christian repertoire in concert halls, cathedrals, festivals and recording studios. He was to be 'especially esteemed' for his interpretation of the Evangelist in the Bach *Passions* and, of course, for his growing number of Handel roles. But all the while there were other influences at work.

That singers specializing in church music will extend their range is, of course, predicated by the music itself. Dramatic elements were present in the very earliest liturgical music but, over the centuries and then especially in the early modern period, the music was filling out. By the eighteenth century the operatic arias that increasingly characterized oratorios ensured that henceforth the great religious works would move forward with secular opera itself. For individual singers this symbiosis, natural as it may seem, was not always easy, especially if the singer had initially been linked with the Church. As his career progressed Robert Tear was often praised for his 'operatic quality' in *Messiah*, and his Handel work generally was thought to have a 'heroic' dimension. And yet critics with specialist interest were often uneasy when operatic elements were brought to early or church music. Various critics thought Tear 'over-dramatic' in a recording of Haydn's *Creation* and 'over-emphatic' in a Bach B Minor Mass. Monteverdi was always the main battleground, with some critics outraged at the deployment of modern 'produced' voices and the preference for 'big names' rather than 'authentic voice production'. The purists had to be won over. In a *Gramophone* review of John Eliot Gardiner's recording of Monteverdi's Vespers, Dennis Arnold thought the soloists 'excellent' but in the case of Tear he had been surprised. He had previously noted how the tenor's 'whole operatic experience has been moving away from the pure line needed for baroque music', but now found that his tone was 'under strict control'.

Robert Tear became a 'big name' in part because of market forces; the age of the oratorio and recital had given way to that of the LP and the opera house. But it was also a question of preference, for the tenor relished the opportunity to act as he sung. In the transition from chorister and soloist to opera star he was to experience a crucial, fascinating and contentious interlude as a member of what he was to describe as the Benjamin Britten 'stable' at Aldeburgh. Undeniably amongst the twentieth-century's greatest composers, one of Britten's concerns had been to extend the tenor repertoire, not least, of course, because of his relationship with Peter Pears. Tear was specifically summoned to Suffolk because of the similarity of his voice to that of Pears. He had sung Quint in the English Opera Group's *The Turn of the Screw* in 1963, but it was in 1964 that the conductor Meredith Davies took him to Aldeburgh to understudy and deputize for Pears in Britten's *Curlew River*, a church parable based on a fifteenth-century Japanese text. Virtually from the outset there was to be what can only be described as a 'creative tension' between Britten and Tear. Humphrey Carpenter, Britten's biographer, has commented on Tear's initial reluctance to identify fully with the central tenor role of the Madwoman in the singing of which he alternated with Pears in Suffolk, London and Moscow, and many authors have relished telling the story of the exchange between Britten and Tear which has become a key anecdote in the annals of modern music. It was during a rehearsal of *Curlew River* at Southwark Cathedral that the composer told Tear that he was 'disappointed' with his work and accused him of 'using my music as a vocal exercise'. Later the tenor was often to reflect on the relative justice and 'cruelty' of that remark. For him Aldeburgh was always 'full of uneasy vibrations and hidden malice'. Britten was clearly a genius but, obsessed with his sexuality and with a sense of himself as victim, he composed operas which Tear thought of as failing to confront his essential dilemma and which were musically 'shallow and brittle'. In one respect Tear held the composer in the highest respect, and mercifully it was an aspect of Britten that suited the singer's career beautifully. For Tear, Britten was 'the greatest illustrator of texts since Purcell'; thus it was that the tenor from Barry was given the opportunity to develop into the finest performer of English texts.

In his introduction to *Peter Grimes* Britten explained that one of his chief aims had been 'to restore to the musical setting of the English language a brilliance, freedom and vitality that had been curiously rare since the death of Purcell'. Many authors have contemplated the highly satisfying relationship between English music and the English language. In *The Singing Church* (1941) C. H. Philips commented on how Latin had 'left the composer to find his own rhythms', but with English 'its elasticity, its dipping dactyls, its feminine endings, its sibilants, palatals and clusters of consonants' forced composers like Byrd and Gibbons to be rhythmically inventive. Then, three hundred years later, in the English musical renaissance, Delius, Warlock, Ireland and Vaughan Williams established English poetry as 'one of the mainsprings' of their work and as presenting what Wilfred Mellers once described as 'the very roots of a musical idiom'. Enter Britten, with whom English song was 'to be born again'. For the six years he was at Aldeburgh and then in his subsequent recording career Robert Tear played a crucial and central role in the re-establishing of English as a musical language. He was in the forefront of the process whereby the vocal music of Britten and other modern British composers became popular and part of every music lover's frame of reference.

At every stage it was inevitable that Robert Tear would be compared with Peter Pears. Peter Evans commented on 'the uncanny similarity in timbre between the voices', a fact that resulted in Britten's *The Prodigal Son* where the roles of the Tempter and his alter ego, the Younger Son, were specifically written for the two tenors. In fact there were vital differences between the voices, and over the years critics were to make their preference clear. Initially one can detect resentment that a young upstart should have the nerve to enter into competition, but gradually the possibility and legitimacy of new interpretations were accepted and eventually the 'brilliance' of the tyro was recognized. In one patronizing review of Tear's recording of Britten's folk-songs in *Gramophone* (April, 1975), John Warrack explained that the songs 'actually lie on the voice' in a specific way because they were written for Pears. This was 'a matter of tessitura' and of 'the invitation to upward portamentos' and, inevitably, 'in the sincerest form of flattery', Tear had fallen back on imitation. What was admired with Pears was his expressiveness, his range of colour and his instrumental quality, but the singer who had once wondered if he was a baritone lacked Tear's flexibility and brightness in the upper register. When Tear recorded his second versions of the *Serenade* for tenor, horn and strings and *Les illuminations* in 1980, Warrack conceded the singer's brilliance, particularly in the latter work. In his use of his own language Britten had been greatly influenced by French song, and in *Les illuminations* Tear's impeccable and beautifully articulated French gave the work a new sheen. It was to be this flair for languages in general that made his recording career so varied.

The break with Aldeburgh came in 1970 when Tear was faced with a choice of singing in Britten's *Owen Wingrave* or Michael Tippett's *The Knot Garden*. He was ripe for departure from the Suffolk hot-house, but what decided matters was that Tippett's new opera was to be performed at Covent Garden. Tear was to create the role of Dov, a white musician in love with Mel, a black writer. This new engagement was a vital and liberating moment for Tear. Tippett was another genius, but one 'with no dark side', and a general outlook with which the singer could empathize. The role was a challenging one in which again vocal dexterity and clarity were essential. Crucially, a link with the Garden had been established; he was to sing there every season for the next thirty years. That Tippett role in 1970 began a remarkable era in which Robert Tear was caught up in an increasingly busy and varied career with concerts, recitals, opera houses and recording studios all playing a part.

This career was sustained by a highly distinctive tenor voice. Unusually, it is a singing voice that reflects many of the qualities of its owner's speaking voice. Robert Tear speaks quite beautifully, without a trace of a Welsh or even Barry accent. It is the controlled voice of somebody moulded by a good school, an ancient university or a profession; it could belong to a cathedral precentor or a public school housemaster. It certainly does not sound like the speaking voice of a man in his early sixties; it suggests intelligence and thoughtfulness but also a youthful enthusiasm, conviction and courtesy. It is not only personal recollection that prompts me to think of him as a perpetually open-faced and eager student. Certainly the singing voice is more mature, an adult masculine voice, firm and rounded in the lower register with a lower pitch than many tenors. He once told Chris Stuart of BBC Wales that, as lyric tenor voices go, it was 'a useful voice' with which he could do anything, sounding big or small according to the accompaniment. Without doubt it is a voice that carries no hint of straining for effect; there is no affectation or sloppy sentimentality. Crucially, tenor voices need to have a pleasing tone and timbre, and that is the foundation on which Robert Tear can build. Over and above that, however, his voice has a brightness, honesty and urgency that convey enthusiasm and suggest spontaneity. The music is being enjoyed and, even more, the words are being relished. With every singer one wonders about the physical aspects of the voice; perhaps with Tear there is a curl of the mouth that combines with the clarity of his diction to give his singing the dramatic emphasis that is his hallmark.

It is his English work that most fully conveys the confidence that he has in his voice, as well as the beauty of his tone and his ability to give full value to every word. In the Haberdasher's song from George Dyson's *The Canterbury Pilgrims* and in Vaughan Williams's *Vagabond* these attributes are displayed to best effect. The advice of his influential singing teacher, Julian Kimbell, had always been to 'sing the line', and in the role of Dov it is the clearness and cleanness of every note that impresses. With *The Ploughboy* by Britten one can sense the singer's pleasure and one knows that he is smiling. That much of his work is great fun is best conveyed in the many Victorian songs he has recorded with his friend, the baritone Ben Luxon. Their versions of old favourites are a delight, not least 'The Dickey Bird and the Owl', 'The Gendarmes' and, above all, Sullivan's Gondoliers duet in which the 'soft serenading' has never been so mellifluous or effortless. Tear has often had to explain just how much serious musicianship has to go into preparing these difficult songs, but most listeners will think that his expertise is more fully conveyed in his marvellous rendering of Copland's songs such as 'Simple Gifts', where the effect relies as much on boldness as on delicacy, on intelligence as much as tone.

He has identified Beethoven's Missa solemnis as the work which most ideally suits his voice; here both the musical and emotional range seem absolutely right. In the popular mind, he is more readily associated with Handel, a composer he finds easy on the voice ('he never does anything you can't do') and whom he always sings in a full-blooded operatic fashion, displaying in works such as *Semele*, *Samson* and especially *Acis and Galatea* a breath control that has been described as 'miraculous'. *Messiah* has been important in his career and, associating it as I do with my own childhood in Wales, I enjoy returning to his delivery of 'Ev'ry valley' in which his boldness ensures our knowing the extent to which 'the crooked' will be made straight and 'the rough places plain'. Gareth H. Lewis, writing in *Welsh Music* in 1989, has pointed out the 'long Welsh connection with the role of Gerontius' and, although Robert

Tear has spoken of his musical and theological objections to Elgar's work, he is one more Welshman who sings it memorably. For me at least, the old Stanford quip about the 'stink of incense' is forgotten as I respond to the singer's utterly relaxed yet heroic and dramatic assertion in the 'Sanctus Fortis' that 'God is three and God is one '.

I have often imagined being a guest on Michael Berkeley's BBC Radio 3 *Private Passions* and selecting my favourites from Robert Tear's 250 or so recordings. Of course I would have to choose Bach, Handel, Elgar, Vaughan Williams and Copland, but perhaps there would be some surprises for those listeners who had not kept up with the range of the singer's opera work. In his writings and in *Artist of the Week* radio interviews with Joan Bakewell in 1998, Tear has named his favourite roles; his range is astonishing and, listening to the recordings, one has to conclude that he has been one of the most dramatically effective tenors of his era. His Loge, which he has sung in London, Paris and Munich productions of *The Ring*, is markedly different from the sarcastic, crafty, scene-stealer whom we are usually offered. The God of Fire has been described as the *The Ring*'s 'only intellectual', and this is reflected in Tear's concept of the god as 'Logos' who brings a warning to the other 'dim' gods, caught up in what the singer describes as Wagner's 'load of tosh'. His Loge is utterly reasonable and is focused on conveying the beauty of the music. He has also sung Mime at Bayreuth. Another speciality is the role of Herod in Richard Strauss's *Salome* and here again he has worked at overcoming a stereotype, for this deranged autocrat is often played 'as a *buffo* character'. As we saw in the WNO production, Tear concentrates on the highly lyrical music as he fleshes out the kaleidoscope of the king's moods. He confesses that by the time a performance ends with those 'final high As and the cruel B flat' he is, on average, four pounds lighter.

More recently Bob Tear has returned to the WNO to sing Captain Vere in *Billy Budd*. He has often made plain his dissatisfaction with Britten's operas, not least their 'tedious' concern with the central character as victim. Vere, though, is 'a joy to sing'. Unusually the WNO programme notes carried a debate in which the producer, Neil Armfield, and Tear himself advanced differing interpretations of Vere. Tear conceives of him as 'a sad, weak vacillating character', somewhat overwhelmed by the tragic fate of Billy and ultimately haunted by the knowledge that he is the one person who could have prevented the hanging. By general consensus the April 1998 performance of *Billy Budd* at Swansea constituted one of the Grand's greatest nights. Clambering over Brian Thomson's stunning nautical set Tear's controlled yet deeply troubled Vere convinced us of this opera's greatness. And yet if one had to choose just one disc to illustrate the tenor's operatic charisma it would have to be Shostakovich's *Lady Macbeth of Mtsensk*. Here he sings the role of the drunken peasant who discovers the corpse. The music of the whole work is gloriously 'vulgar', and Tear's voice becomes one more instrument as it takes on the huge frenetic orchestra with augmented brass and percussion. This is modern opera at its most urgent and thrilling.

One can only envy Robert Tear's access to such a wide range of music, and one can sense the pleasure he has taken in so many fortuitous discoveries. And yet nobody has written so dispassionately about the commonplace daily routine of professional singing. His voice, he explains, has 'a life of its own', and it is a thing not always to be trusted. Both travelling and rehearsing can be tedious; at concerts there can be mishaps and in the opera house there will be rows, if not over interpretation then certainly over wigs. Even more frustrating is the perpetual sense that as a singer one is a merely 'a commodity', a member of a profession which 'rests on the margins of frippery, chicness and downright uselessness'. The public is invited to 'roll up, roll up' to witness the freakish talent. The inescapable fact is that the singer is merely an interpreter engaged in an occupation that, as he told Joan Bakewell, 'does not provide for thinking originally'.

Tear, however, does a great deal of thinking, for there is far more to his life than singing. He has been a pianist since his schooldays and his Steinway (acquired from a Barry friend) is a treasured possession. Making his debut in 1985, he has conducted many first-class orchestras including the Philharmonia and the London Mozart Players. He is Honorary Fellow of King's College Cambridge and holds the Chair of International Singing at the Royal College of Music. At his family home in London he retreats into his 'real' self. As befits the Cambridge English graduate and student of F. R. Leavis, he is a writer and metaphysical poet; Dylan Thomas, Auden and Emily Dickinson have all been influences. He is also a painter and illustrator.

Early in his career Robert Tear read *The Wisdom of Insecurity* by Alan Watts and his life was changed when he became a Zen-Buddhist. That conversion had occurred in Los Angeles; some years later in San Diego he was to experience an 'exquisite blinding light' in which he lost all sense of self and which left him convinced that most things, including music, were trivial. Once he realized that music was not everything, it could indeed become fun. All the rows and cruelties of the past could be dismissed as ephemeral emotion. He can now cast off anything that is not essential.

His countless listeners and admirers have no reason to make anything of Robert Tear's Buddhism other than what he is prepared to reveal. One senses that the young singer was reluctant to abandon ethics learned in church, something confirmed by his suggestion that the historic Christ had more in common with Eastern religions than the Western hierarchy is prepared to admit. One suspects that the working-class lad from Barry, who was first plunged into the midst of the English academic and musical establishments and then the rat race of international music, needed to buttress his own identity and find a base on which to build his confidence and self-control. What really matters is that his faith has not only given him the energy to sustain an astonishing forty years of professional work but also enabled him to inject his natural eagerness and vitality into all that work. His voice thrills; his intelligent commitment to the meaning of the words always exhilarates. With utter conviction he is able to tell Jerusalem and, indeed all of us, that our 'warfare is accomplished'.

Acknowledgements
For this essay I have drawn extensively on reviews and debates in *Gramophone*, *Opera* and *Welsh Music*. The following volumes have been particularly helpful.
Robert Tear, *Tear Here* (London, 1990).
Robert Tear, *Singer Beware* (London, 1995).
Humphrey Carpenter, *Benjamin Britten* (London, 1992).
Howard Goodall, *Big Bangs: The Story of Five Musical Discoveries that Changed Musical History* (London, 2000).
Michael Trend, *The Music Makers: The English Musical Renaissance from Elgar to Britten* (London, 1985).

Dennis O'Neill

Frank Lincoln

In a radio interview that I did with Dennis O'Neill to celebrate his fiftieth birthday in 1998, I asked him why he thought that he had made it as a successful international tenor while other promising singers of his generation had not. His answer was revealing not just of his passion as a singer but of his honesty as a man:

> I'm a tenor, and the market is with me, there are so few remotely good tenors. That's part of the explanation. Perhaps I worked harder, I practised harder – that's not Victorian morals – I had to, I had no choice, I was addicted to the vocal art and the music. Being famous wasn't the issue, but I wanted to be the best, and you don't have the faintest chance of being the tenth best tenor if you don't want to be number one. I think that I got that by nature – the drive, the satisfaction of getting better year by year. That was something that came from God really. My nature.

These words reminded me of Caruso's recipe for success: 'A big chest, a big mouth, ninety percent memory, ten percent intelligence, a lot of hard work and something in the heart.' However, as well as perseverance, passion, genetic and physiological gifts, most singers also seem to agree that you need something else as well – luck. Indeed, that knack of being in the right place at the right time is something that Dennis O'Neill has managed to achieve throughout his career. Some might call it 'the luck of the Irish', which all started with his father's arrival in Wales. This, in itself, is an episode which illustrates a 'force of destiny', a serendipity all of its own. His father graduated as a doctor in the 1940s, but employment prospects at the time were not good in his home town of Cork. So, he decided to take up his younger brother's invitation to join him in Wales, where he was a teacher in a school in the Bryn area – a little village in Carmarthenshire, half way between Llanelli and Pontarddulais. 'The Doc', as he was always called in the family, duly arrived in the Bryn, only to find that his brother had quarrelled with the headmaster a few days previously and had left for London without leaving a forwarding address. Stranded, 'the Doc' had no alternative but to walk and walk to he knew not where. He duly arrived in Pontarddulais, where lo and behold the local doctor was looking for a locum. He took the work just to tide him over for a while, but he was never to leave the village again. It had not taken him long to fall in love with the place and its people, and in particular with the beguiling charms of Eva Rees. They were soon married, and six incredibly talented children were born to them – gifted perhaps by the 'marriage' of two Celtic spirits – the Welsh and the Irish.

Dennis James O'Neill, the eldest of the children, was born on 25 February 1948 (a birthday which he shares with Caruso). If Gigli could say of his upbringing that 'the uninhibited delight of singing out loud is a very Italian characteristic', so certainly singing and performing were an essential part of everyday life in Pontarddulais in the 1940s and 1950s when Dennis O'Neill was growing up. He remembers singing in public for the first time at the age of four – a song about a teddy bear. He forgot the words apparently, a trait which he says has stayed with him ever since. At about the same time he started to take piano lessons, and loved them. Meanwhile he had been diagnosed as asthmatic and advised to have singing lessons to help with his breathing. It was not long before he was being 'strongly encouraged' by his mother to 'enjoy' the eisteddfod circuit, and all the competing that it entailed. From an early age he thus got used to appearing in public, and he was exposed to a very wide repertory of vocal music. At one eisteddfod, when he was about six, he remembers hearing an aria from *Tosca*, and although he did not know what he was hearing, he knew that 'it was wonderful'. At fourteen, and with his voice just broken, he heard 'Cielo e mar' being sung at the Llanelli National Eisteddfod, and wished that he too could sing the exhilarating top note at the end. He knew then that he wanted to be a tenor. There were never any daydreams about being a train driver or cricketer; the ambition was always one and the same – to be a singer.

But making the dream a reality was not an easy task, and he was not to know that the difficult formative years were to be so important in his development as a singer. Under parental pressure he went to Sheffield University, but the academic study of music was a terribly unhappy experience for him, although it did make him a very proficient all-round musician. In reality, he spent much of his time hitch-hiking to the Royal Northern College of Music in Manchester where one of the legendary teachers of voice, Frederick Cox, had taken him under his wing. Cox was to have an enormous impact on O'Neill's life and career, although much of what he had to say and teach did not make total sense to O'Neill until later. A psychologist by training, Cox was someone who found it difficult to be impressed by voice and technique alone. He was always looking for the 'complete package', the personality that wanted, indeed needed, to express and communicate emotion and drama to an audience. His aim was to develop the personality alongside the voice so that they became inseparable. O'Neill recalls that one of the first things that Cox ever said to him was 'there's a voice there, but you're not much of a singer are you?'. However, a few years later when the career was beginning to take off, *The Observer* nominated O'Neill as one of the up and coming singers in the operatic world, and they asked Cox what he had thought of him at their first meeting. He replied: 'Overdressed, in his best suit and shirt, a typical little Welshman with a Neapolitan trying to get out.' Prophetic words indeed.

There was little work for O'Neill at the start of his career. He had six months with the BBC Singers, otherwise the only way to pay for a dreadful flat in Crystal Palace was to teach English to foreign students, play the organ in an orphanage, and coach 'O' level students in music. He also gave piano lessons to ambassadors' children who arrived at the flat in chauffeur-driven Mercedes cars! Times were hard.

It was one of those uncanny strokes of luck, which I mentioned earlier, that would kick-start the career. In 1972 Scottish Opera For All was suddenly desperate for a tenor. O'Neill auditioned and got the job. It was August, and he is convinced to this day that he was successful only because everyone else was on holiday. Amongst themselves the cast referred to the company as 'Opera for Nothing', but it was invaluable experience for him, touring the Western Isles, to Shetland and Orkney, singing roles as diverse as Ramiro in *La Cenerentola* and the Duke in *Rigoletto*. The cast of 'unknowns' also included Malcolm Donnelly, John Tranter and Phyllis Cannon. Someone had an ear and an eye to the future.

In 1974 O'Neill joined the Glyndebourne Chorus, but also sang Triquet the music master in *Eugene Onegin* for Glyndebourne Touring Opera. A small part, yes, but a performance that drew warm praise from the press: 'A special bouquet for Dennis O'Neill's gorgeous cameo'. At that very moment Myer Fredman, the music director of the touring company, just happened to become music director of the newly formed State Opera of South Australia (that luck again!), and was looking for a 'house' tenor; he knew instantly that he need look no further than the young Welsh singer who was beginning to woo audiences with the beauty of his voice. But it was still a small, underprojected voice, with quite a few problems at the top, which in his own words was 'hopelessly limited'. Slowly, over a period of time, he found a way to get through without cracking the high notes. They may not have been terribly exciting and he did not hang around on them, nor could he always guarantee them, but they were there. His time in Australia provided an all-important breathing space – time to work on his repertoire and his technique. But years later, and well into a successful career, O'Neill realized that still more work was needed on that technique, and he embarked on further study with Ettore Campogalliani in Mantua, and Luigi Ricci (who had been Gigli's pianist) in Rome. It was Ricci who got the passaggio right – the natural modification of the voice as it goes from one register to another. The final piece of the vocal jigsaw was provided still later by Sherrill Milnes when he and O'Neill were working together in a production of *Rigoletto* at Covent Garden. Milnes had the courage to take O'Neill aside and tell him: 'You have to stop smoking!' Unbelievably, the aspiring international tenor who already suffered from asthma, was a heavy smoker. He heeded Milnes's advice, and it made a considerable difference vocally. They have been great friends ever since.

When he returned to Britain from Australia, O'Neill auditioned for Sir Alexander Gibson and the main Scottish Opera Company. Now does this sound familiar? They were in a quandary, because their 'house' tenor had suddenly left at short notice. And who was in town and available to take advantage of the situation? You've guessed it! At the end of the audition Sir Alex, who was to become a great friend and an ardent admirer, jumped on to the stage and asked in *Welsh*, when could he start. (The language expertise was because Sir Alex had once been engaged to a Welsh girl.)

And so started one of the most important and happiest periods of O'Neill's career. Both his children were born in Glasgow; he felt at home with the Glaswegian sense of humour, which reminded him so much of the Welsh humour that had surrounded him in his youth. They were happy days too, because the major national newspapers and music journals began to trumpet the arrival of a highly promising talent on the operatic scene. The *Daily Telegraph* loved 'the youthful ardour' of his Fenton in Verdi's *Falstaff*, and his 'burnished, passionate account' of Belmonte in Mozart's *Seraglio*. In *Music and Musicians*, Noël Goodwin wrote: 'Hearing his Rodolfo I was reminded of Carreras and sometimes Pavarotti'. Not long afterwards, Hugh Canning thought that O'Neill's timbre had the darker tones of a Bergonzi, and with few others left to compare him with, inevitably Domingo's name was also mentioned by someone else. To be fair to the American critics, when he made his début at the Met some years later, at least they came up with a new, and surprising name to add to the list of comparisons – Jan Peerce – an American tenor and an idolized Alfredo at the Met. Now I fully appreciate that all these comparisons were a mark of great respect, and an attempt at conveying the impact of Dennis O'Neill's emergence as a singer of importance, but could he really have sounded like all those other singers in the space of a few years, or even weeks in some cases? It just goes to prove that voices like wine, are amazingly difficult to describe and define. It did not take the magazine *Opera* long to find a way of avoiding the problem altogether. Covering the Wexford Festival, they simply reported that 'his voice has a nice *Italianate* ring to it'. The *Daily Telegraph* was not long in following suit – 'a vibrant *Italianate* tenor', and describing a performance of the Verdi Requiem at the Royal Albert Hall, it simply said that 'Dennis O'Neill, a late replacement, was passionately *Italianate*.' Twenty-five years later and they are all, give or take a few, still at it. There is hardly a review of his singing which does not contain somewhere a reference to 'our own' or 'our most' Italianate tenor.

It was in the Italian repertoire that I personally remember becoming aware of O'Neill's remarkable talents. Coming from Llanelli, of course I knew of him and had heard him sing. Although I liked what was then a small but quite pretty voice, I would not have honestly predicted an international career for him. So I was totally unprepared for what I heard in the New Theatre, Cardiff, in September 1979 on his Welsh National Opera début in *La traviata*. His Alfredo literally bowled me over. I was the one without a voice at the end of the performance. Along with most of the audience I just had to bawl my approval. At his first entrance, you knew that here was a world-class voice – focused, and with wonderful rhythmic attack. The tone was juicy and generous, combining honeyed mezza voce and dramatic 'ping'. I do not know if singers realize this, but if an audience feels concerned about a singer's ability to perform a role, it too can become nervous and edgy on his or her behalf, but there were no such tensions on that September night. You could relax, everything was under control; this was of a quality that up until then I had only heard on records! The 'Libiamo', 'Un di felice', 'Dè miei bollenti spiriti', and the duets poured out with full-throated ease. The top C in the second act (which O'Neill swears he found how to sing in the shower prior to the performance), was hair on the back of the neck tingling time – this is what opera was all about! On top of everything he could act as well, with that touch of danger and arrogance that made the confrontation in Flora's house more believable than I have ever seen it since. He looked dark and brooding. Dare I say it? He looked Italian and sounded it! At the end, and I know that this may sound terribly Welsh and parochial, I was proud that he was a fellow countryman and from my neck of the woods as well. Overnight he became an established favourite, and ever since the Welsh public has shown him enormous love and affection. Later, the Covent Garden audience also took him to their hearts; I will always remember that at the recital he was invited to give there to mark the closure of the House prior to its refurbishment in 1997, members of the audience held up a placard that read 'O'Neill touches the hearts that other tenors cannot reach.' That is the personality, the communication skills that Freddie Cox was on about.

In that Welsh National Opera production of *La traviata*, Violetta was sung by Suzanne Murphy, and hers also was an immensely moving and outstandingly well-sung performance. This was the beginning of a wonderful partnership that heralded one of the Company's golden eras of singing and production. Bellini's opera *I puritani* was a triumph for both singers: 'A life enhancing evening', wrote Desmond Shaw Taylor in *The Sunday Times*, and 'Dennis O'Neill was knocking up high notes like a cash register'. In Verdi's *Un ballo in maschera* he made me think of Gigli (there, I'm at it now), and later *Tosca* and *Lucia di Lammermoor* were also great successes. It was some years later that *La fanciulla del West* was added to the list – the first time that I remember the critics openly referring to O'Neill's physical stature. Almost all of them praised the singing, but some thought that his lack of height was a problem in his portrayal of the bandit Dick Johnson. Interestingly, of course, the part had been created by Caruso – and O'Neill is exactly the same height as he was.

It was during the 1980s that O'Neill became an established favourite at Covent Garden, graduating from the small part of Flavio in *Norma*, to the major roles of Italian opera, with the very occasional sortie into a different repertoire, such as Matteo in *Arabella* or the comic role of Alfred in *Die Fledermaus*. Occasionally, too, qualities that had been considered strengths were perceived as weaknesses by the critics. Alan Blyth could detect *bad* Italian habits – 'too much of a tear in the voice' and another thought that he 'made a meal of Macduff's aria' and to yet another was 'too aggressive by half'. But the vast majority of reviews were very favourable indeed. In 1987 the first of his many BBC network television series proved a huge popular success, and the CD which was released, based on the series, was at number one in the Classical Album Charts for a record number of weeks. Rodney Milnes expressed what many felt, 'Now is the time to confiscate his passport!' But soon O'Neill was a busy traveller, in demand at the Met, San Francisco, Chicago, Barcelona and Hamburg, working with conductors such as Abbado, Muti, Solti and Sir Colin Davis. The other centres of Munich, Vienna, Rome, Venice, Parma, Florence and Paris were to come later. Critics the world over could once again prove their originality, writing, as some did, that they had heard the 'British Pavarotti'!

Fate, however, still had one major trick to play. O'Neill has never considered himself to be ideally suited to the operas of Rossini (even less suited to Mozart), but in 1986 very much against his better judgement, he was persuaded to play Count Almaviva in *The Barber of Seville* at Vancouver Opera. There he met someone, who to this day he still describes as 'the most beautiful woman I have ever seen'. Her name was Ellen, and she was to become his second wife. Not only did she change his life, but she also had an amazing effect on his singing. He feels that she gave him a new perspective, a contentment and, as a result, singing was not quite as important as it had been before and therefore much easier. Frederick Cox's words, spoken all those years ago, now made sense – singing is really about the person, the maturity and the happiness of that person – it is not just about technique, it is 'the complete package'. The sense of security within the person brought with it a confidence within the performer.

Yet the end of the 1980s could have been a period of crisis for his career. A tenor cannot hope to sing a role like Rodolfo in *La bohème* forever – the voice and the physique inevitably change. Many singers find that their careers simply come to an abrupt end because they cannot make the move into a new repertoire. In 1990, O'Neill sang a role that opened up undreamed-of possibilities. The role was that of Foresto in Elijah Moshinsky's dramatic production of Verdi's *Attila* at Covent Garden. The critics raved. 'When did a British tenor singing Italian opera last receive and deserve Domingo-like applause?' asked the *Sunday Telegraph*, while Hugh Canning thought that O'Neill had provided the Royal Opera House with 'some of its finest Verdi singing in years'. With great perception, Max Loppert wrote: 'The personality has gained maturity, and the voice power without monotony'. Foresto was the role more than any other that helped establish O'Neill as one of the great interpreters of Verdi. By now he has sung in no fewer than twenty-one of Verdi's operas – is there any other tenor in the world who has sung more?

In the television programme devoted to the recital that Dennis O'Neill gave to mark the closure of Covent Garden for refurbishment, I had the opportunity of asking one of the finest Verdi conductors, Sir Edward Downes, about the qualities that made O'Neill such an ideal singer of the composer's work. His response was revealing:

> A Verdi tenor is someone who can sing a beautiful legato line when required, but can also make an heroic sound when that is required. It is not uncommon to find a tenor who can sing a sweet line, but they usually sound strangulated and eunuch-like when they have to be heroic. Alternatively, you can find lots of tenors who can bawl like a bull, but are utterly unable to sing anything lyrical. One of the great things about Dennis, and essential to be considered a real Verdi tenor, is that he can do both.

Those words came to mind when I heard O'Neill singing Manrico in *Il trovatore* at the Staatsoper in Munich – another house to welcome him back time and time again. In Act III 'Ah si, ben mio, coll'essere' sung with amazing, melting lyricism, was followed by a truly heroic 'Di quella pira' sung in the original key (most tenors transpose it down a tone) and with a held top C at the end that brought the house down. No, the voice does not have the leonine power of Franco Corelli for example, but it is focused, with great carrying force. The top is in healthy shape, still bright and vibrant, and the lower register is growing ever richer. He is also so reliable and consistent, and the stamina is amazing – how fresh he sounded after singing both tenor roles in *Cavalleria rusticana* and *Pagliacci* on the same night for Welsh National Opera. Perhaps, because he had to work so hard on his technique at the start of his career, he now knows exactly why something works, exactly how he produces the voice – it isn't hit or miss. He is totally skilled in his craft. When the time comes, I am sure that he will make a wonderful vocal teacher. Looking back, it is amazing to think that the 'under-projected' voice of the Australian years, should now include in its repertoire, not only Calaf (which I was privileged to hear at the Met in 2000) and Manrico, but also Radames and, perhaps the greatest test of all, *Otello*. How wonderful, if Welsh National Opera were able to revive Peter Stein's production, so that Cardiff audiences could appreciate O'Neill's interpretation of the Moor, which so far has only been seen at Covent Garden and Hamburg, and in Munich to glorious effect under Zubin Mehta. Welsh National Opera has made ample use of his talents over the years, and his commitment to them has been total, but a chance to hear his passionate Otello in Cardiff would be something special.

Then again, he is totally committed to most things in his life – his singing, his family and friends, Wales, even cooking for his famous dinner parties at his Cardiff home. As a trustee of the ill-fated Cardiff Bay Opera House, he was passionately angry about what he saw as the political manoeuvring that brought about its demise. I wonder how much longer we shall have to wait for an opera house that is truly worthy of the world-class opera company that we have in Wales. Will it be in time for Dennis O'Neill to grace its boards? Have no fear, the voice will be there for years to come, but I wonder for how long he will be able to sustain the energy required to fly around the world from country to country (particularly as he literally hates flying), and living in one hotel after another. I am certain that the opera house will be built eventually, but I am also certain of this: whoever the young tenors fortunate enough to sing from its stage, they will have a tough act to follow. Dennis O'Neill has set the standards by which all our young tenors of the future will be measured, because without doubt, he is one of the greatest Verdi tenors of his generation.

Acknowledgements
Dorothy Caruso, *Enrico Caruso* (London, 1946).
Beniamino Gigli, *The Memoirs of Beniamino Gigli* (London, 1957).
'Dennis O'Neill at Fifty' (BBC Radio Wales).
'Y Datganiad Olaf' (Sir Edward Downes) (Avanti/S4C).

Bryn Terfel

Geraint Lewis

To start a chapter like this on Bryn Terfel without resorting to cliché is difficult. Less than five years after his operatic début at Cardiff's New Theatre in 1990 he had the opera houses of the world at his feet, and as the twenty-first century dawns he strides their stages like a Colossus and calls the tunes of his career. Bryn Terfel is not just the hottest property of the singing world but he has also become the international embodiment of Wales and the nation's unofficial ambassador. The clichés are perhaps worth parading simply because they happen in this case to be true – Bryn Terfel is unique and his success a phenomenon rare at any time.

Given the contents of this volume it might be thought that such success in a singer is something Wales has seen many times before. But I wonder if this has ever been true in quite the same way? The singers of previous generations who enjoyed truly international reputations – Geraint Evans and Stuart Burrows, Margaret Price and Gwyneth Jones, Dennis O'Neill and Della Jones – came from a cluster of industrial valleys in the south Wales coalfield. Bryn Terfel's family background – and the inextricable background to his singing – is rooted in the hill-farming rural communities of Gwynedd in north Wales, specifically at Pant-glas, some twelve miles to the south of Caernarfon where his parents have a farm and where he was born on 11 November 1965. It hardly needs saying that both areas have richly indigenous musical traditions, but they are quite different in kind and this difference lies at the heart of Bryn's development as a singer.

The crucial distinction is perhaps that of language and the depth and continuity of tradition. The twin training grounds of chapel and eisteddfod have nurtured generations of performers and, significantly, both have provided platforms for children. This has engendered a spontaneous ability to communicate and a self-confidence in projecting both words and music. In the south Wales valleys the remarkable burgeoning network of bilingual schools established since the 1960s has, alongside the Urdd Eisteddfod, brought cultural regeneration to an area where the Welsh language was in decline and in which the chapel tradition has in fact virtually disappeared. A new culture has effectively been grafted onto the old. In contrast, the roots of that culture still flourish in extensive areas of north Wales and sustain a living and healthily self-generating tradition.

Singing in such a rural, farming community is part of the fabric of life and for a young schoolboy no more unusual than the everyday kicking of a football. The focus for singing is the home – but singing also belongs to school and chapel life as naturally as walking and breathing. There is therefore no element of the self-conscious in relation to singing here and it is as much a masculine as a feminine activity, arguably even more so than in industrial south Wales. Another critical difference is the intrinsic link with folk-singing and *canu penillion*. In the north in particular (as well as the west) these flow as if in the blood, and projecting the marriage of words or poetry with music becomes second nature. Taking to the stage under the age of six or seven is commonplace and creates an immunity to stage-fright, memory loss and so many of the hazards of performance which can bedevil singers in maturity. This early plunge also cultivates an instinctive musicality and command of an audience, alongside a keen sense of competition as well as fellow-feeling for other performers – all qualities which become essential for the mature performer.

There are plentiful reels of television film from eisteddfodau held all over Wales in the 1970s and 1980s on which the early career of Bryn Terfel was unintentionally well documented. He sings folk-songs, *penillion* and international art songs with equal ease and as a treble he can be heard to have a natural sense of musical ebb and flow. Such characteristics, as well as the same basic cultural background, are also evident in performances by two Anglesey stalwarts of the eisteddfod stage at roughly the same time – Gwyn Hughes Jones and Aled Jones. The transition to the adult voice and negotiating the breaking of the boy's voice can be a traumatic experience, particularly in the Anglican cathedral tradition, to which Aled belonged for some years. This was not a form of music of which Bryn, or Gwyn for that matter, had any knowledge, and for Bryn the vocal transition happened early and without difficulty. His bass-baritone was soon to be heard at eisteddfodau, singing the same wide repertoire as before.

It is important to stress that singing for Bryn, as within this tradition in general, was a natural form of expression. He acknowledges with pride that as far as any sense of vocal technique was concerned he was not so much self-taught as untaught. This freedom of expression remains a hallmark of his mature singing. He was, however, taught thoroughly in the art of *cerdd dant* and *penillion* by Selyf (Dafydd G. Jones) – a legendary authority whose concern, like that of so many others in this field, was to transmit the subtleties of interpretation and the nuance of expression. Indeed, the voice itself is largely taken for granted, and another noteworthy characteristic is that singing in this idiom is not tied to notes on the page and a mechanistic sense of rhythm. It encourages flexibility and natural breathing and a seamless integration of the meaning of words with the musical line – if anything the communication of words is paramount, feeding as it does the music itself. Does it ring a bell therefore when we read Bryn in 2000 declaring, 'I'm obsessed with diction. My voice works with diction, developing colours to suit the scope of the words. I cringe when I hear of singers who sacrifice words to the line and the beauty of tone.' The child is father of the man . . .?

These qualities immediately impressed me when I first heard Bryn sing – he was then about seventeen. Bryn himself recalls how as an A-level student he was fortunate to be sent to a local singer with linguistic expertise in preparation for the practical A-level exam. These sessions with Pauline Desch were not concerned with vocal technique so much as interpretation, projection and the rudiments of exam technique. As a young lecturer who had just arrived in Bangor's Music Department in the days of William Mathias in the early 1980s I was fortunate enough to accompany several of these sessions – but nothing prepared me for the sheer force, colour and character of Bryn's voice. As I remember it, he sang some Handel and Schubert with uncannily natural phrasing and seemingly limitless power. A commanding presence, nearly as tall then as he is now, it was both daunting and thrilling to imagine the potential of this voice and how that potential might be realized. That path led on to the Guildhall School of Music and Drama where he studied with Arthur Reckless and Rudolf Piernay. (It says much of both singer and teacher that Bryn still returns to Piernay for regular sessions on repertoire.) In recalling the years at the Guildhall Bryn refers particularly to the thrill of learning a large repertoire, but also of getting under the skin of the music and of immersing himself in the languages of the songs and their pronunciation. The other aspect of the training which he clearly found invaluable was the dramatic dimension of the opera course, of putting expression into action. Significantly, he does not emphasize any major technical interference with the voice itself; its scope was retained while its nuances were widened. Technique for its own sake did not interest him (or his teachers) and neither was it necessary. This voice if any is God-given.

The story now becomes part of singing history. In 1988 Bryn won the prestigious Kathleen Ferrier Scholarship which traditionally alerts the rarefied world of singing cognoscenti to the presence of a major new voice. One requirement of the competition is the performance of a song by a living composer. Bryn rang up the doyenne of Welsh song-composers, Dilys Elwyn-Edwards, at her home in Caernarfon and asked if she had anything for bass or baritone. (Most of her well-known and published songs are for high voice.) After some searching she produced a song written some decades earlier and kept in her folder – a ravishing setting of W. B. Yeats's 'The Cloths of Heaven' which, following its inclusion in Bryn's first recital for Radio 3, following the Ferrier, has entered the repertoire. She went on to compose two songs for him to perform at the 1989 Cricieth Festival – 'Eifionydd' and 'Berwyn' (*Caneuon Bro a Mynydd*). This was the year when he was awarded the Gold Medal on finishing his studies at the Guildhall and then embarked on a professional career immediately.

During his years in London Bryn had maintained an active performing career in Wales. He appeared at a wide range of concerts, took oratorio parts and made several recordings – mostly of Welsh repertoire – for the Sain label with whom he won a *Gramophone* award for his Schubert *Schwanengesang*. He remained loyal to Sain until he was offered a contract by Deutsche Grammophon, the most prestigious recording company in the world. His exceptional talent had now been widely noticed and when he won the Young Welsh Singers' Competition organized by the Welsh Arts Council he became the obvious choice to represent Wales in the Cardiff Singer of World Competition in 1989. Patriotic hopes were naturally high but the final outcome was, in itself, a competition which in sheer drama and quality went a long way to seal the success of the event as arguably the world's premier song competition. Much ink has been spilt on the unforgettable 'battle of the baritones' as Bryn duelled metaphorically with the gloweringly magnificent Dmitry Hvorostovsky. Most impartial spectators would have said that it was a close call, and although many were disappointed when the Russian triumphed there was no sense of Bryn's being 'second' in carrying the competition's prestigious and discrete Lieder Prize. Bryn himself has always generously acknowledged Hvorostovsky's success – but all sensible musicians (as opposed to competition freaks) understand that competitions can be transitory in what they reflect and somewhat voyeuristic in the enjoyment they afford. More significantly they open doors to concert halls and opera houses the world over.

The operatic début came swiftly, as Guglielmo in Mozart's *Così fan tutte* with Welsh National Opera in Cardiff's New Theatre in 1990 and subsequently on tour. This was quickly followed by the role of Figaro in *Le nozze di Figaro* for WNO, which he went on to perform in English for English National Opera in 1991. These were the ideal roles to launch an operatic career and it was noticed, of course, that Bryn had slipped naturally into Geraint Evans territory. The maestro, now retired, was happy to give advice to his young compatriot but some made too much of the inevitable comparisons. My own recollection of the Cardiff performances was of a natural stage-craft which animated the singing unobtrusively. The real joy was of encountering such a marvellous youthful actor whose every move illuminated the music. One trait only seemed to bring Sir Geraint vividly to mind – the occasional wonderful, expressive rolling of the eyes! Bryn is blessed with such mobile and memorable eyes that it comes as no surprise to find that he can bring the tiniest musical gesture to life with a suggestive glance, a glance too that can carry to every corner of the theatre.

By 1992 Salzburg had beckoned with a debut as Jochanaan in Strauss's *Salome*, a role soon repeated at Covent Garden and on record. It seemed a part tailor-made for the stream of glorious sound which emanated from the underground vault – a post-Wagnerian musical flow which whetted international appetites for a Terfel Wotan and much else besides. Since the early 1990s Bryn's operatic career has followed a notably pragmatic and sensible approach to repertoire. He has taken three roles in Mozart's *Don Giovanni*, as the libidinous Don himself (recorded under Solti), Leporello (recorded with Abbado) and Masetto; in Verdi's *Falstaff* he has been both Ford and Falstaff; from Puccini he has taken Sharpless (*Madama Butterfly*) and Scarpia (*Tosca*) and recorded Angelotti in *Tosca* under Sinopoli while Wagnerian roles include Donner (*Das Rheingold*) and Wolfram (*Tannhäuser*). His roles in Vienna have included the four villains in Offenbach's *Tales of Hoffmann* with a recording of the Baron in Lehár's *The Merry Widow* with John Eliot Gardiner. Twentieth-century roles have included Captain Balstrode in Britten's *Peter Grimes* and Nick Shadow in Stravinsky's *The Rake's Progress*. The spectacular story behind this snapshot of his repertoire is the role-call of opera houses in which he has appeared. From Salzburg the path led to the Royal Opera Covent Garden, La Scala in Milan, the Vienna State Opera, the New York Met, Chicago's Lyric Opera, the Monnaie in Brussels, the Chatelet and Opéra Nationale in Paris, Santa Fe, Netherlands Opera Amsterdam, the Bavarian Opera in Munich, Hamburg, Lisbon, Australian Opera and San Francisco. Few singers can ever have conquered the operatic world so effectively in less than a decade, and not since Caruso and Callas has a singer created quite such a sensation on the front pages of the New York papers. For a singer with the world thus at his feet it is sobering to find in Bryn a singer with his feet so firmly on the ground!

It is perhaps natural to emphasize the operatic triumphs in a career for they stand out like milestones along the path. In Bryn's case he has 'become' the Figaro of his generation, singing alongside a colleague like Cecilia Bartoli as his Susanna in Jonathan Miller's production at the Met. The long-awaited reopening of the Royal Opera House came with a new production of Verdi's *Falstaff* created by Graham Vick as a vehicle for Bryn Terfel in the title-role and conducted by Bernard Haitink. Significantly, he has forged lasting partnerships with the leading conductors of the world, notably James Levine at the Met who exceptionally acts as pianist for him from time to time. His recordings have also given audiences a taste of things to come, particularly of Wagner and Verdi arias and a spectacular disc of Handel operatic and oratorio arias with Handelian specialist Sir Charles Mackerras. By working in concert hall and recording studio with the world's major orchestras and conductors Bryn has committed an impressive range of the oratorio and symphonic vocal repertoire to disc, a range which shows clearly his versatility. His performance in Monteverdi's *Vespers* of 1610, recorded with John Eliot Gardiner and his Monteverdi Choir and

Orchestra in St Mark's in Venice, captures a particular authenticity with thrilling immediacy, and there are few singers who are equally at home in Walton's *Belshazzar's Feast*, where the singer's obsession with diction raises the hairs down the back of the neck. Another highpoint is the role of Elijah in Mendelssohn's oratorio with the period-instrument forces of the Orchestra of the Age of Enlightenment under Paul Daniel, an interpretation which brings out all the latent drama of the role, removing layers of later Victorian varnish with a vengeance. One major work, which Bryn has performed incomparably in the concert hall but has yet to record, is the role written for Dietrich Fischer-Dieskau in Britten's *War Requiem* – just one instance of glories still to come.

Mention of Fischer-Dieskau brings another facet of Bryn's versatility to the fore. The critic Richard Wigmore has written of his 'reputation as one of the most exciting and probing lieder singers of the day, hailed by the Germans themselves for his flawless command of language and idiom, and provoking comparison with two of his idols, Hans Hotter and Dietrich Fischer-Dieskau'. And yet Terfel's interpretations of Schubert and Schumann lieder, in particular, superbly partnered by the pianist Malcolm Martineau, are entirely his own, coloured as they are with greater light and shade than is normally found on the recital platform. As the distinguished vocal critic John Steane once wrote in a review: 'There is a boldness about Terfel's art that could be perilous, but which, as exercised here, is marvellously well guided by musicianship, intelligence and the genuine flash of inspiration.' He was writing about a disc that brings together some of the finest songs in the English language – by Vaughan Williams, Butterworth, Finzi and Ireland. These passionate songs have survived generations of English performances characterized by a certain stiff upper lip (with notable exceptions!), but it is quite a day when English critics have to re-evaluate the finest settings of Shakespeare, Stevenson, Housman and Masefield because a Welsh singer has brought their poetry alive in a way quite unlike any native Englishman. And why? Well again, the obsession with diction for one thing – and a similar obsession with the meaning of the poem. Here is a singer who can get right to the heart, or uncannily under the skin, of the poetry and thence the music.

The intensity and passion of these interpretations have everything to do with the art of communication and of identification with the music.

It is no surprise to find the same hallmarks in a remarkable disc devoted to the songs of Meirion Williams – romantic songs which have often been treated as eisteddfod war-horses in performances which can paradoxically blunt their musical qualities. It took Bryn to devote the same care and devotion to these works on disc (as in public performance) as he lavishes on Schubert or Debussy and to awaken his compatriots to a long-neglected cycle, *Adlewych*. As Kenneth Bowen said when he presented him with the John Edwards Memorial Award of the Guild for the Promotion of Welsh Music in 2000, 'I cannot think of any other soloist who has sung the songs of Meirion Williams in recital at the Wigmore Hall, La Scala, Vienna's Musikverein and the Carnegie Hall in New York.' For us in Wales opportunities to experience the full magic of Bryn in recital are all too rare – song recitals are rare in themselves and there are few ideal venues. But the magic when unleashed is unforgettable. When in 1992 I took over the directorship of the North Wales Music Festival following the untimely death of its founder William Mathias, I invited Bryn to give the opening concert of the 1993 Festival. St Asaph Cathedral was once famously described by the leader of the Amadeus Quartet as 'one of the finest concert halls in Europe' and on this occasion it was packed to the rafters. A solo singer on stage has to win the hearts of an audience. With Bryn the charisma goes without saying, but what matters is that alchemy which soon has an audience in the palm of his hand. It is noticeable that those eyes have a capacity to embrace 700 people as if with a single individual glance. Here, alongside his pianist Annette Bryn Parri, was music-making of a rare distinction – a spellbound audience would happily have sat there all night.

Versatility . . . I could go on and on! One aspect of Bryn's repertoire which deserves mention is his championing of show-songs by Rodgers and Hammerstein and Lerner and Loewe. In an age when the term 'cross-over' as applied to so-called 'classical' artists is generally derogatory, Bryn is an artist to whom such divisions simply do not apply. Anyone familiar with the range of his Welsh repertoire would understand instinctively how he could sing his heart out in the classics of the Broadway stage. What is typical too is his impeccable approach to accent and pronunciation, so much so that the American coach Peter Howard, who worked with both Rodgers and Hammerstein waxes lyrical about 'eliminating the classical singer's rolled letter "r". I knew we were on the right track when he mastered the phrase "When I take you out tonight with me . . . honey, here's the way it's goin' to be." Here suddenly was Curly singing to Laurey on an Oklahoma farm.' That obsession with diction again – and also with character!

Bryn particularly relishes the opportunities of working with opera producers as a member of a team of singers who are dedicated to understanding how a theatrical experience gels. Gone are the days of star singers flying around the world's opera houses with their personal costumes, expecting to slot into any production without rehearsal. The weeks spent forging characterization are among the most productive of all for a singer obsessed with those elements which make a character tick – both on his own and in ensemble. A similar passion for communication lies behind the establishment of the Bryn Terfel Faenol Festival, a few miles north of Caernarfon, and launched in August 2000. Here, on a large canvas, he can invite an eclectic mix of the finest singers in the world to join him in providing a feast of big-boned music for a warm-hearted audience – a perfect blend which enshrines an ability to cross boundaries and to break down barriers in the urge to communicate. The same committment saw Bryn singing at the 1999 National Eisteddfod with the National Youth Choir of Wales (of which he was a founder member, now president) and in 2000 fronting the BBC National Orchestra of Wales and massed choirs in the première of a major new work, *Y Groesffordd*, by Pwyll ap Siôn. In 2001 we find him insisting on inviting the youthful and inspiring players of the Cardiff Bay Orchestra under its founder, WNO's Gareth Jones, to support him in Brahms's *Ein deutsches Requiem*.

Bryn's dedication to Wales is that of a practical patriot. He can persuade his multinational recording company to record a disc of traditional Welsh music with the orchestra of Welsh National Opera and so boost his natural role as a world-wide ambassador for Wales. He makes his home in Bontnewydd near Caernarfon, where his three sons can enjoy a Welsh upbringing and education in close proximity to his family and that of his wife Lesley. The walls of his house are filled with vivid paintings by Welsh artists and he has created an open-air festival extravaganza for north Wales. Yet his horizons are wide and he responds to many of the requests for his patronage, some outside the worlds of music and of Wales, such as the presidency of the International Performers' Aid Trust, a charity which developed out of Equity's International Committee for Artists' Freedom.

But there are also practical limits. I remember his most recent appearance with Welsh National Opera when he sang Nick Shadow in *The Rake's Progress* under Mark Wigglesworth's acute musical direction in 1997. This was a period when one attempt to build a Cardiff Bay Opera House had just foundered and another was attempting to get off the ground. Bryn's magisterial performance at the New Theatre underlined just how inadequate WNO's Cardiff home has been. With a realistic assessment of his own straining against these limits he declared that he would no longer feel able to sing opera in Wales until . . . This gesture is one that he could afford to make on behalf of all the other Welsh singers who did not have his bargaining power. It also recognized the fact that few if any of the international singers who shared his productions in New York, Vienna and London would dream of working in such inadequate conditions – theatrically, as in Cardiff, acoustically, as in Llandudno, and both in Swansea. In depriving the people of Wales of his operatic presence he was able to throw a meaningful challenge at the door of the 'powers that be' (such as they are) – when you provide adequate resources and build the opera house this company and Wales deserves I will come and sing here again.

That his diary has included the title-role in Wagner's *The Flying Dutchman* with WNO at the Wales Millennium Centre originally for 1 March 2000, then 1 March 2001 speaks volumes. Each rubbing-out is testimony largely to political accident, vacillation and lack of vision – at a time when both Millennium Commission and Arts Council have repeatedly pledged funds and support. When I first wrote this in April 2001, Bryn had just issued a heartfelt plea endorsing the Centre as a project not only essential for Wales's confidence and self-respect in the world but also crucial for him as a North Walian as the realization of a unique dream in his nation's capital. It is now four months later and still not a spadeful of earth has been turned, after more than six years of painstaking preparation. Moreover, it now looks as if even 1 March 2004 is set to disappear from the diary. The faithful, however, must not only hold fast to the ambition but also continue to lobby those politicians who sit on the putative Centre's doorstep in Cardiff Bay and who enjoy the power to vote on its creation – so that we can at length see and hear our greatest singer in all his glory in his own country.

Acknowledgements
I am grateful to Bryn Terfel for his time and generosity in the preparation of this chapter.
'Bryn Terfel: a Born Communicator' sleeve notes to *Schumann, Liederkreis Op. 39*, Deutsche Grammophon, CD 447042–2.
Sleeve notes to *Something Wonderful – Bryn Terfel sings Rodgers and Hammerstein*, Deutsche Grammophon, CD 449163–2.

The Choir – Côr Meibion Treorci

Gareth Williams

The valley's classic sound, the great distillation of the strength and comradeship of our people, has been the male voice choir. The voices of men raised in full choral cry is what a stranger would take away as the clearest revelation of our talent and character. In all this great garment of harmonious sound no thread has been more golden that that of the Treorchy Male Choir.

Gwyn Thomas

It was the night of 8 August 1964 and Treorchy was *en fête*. The Cardiff Arms, Con Club, RAFA Club and Stag Hotel all delayed their closing times and celebrating crowds continued to mill around the main street into the early hours. The occasion was the triumphant return from Swansea of Treorchy's pride and joy, the male voice choir, after one of the most compelling, nerve-tingling contests in the whole history of the National Eisteddfod. The night editor of the *Rhondda Leader* had already decided on the front-page headline of the next issue: 'Drama in Battle of the Giants: Sick man leads choir to "Finest Hour".'

It had been no ordinary week for Swansea or the Rhondda. The Eisteddfod, taking its cue from Glamorgan's historic victory over the Australians at St Helen's earlier in the week, was favoured by warm weather and record crowds. Despite its own borough council's petty refusal to make any financial contribution to the Eisteddfod, Rhondda representatives did the valley proud. Pentre-born Rhydwen Williams won the Crown, the Mid-Rhondda Workmen's Band snatched the major brass band prize of £500 from under the noses of their rivals Parc and Dare, Cory and Tylorstown, and the renowned competitive tradition of Rhondda choralism had been upheld by Porth Choral Society, Wattstown OAP Choir, the Ferndale Imperial Singers, and the Pendyrus Male Choir, named after a signal box (there is no such place as Pendyrus), and led by the flamboyant Glynne Jones. Under his predecessor Arthur Duggan, Pendyrus regularly electrified audiences but rarely satisfied adjudicators. Glynne Jones aimed for greater discipline and more finesse without sacrificing the full-blooded Pendyrus sound. He would achieve it at Aberafan in 1966. Here in

Swansea in 1964 he was up against a champion of the Eisteddfod arena from whose belt swung the scalps of all the leading Welsh choirs, including the redoubtable Morriston Orpheus, Manselton, Beaufort and Rhos, as well as Pendyrus. He was up against Treorchy.

The competition for male choirs of more than eighty voices attracted for an unprecedented £500 prize the six biggest names in Welsh choralism, in the order in which they were to sing: Rhos, Treorchy, Morriston, Pendyrus and Manselton, all previous winners, joined now by the young Turks of Pontarddulais, resplendent in green blazers and with a bright, incisive top tenor sound they might have learned from Treorchy. They had; Bont's Noel Davies has always unstintingly acknowledged the personal and musical influence of Treorchy's John Haydn Davies on his own and his choir's development.

In time-honoured fashion this was the closing competition that would bring the Eisteddfod to its climax. The pavilion was packed to its 8,000 sweaty capacity: another 30,000 strolled the field, basked in the Swansea sunshine, or clustered around the loud speakers that relayed the activities on stage to the enthusiasts outside. But few among those thousands were aware of the drama that might even now prevent Treorchy from appearing. For the past week their conductor John Haydn Davies had been the victim of a severe chill and high temperature, and unable to attend any practices: the all-important pre-competition rehearsal on the Saturday had to be cancelled. Whether John Haydn or his choir could make it at all was doubtful, except to John Haydn; as his wife Olwen later confessed, 'If I had not allowed him to go to Swansea it would have affected him mentally'. So while six coaches of choristers and supporters headed west the conductor crawled from his sick bed and was taken to the Eisteddfod by car which was waved through the main gates – a privilege denied even the archdruid – to the rear of the stage.

At 4.45 p.m. 'this diminutive but mighty maestro of the baton' (*Rhondda Leader*) mounted the podium and surveyed his choir. A third of them still worked in coal-mining and its associated industries, but no miners ever entered the cage to meet the challenge of the shift underground more apprehensively than the ninety-eight Treorchy choristers who filed on stage that August afternoon. They felt more like martyred Christians than Roman gladiators but they returned his gaze tensely confident, relaxed but every sinew straining with anticipation. If they were nervous it was not for themselves but for their conductor: surely the previous two and a half months of unremitting rehearsal three times a week, at the expense of all other engagements and diversions, would count for something? At John Haydn's signal conveying the required rhythmic urgency, three bars of energetic piano accompaniment from the dependable Tom Jones introduced William Mathias's spirited treatment of 'Y Pren ar y Bryn', which the choir attacked with gusto. The modulation from the perky playfulness of Mathias to the reverential tranquillity of Tomás Luis de Victoria's motet 'Arglwydd Da nid wyf deilwng' ('Domine non sum dignus') was not easily managed – this was the Eisteddfod Pavilion not the Escorial – but manage it John Haydn did, though he was visibly wilting by the end of the last piece, a robust setting by Granville Bantock of Robert Browning's 'Paracelsus'. He literally staggered off at the end to be bundled into the waiting car that whisked him back to Treherbert and bed, where news of the result reached him within minutes of its announcement around 6.30.

He never heard the other choirs, nor the arguments among the enthralled audience. Had the sonorous Rhos basses done enough to off-set the bright-toned young tenors of Bont? The mellow influence of the late Ivor Sims could still be heard in the uniquely burnished sound of the Orpheus, while Glynne Jones had so authentically recreated the suave polyphony of the sixteenth century as to suggest that ripples of the Counter-Reformation had eddied even as far as the Rhondda Fach. While the arguments went on, the only cardinals who mattered, the adjudicators, went into solemn conclave: the eminent choral and orchestral conductor Meredith Davies, Peter Gellhorn, director of the BBC Chorus, and Elfed Morgan, music organizer for Carmarthenshire. Gellhorn stepped to the microphone to say 'Canu bendigedig' ('Wonderful singing') and Elfed Morgan delivered the adjudication. The cleanness of Treorchy's reading of the motet was much admired, so was the resonant, consolidated sound they produced in the Bantock. And it was the Mathias that showed their 'fine rich voices' to the best effect, putting them three marks ahead of a jubilant, because still apprentice, Pontarddulais, with a chastened Pendyrus third just ahead of Morriston. Thus it was that while a crowd of 2,000 had welcomed the choir back from their northern triumph at Caernarfon in 1959, now twice that number – nearly half the population – came out on to the Stag Square to greet the heroes of Swansea. The accolade that most delighted their conductor, however, came the following week in a letter from William Mathias: 'It thrilled me considerably', he wrote, 'to hear "Y Pren ar y Bryn" so finely done . . . It had musicality, excitement and that necessary bit of dramatic point. Above all I admired the flexibility of the choir which, while taking in the various tempi, nevertheless allows it to sing and react to your beat as though it were one man.'

When Treorchy exposed a London audience to this piece, in a varied programme ranging from Palestrina to Bruckner's 'Consolation of Music' at a regal concert in the Royal Albert Hall in November 1966, they received the plaudits of the national press too. *The Times* commended their 'unshakeable intonation, precise and unfussy discipline and richness of sound in whispered pianissimos', while the *Daily Telegraph* thought the Bruckner 'gave the basses an opportunity to produce a sonority which bade fair to rival the organ'. That gala performance is still regarded by veteran choristers of the time as perhaps the finest performance Treorchy has ever given. A hundred and four strong, they were clearly 'up for it', and if the stimulus was the presence of royalty, then this was because a royal occasion seventy years earlier was stitched into the fabric of their mythology. For when Treorchy won again in what was to be their last competitive appearance at the Bala National Eisteddfod in 1967, they had established an unprecedented record of eight firsts out of eleven at the National, fourteen out of sixteen semi-nationals, and five out of five at the Miners' Eisteddfod. It was their competitive success that had once again earned the Treorchy Male Choir the seal of royal approval first extended to them in 1895.

* * *

When choral competitions first became a feature of the National Eisteddfod in the 1860s there were no Rhondda entrants for the simple reason that there was, then, no Rhondda choralism to speak of. This would soon change as the rapid industrial development, which made these two valleys the most famous coal-mining region in the world, began gathering steam and the steepling graph of its population growth expressed in a vibrant cultural and recreational life.

The inhabitants of the Rhondda more than doubled (from 23,950 to 55,632) in the decade after 1871, the Upper Rhondda especially becoming a magnet for droves of incomers from west Wales, who brought with them elements of the associational popular culture of Welsh Nonconformity. In 1891 two-thirds of the residents of Dumfries Street, Treorchy came from south-west Wales, and 35 per cent of those were young unmarried men, lodgers who were usually given the room nearest the front door through which they went in search of more congenial companionship and rewarding recreation than that found in the local public house. There were in the Rhondda in 1891 roughly 50,000 men to 38,000 women – who themselves worked seventeen-hour unpaid shifts of unremitting housework – a gender imbalance that goes far to explain the patriarchal nature of valleys' society and its male-orientated recreational life.

In 1883 a group of some twenty of Treorchy's young men aged between eighteen and twenty-two who used to meet up at convenient outdoor locations like the Stag Square, Cardiff Arms Square and Tylacoch to sing, won the handsome prize of one pound for the best rendition of 'Myfanwy' in an eisteddfod at the Red Cow, and won again later that year in Treherbert on another Joseph Parry favourite, 'Codwn Hwyl'. Now enters William Thomas (1851–1920), originally from Mountain Ash where he had led a choir to victory at a local eisteddfod at ten years of age. A member of Caradog's South Wales Choral Union, he came to Treorchy in 1873, soon after the Côr Mawr's second Crystal Palace triumph, and in 1885 was invited to conduct the Treorchy songsters who had been so gratified by their victory at the Red Cow that they made it their meeting place. Deacon and choirmaster at Noddfa Baptist Chapel and attendance officer of the local school board, William Thomas agreed to conduct them so long as they quit the pub for the schoolroom in Glyncoli Road, which they did and where, remarkably, they still are. The first piece they performed competitively under him was Adolphe Adam's 'Comrades in Arms', which they still sing too, at a Whitsun eisteddfod at St Fagans in 1885, with Caradog himself adjudicating. Following this, more eager young men came forward, bringing the choir up to eighty in number. Victories at local eisteddfodau throughout Glamorgan paved the way for their first National success, at Brecon in 1889, and after being shaded by Pontycymmer in a titanic five-hour contest at Swansea in 1891 the choir won again at Llanelli in 1895 when Joseph Barnby of the Royal Choral Society adjudicated Treorchy's performance to be 'the finest specimen of singing I have ever heard'.

Two years earlier though, the prize that William Thomas really coveted had eluded him. Treorchy's great rivals were the Rhondda Glee Society, conducted by Brynaman-born Tom Stephens (1856–1906) who, like William Thomas, came to the Rhondda from the Cynon Valley, where he too had sung in the Côr Mawr. William Thomas's choir was drawn from Treorchy and Pentre, Tom Stephens's territory was Ton and Ystrad, and the rivalry between them was as ferocious as any of the bloodthirsty items in their repertoire, a feud intensified by rival choristers living in adjoining streets and often working alongside each other. At the Porth eisteddfod on Mabon's Day 1890, members of the Glee Party attacked some of the victorious Treorchy choristers as they left the marquee. At Pontypridd in 1893 Tom Stephens's one-point victory over William Thomas's choir was enough to guarantee the Gleemen their passage to Chicago where they won immortality – and caused apoplexy in Treorchy – at the World's Fair Eisteddfod.

This convinced Tom Stephens that the summons which arrived in the Rhondda to a Royal Command performance at Windsor Castle on November 1895 had gone to the wrong choir. But there was no mistake. Treorchy were the current National winners, and William Thomas's 77-strong choir prepared a programme designed to delight Queen Victoria and *her* 60-strong entourage that comprised several members of the royal family, assorted aristocrats, the queen's Welsh-speaking head gardener Owen Thomas, and – a wise precaution given the distinctly martial fare on offer – the royal physician Sir James Reid. The encounter between 'a Rhondda school attendance officer and the Queen Empress' occasioned much comment back home, but William Thomas later admitted that an audience with William Jenkins of Ystradfechan, director and general manager of the Ocean Coal Company, was far more terrifying.

The Treorchy choir of the late nineteenth century turned on an Ocean–Noddfa axis, an alliance personified by choir secretary W. P.

Thomas (1861–1954), William Jenkins's protégé who rose from office boy at the Ocean Coal Company to become one of its directors. A local politician of influence and controversy, W.P. appreciated how well the coal owners were served by a sober, contented, respectable work-force; he was uncommonly pleased by reports that 'the Treorchy boys at Windsor' – the title of a souvenir brochure marking the occasion – had 'behaved like gentlemen and sung like angels'.

In the event William Thomas himself proved to be as ruthless as his namesake. Once his choir was granted the right to adopt the designation of the Royal Welsh Male Choir, he withdrew them from the competitive stage to devote themselves entirely to concerts, and in order to fit into the often confined venues in which they were required to sing, severely pared them down to around twenty-five in number; this select band he took to North America in 1906–7 and on a staggering 50,000-mile world tour of 310 engagements in 1908–9. 'Such precision, such volume, such grandly perfect harmony' had never been heard by one South African scribe, 'there are no rivals to this superb combination. They stand alone.' Not so lonely, though, as the despondent rump left tour-less in Treorchy; conductor-less too, they disbanded in 1897.

For two decades there was no male choir in Treorchy. But to adapt H. W. Longfellow's words in Daniel Protheroe's rousing setting of 'The Nun of Nidaros' (1902), the dawn was not distant, nor was the night starless, love is eternal. Treorchy's devotion to male choralism could not be denied, and in 1917 the Treorchy male choir was reformed under John Pugh, who was followed five years later by Gwilym Jones of Cwm-parc, a former conductor of the Royal Welsh, who instituted three practices a week to accommodate shift work in the collieries. In building the strength of the choir up to 140, Gwilym caused resentment by bringing some of his Royal Welsh choristers with him, placing them in the first two rows and paying them.

Treorchy's Rhondda rivals now were two of Wales's finest, the mighty Williamstown, founded during the Cambrian lock-out of 1910, and the more recent Pendyrus (1924), against whom Treorchy first competed in 1927 at Pontypridd semi-national eisteddfod (Treorchy won and Pendyrus came sixth). The following year, under John Isaac Jones, a choir member who took the baton when Gwilym Jones resigned in 1927 to take his beloved Royal Welsh to South Africa, they had to settle for third behind Williamstown and Pendyrus. Choral singing has been represented during times of hardship as 'a culture of consolation' but the consolations of music were not always evident in the Rhondda of the 1930s. Williamstown was forced into closure, and while competitive regulars Pendyrus scored just one National victory at Caernarfon in 1935, Treorchy's record was worse, coming eighth at Port Talbot (1932), fifth at Neath (1934), and fifth and sixth in successive years at Fishguard and Machynlleth. At this time the two great Morriston choirs, the United and the Orpheus, from a Swansea Valley less ravaged by the Depression, were in the ascendant. In 1937, 92 per cent of Treorchy's choristers were unemployed, a grim statistic which at least provided conductor Arthur Davies who had taken over from W. D. Evans of Maerdy (1933–8) with enough opportunities for rehearsal. Davies though, 'a man of culture from Swansea', was not well-disposed to competition; what he *did* do, with momentous consequences, was appoint in September 1938 a deputy conductor and deputy accompanist. The new appointees were John H. Davies and Tom Jones. In May 1940 J. H. Davies led them to second place behind the celebrated Morriston United, but military call-up was depleting the ranks, and the choir's last performance was at a local Whitsun eisteddfod in 1943 when they beat Pendyrus on 'The Crusaders'. That summer they disbanded once again. The pre-history of Côr Meibion Treorci was over; its modern history was about to begin.

*   *   *

If the war had disrupted musical activity in Treorchy, peace brought new opportunities. In 1947 the Rhondda miners produced a souvenir publication entitled *Rebirth of the Rhondda*, to celebrate the national-ization of the coal industry, the introduction of the welfare state and a return to full employment. The Treorchy choir's own revival was part of that process of recovery.

As a result of a meeting in October 1946 of members of the disbanded choir, John H. Davies was approached to resurrect it. Born in Blaen-cwm at the top of the Rhondda Fawr in 1905, his family roots in Rhydlewis (Cardiganshire) and the Cynon Valley, he had studied tonic sol-fa and the violin. Qualifying as a teacher at Caerleon Training

College, eventually becoming headmaster of Bodringallt Junior School, his vocation was education but his life was music, and in 1933 he became conductor of the Blaenselsig Male Voice party, a colliery choir that met at the Glenrhondda Institute, Blaen-cwm. Two years later he became leader of Blaen-cwm Choral Society, a position he held until 1947 by which time his career had taken a turn that would spread his fame far beyond the coal-tipped confines of the Rhondda.

There was no shortage of new recruits to the reformed Treorchy and District Male Choir, mostly demobbed young men anxious to recreate some of the companionship they had known in the Forces but with little knowledge of what being a chorister entailed. Half were in the first bass section, friends standing together irrespective of vocal compass. John Haydn set about organizing them. He would sing a note and say, 'All those who can sing that are top tenors – stand there', and repeat this procedure for each section. He put the stronger voices in the back, the lighter in the front. The word spread and by the time their conductor reckoned they were ready for their first public appearance, in Ramah Chapel, Treorchy, on 20 July 1947, they numbered 154, the great majority between twenty and thirty years of age and 90 per cent of them employed in the coal industry. Numbers fluctuated; in 1948 membership was withdrawn from eighteen absentee choristers, and the following April the entry book was closed as choristers were now in excess of 170.

There were other decisions to be made too. A full complement of officials was appointed including, as president, councillor and future MP Iorwerth Thomas, who in the election for the post defeated his long-standing adversary W. P. Thomas. John Haydn also moved quickly to eliminate pre-war bad habits: no choristers from outside were to be paid for attending a couple of rehearsals before a competition and allowed to stand in the front row; and no guest accompanist to be brought in for major occasions – whatever the event, the choir's regular pianist would always accompany them, such was John Davies's faith in Tom Jones. They had joined the pre-war Treorchy Choir at the same time in September 1938 and their friendship went back to their days in junior rugby. While Tom went on to represent Treorchy, John Haydn played for Tynewydd in virtually every position behind the scrum, a versatility that stood him in good stead when he had to sing all four parts to the choir in rehearsal. The material legacy of the disbanded choir was five pounds and a battered suitcase-full of music, and the repertoire in those early years was the familiar mix of hymn-tunes, opera choruses, spirituals (like 'Steal Away') and part-songs (such as 'Close Thine Eyes') which, given their natural appeal and the intrinsic conservatism of the medium, are still widely sung today.

The sheer youth of the choir at this time could be illustrated in various ways. There were, for instance, many active sportsmen in the ranks, like top tenor Ross Richards, soon to become Aberavon's full back, Eddie Thomas who would have plenty to sing about when he helped Cardiff beat the All Blacks in 1953, and the captain of Treorchy RFC. Several choristers played for Welsh League side Cwmparc AFC who helpfully arranged kick-off times to suit the choir when there was a clash of 'fixtures'. Thirty members belonged to Treorchy Boys Club, and there were even a few members of the local Tennis Club. Another indicator was that an early issue of the choir's magazine *Excelsior*, founded in April 1948, congratulated six choristers 'on reaching the state of paternity'.

With youth on his side, John Davies embarked on what would be twenty years of competition, since this, 'rightly used, shall stimulate us on the road to technical and artistic excellence'. Following success at local eisteddfodau the choir was 'soberly confident' when thirteen coaches (eleven of them for supporters) nosed north to the 1949 National Eisteddfod at Dolgellau – the logistical headache involved in organizing 310 lunch reservations at Machynlleth as much a strain as the competition itself – which saw Treorchy come second behind Ivor Sims's Morriston Orpheus, winning for the fourth successive time. Defying the slings and arrows of outrageous adjudicators – like J. Morgan Nicholas, who consigned them to fourth place at Sennybridge in May 1950 – Treorchy were 153 on stage at Caerffili in 1950, coming second this time to Manselton, whom Mr Nicholas had placed fifth at Sennybridge. When at Aberystwyth two years later they won, it was the Treorchy Male Choir's first National victory for fifty-seven years. Singing first, Treorchy adopted the risky strategy of interpreting literally the *adagio* marking on the copy of Schubert's 'Salm 23', so that it took more than five minutes to perform and to overwhelm the adjudicators. 'It is only once in a century one hears such marvellous singing', remarked W. Matthews Williams, announcing the result. 'If there is singing like this in heaven then I cannot get there quick enough.'

Treorchy's heavenly host – by definition a male choir, according to John Haydn, since all the angels have men's names – continued in this vein throughout the 1950s, winning at Ystradgynlais (1954), Aberdare (1956), Ebbw Vale (1958) and Caernarfon (1959). It was only to allow younger choristers to be absorbed into the ranks that the choir did not compete at Cardiff in 1960 but by 1961, when only twenty of the 114 choristers were aged over forty (ninety-six of the choir's current 105 are in that category), they were ready for Rhosllannerchrugog and won again on the evergreen 'Nidaros' and Elgar's challenging unaccompanied setting of Bret Harte's poem 'The Reveille'. Forty years on I can still recall the exultant declamation of 'My chosen people, come' that brought premature applause from a rapt audience, and victory over Morriston. John Haydn was magnanimous in victory, generous in defeat. He told his choristers when they lost to say little, when they won to say less, and his own actions spoke for themselves. When Rhos, absent on their own patch the previous year, came south to bring off a stunning victory at Llanelli in 1962, the first on stage to congratulate Colin Jones, the gifted young collier-musician who conducted them, was John Haydn Davies of Treorchy who had to settle for second.

In repertoire terms he was similarly receptive, seasoning the traditional fare of hymns, part-songs and blood-and-thunder with German folk melodies that he himself discovered and set to Welsh words. He conducted one of the earliest performances in Wales of the Cherubini D Minor Requiem in 1955, and, at the Miners' Eisteddfod in 1959 'The Coronation Song' from *Boris Godunov*, sung in English for the first time in the UK and transcribed into sol-fa by himself. For the Llandaff Festival of Music that year he commissioned from Mansel Thomas, Rhondda-born head of BBC Welsh Music, a setting of Psalm 135 for male chorus and contralto soloist (Helen Watts, on its première). From outside Wales, the eminent Communist composer Alan Bush dedicated his 'Owain Glyndŵr' and 'The Dream of Llewelyn ap Gruffydd' to the choir who in 1957 had exchanged musical greetings with the legendary but at that time outcast Paul Robeson via a telephone link-up from the Miners' Eisteddfod at Porthcawl to a studio in New York. For this was a choir so firmly rooted in the turbulent history of the south Wales coalfield that when they established a friendship with the Glasgow Police Union, a Scottish correspondent regarded the bringing together of a police choir and one from the mining community as 'a bloodless revolution'.

A regular radio broadcaster on the home and overseas services of the BBC, in 1965 Treorchy appeared in the first television programme to go out from Wales on BBC2, from the Memorial Hall, Barry, prompting William Mathias to compliment the choir on its 'professional perform-ance'. 'Professionalism', he wrote, 'is . . . an attitude of mind . . . an insistence on the highest standard of musicianship and performance . . . Music should never be just sound but always meaningful sound and your singing was full of the latter.'

Since making their first commercial recording for Qualiton Records (Pontardawe) in 1956 – 'Sospan Fach', incongruously recorded in Bethlehem Chapel, Treorchy, and soon to penetrate Welsh homes as the signature song of a Saturday night sports programme – the choir's discography extends to fifty releases. Recent converts to the Treorchy sound may owe their re-education to the 1990 CD *Showstoppers*, but older addicts still cherish their early seven-inch 45 rpm extended play recordings of 'Llef' and 'Hyfrydol', of the now politically incorrect saga of the American West 'Crossing the Plain' ('To hunt white men by day or night, to take their scalps is our delight', written about the time Buffalo Bill Cody's Wild West Shows were touring south Wales), and 'The Silver Birch' ('Y Fedwen Arian', Welsh words by Wynne Lloyd), Alexdrof's arrangement of a Russian folk-tune that is found also in Tchaikovsky's Fourth Symphony.

From the mid-1960s John Davies gradually withdrew from the conductorship, officially retiring in January 1969 to return to the violin and help found the Rhondda Symphony Orchestra. He died on 17 June 1991. 'He was', said Arwel Hughes, 'a master of all the tricks of the trade, a *rallentando* here and *accelerando* there, and a touch of vibrato thrown in for good measure, putting to shame many an orchestral conductor of greater repute.' His successor was John Cynan Jones, born in Pentre in 1933 with family ties to Brithdir (Dolgellau) and Carmarthenshire. From conducting as a teenager a glee party called the Lydian Singers he progressed to the music department at Aberystwyth where he was a contemporary of William Mathias, conducted the

College Madrigal Society, and took his M.Mus. in 1956. Formally more qualified than John Haydn, he never had anything less than unqualified praise for his predecessor's 'kindness, humility, patience, dedication to his art and a most uncanny sympathy with composer, chorister and audience', and John Cynan would over the next twenty-two years, demonstrate those qualities himself. Where John Davies's roots were in the cultural traditions of Nonconformity, John Cynan was inspired by Anglicanism and the organ loft; by a nice coincidence, when Treorchy won at Aberystwyth in 1952, he had taken first prize in the organ solo earlier the same day. Head of music at, successively, Pentre Grammar, Cyfarthfa Castle and the Upper Rhondda Comprehensive School, he had been appointed assistant conductor in 1965, when the choir was not greatly different from what it had been at its re-formation. Of the 106 choristers, twenty-eight were founder members from 1946. A third of the choir was still employed in the coal industry and about the same number Welsh-speaking. Of the choir's thirty-five engagements that year, only two were outside Wales.

But as in 'Comrades in Arms' on the breeze a sound was stealing, the sound of change. The year 1966 saw the death of MP and choir president Iorwerth Thomas, to be succeeded by Clifford Taylor (1915–98), a native of Barry who was managing director of Polikoff International, a clothing factory which would soon be the major employer in the locality. In 1967 the steadfast Tom Jones felt too unwell to accompany the choir at the Bala National, and Goldsmiths' university student Marion Williams, home in Treorchy on vacation, not only deputized but played the diabolically difficult 24-bar introduction to Bach's 'Moliant Fo i Dduw Anfeidrol' ('Praise Be to Immortal God') from the *Christmas Oratorio* so well as to be singled out, as Tom Jones had been in 1952, for especial mention by the adjudicators. When Tom Jones died in 1971 he was replaced by Jennifer Jones, a harpist as well as pianist, who would accompany until 1989 when Marion Williams who had moved to Kent, returned before being in turn succeeded in 1998 by one of her own pupils Rhiannon Williams, who travels to rehearsals from Barry two, often three times a week. John Haydn stood in for John Cynan at rehearsals and concerts until well into the 1970s and Jennifer Jones herself took the baton on occasions.

Here was another 'bloodless revolution', the humanizing of a choir of potentially uncompromising chauvinism. There were clear undertones of misogyny in an article in the choir's magazine of 1948 lamenting the infiltration by women of many musical activities which were once purely male, prophesying that

> Before long we shall see them in our Brass Bands. The last refuge for that displaced person, the musical male, will be in choirs like ours. Women may be able to blow trumpets and trombones . . . we challenge them to sing bottom bass. But do not interpret this as an attack on the ladies (God bless them!). Let them run riot in their ladies choirs, sewing guild and tea parties.

By the 1970s such an archaic atttitude had been overtaken by events, not least an increasingly female work-force, a development that had long-term consequences for the choir. The months of July and August had now to be ring-fenced for summer holidays and the choir has not competed anywhere since 1967; under John Cynan the choir changed from being a competitive to solely a concert choir. He also responded to socio-cultural shifts by adapting the repertoire to reflect them. He added Brahms, Vierne and Fauré, but recognizing new expectations and a changing taste among his choristers as well as their audiences, he also began extending the classical Welsh and operatic chorus base with songs from the shows. Musicals rubbed shoulders with Mozart and by the 1980s Andrew Lloyd Webber, Paul Simon and Stephen Sondheim were featuring more prominently than Daniel Protheroe and Joseph Parry – barring 'Myfanwy' of course, who could and can always be relied upon to irrigate the tear-ducts of time-warped exiles to whom the compositions of Brian Hughes, Gareth Glyn, Robert Arwyn and even Ryan Davies, regrettably, are as unfamiliar as perhaps they are to the Treorchy Male Choir itself.

Undoubtedly the choir's international reputation grew as it appeared on TV spectaculars as backing to Tom Jones, Julie Andrews and Ella Fitzgerald, but to more traditional followers reared on crusaders and comrades in arms the preference for 'My Way' (the choir's signature tune) over 'Martyrs of the Arena' was truly to 'send in the clowns'. Yet there was no denying the popular appeal and commercial success of this modernized repertoire, and John Cynan's inherent musicality, tasteful arrangements, good working relationship with other arrangers like

Mike Sammes and his keen interest in EMI's advanced digital recording technology ensured the maintenance of standards as the choir reached out to new audiences. By the 1980s half their engagements each year took them to the other side of Offa's Dyke; they have visited north Wales only once since 1967.

The immediately recognizable Treorchy sound, notably the ability to generate a well-balanced tune at all dynamic levels, remained as distinctive as ever. When the choir appeared on Tom Jones's 1969 Christmas Show at ITV's Elstree Studios, the chief sound engineer said the internal balance of the choir was so nearly perfect he could record them with one microphone. Tonal brightness has always been a feature of their top tenors and bottom bass, but the mark of a good choir is when the inner parts too are of comparable quality and power. John Cynan inherited this from John Haydn, as well as his gift for creating sensitive, colourful and often dramatic portraits, especially in unaccompanied singing. 'The 90-strong choir performed with superb discipline, imagination, commitment and authority', noted the music critic of the *Hull Daily Mail* after a concert there in 1979, 'its tonal resources are quite prodigious.'

Under John Cynan Jones the choir extended its geographical as well as its musical range. Their tour of Canada in 1980 was their first beyond Europe, and their first ever since Switzerland in 1963. When they returned in 1985, a full house of 2,800 at the Roy Thompson Hall, Toronto, included a thousand exiles, eighty of them from the Rhondda. It was as well that their 1986 tour of Australia, where they became the first Welsh choir to sing to another capacity audience at the Sydney Opera House, was sponsored by James Hardie Industries, 'manufacturers and distributors of building and construction materials', for Treorchy's reputation for bringing the house down was well-founded: a performance of Mascagni's 'Easter Hymn' at Walsall Parish Church in 1980 dislodged some pieces of masonry from a window in one of the side chapels and brought it crashing to the floor.

In May 1991 pressure of work brought about the collapse and enforced resignation on medical advice of John Cynan Jones himself. In the mid-1980s he had virtually reconstituted the choir after a decline in membership and the 1984–5 miners' strike, which affected a number of choristers personally, and because dwindling coal supplies reduced the choir to practising in overcoats. With another overseas tour already arranged and imminent, they were fortunate to obtain the services of John Jenkins from Cwm Nedd, musical adviser for West Glamorgan and noted for his keen involvement with youth bands and orchestras, who was appointed in July 1991, took them to the USA three months later and remained for five and a half years. They made a flying visit to Atlanta, Georgia, in February 1993 as an advance party for David Wyndham Lewis's ill-fated World Choir, and crossed to the west coast the following year. Visiting Carmel, California, they encountered cinema diva Joan Fontaine celebrating her birthday, and according to Welsh journalist Byron Rogers who happened to be there, 'when she stood among them they spontaneously burst into song, leaving her in tears. Our mines have closed, our rugby teams may no longer win but boy, we can still make them cry'.

Treorchy could be seen now more often on American TV than on S4C, but if their Welsh was slipping their Finnish was picking up. In 1992 they became the first British choir to perform Sibelius's choral symphonic poem *Kullervo* in the original language with the Royal Philharmonic Orchestra conducted by Owain Arwel Hughes at St David's Hall, Cardiff. Nothing if not versatile, the choir then proceeded to shake the world of choral music once more by selling 7,000 copies in two months of their rock CD *Treorchy Sing Queen*, recorded at EMI's Abbey Road studios with every chorister wearing headphones. Clearly the choir had come a long way since marching through the streets of Zurich in 1963 in NCB overalls and miners' helmets; Myfanwy had embraced Freddy Mercury. 'Good grief, these guys can sing', was the stunned response of Queen's Brian May on hearing the choir's tribute to his famous band.

Andrew Badham, deputy-conductor 1991–3, took over when John Jenkins resigned through ill-health in March 1997. Continuity with the past was confirmed in that Andrew like William Thomas a century earlier is from Mountain Ash, and as conductor of the Cwmbach Male Choir no stranger to male choirs. A civil servant and graduate of the Welsh College of Music and Drama who studied conducting with a pupil of Kodály, in 1999 he took the choir on a four-week tour of Australia where they performed twenty-one sell-out concerts.

Still 105-strong, still standing through every rehearsal, the Treorchy Male Choir of today is clearly a different organization from the one that re-formed in 1946. Members' annual subscription is now thirty pounds not sixpence. While a few travel from as far afield as Porthcawl the great majority of them still live within a five-mile radius of their unpretentious rehearsal room in Glyncoli Road; none of the choir is a miner, since there are no coal-mines left in the Rhondda, though several work at the Royal Mint in Llantrisant. Most of the choir are clerical or skilled blue-collar workers. Half are retired and the average age is no longer between twenty and thirty, but fifty-eight. Barely half a dozen are Welsh-speaking, but many more will sing it confidently and with ease. The furthest the choir travelled in 1955 was to the Workmen's Hall in Abertridwr: nowadays, while their schedule is still typically around thirty engagements a year, half of them are in England where their audiences are more comfortable with the *Titanic* theme-song 'My Heart Will Go On' than with 'Calon Lân'. But their historic qualities of internal balance, superb discipline, security of intonation and harmonic quality have never lapsed. Their singing is still intensely powerful. After a concert in Lincolnshire in 1994 a critic noticed how 'valley' unaffectedly came across as 'varlee'; more to the point, 'the phrasing was beautifully controlled, the diction always crystal clear. "Were You There" was sung with so much control yet so much intensity of feeling that I found it almost unbearably beautiful. There are moments when music transcends the ordinary and achieves a communication of emotion which words can never convey.'

We can be sure that the future contains many more such moments and that there are many audiences still to be thrilled by the resplendent sound of Côr Meibion Treorci – the Treorchy Male Choir.

Acknowledgements
I would like to thank Norman Martin, registrar and honorary archivist of the Treorchy Male Choir, and Dean Powell, former publicity officer, for their help in preparing this chapter.
Hywel Teifi Edwards (ed.), *Cwm Rhondda* (Llandysul, 1996).
K. S. Hopkins (ed.), *Rhondda Past and Future* (Ferndale, 1975).
E. D. Lewis, *The Rhondda Valleys* (London, 1959).
Dean Powell (comp.), *Musical Rhondda* (Stroud, 2000).
Gareth Williams, *Valleys of Song: Music and Welsh Society 1840–1914* (Cardiff, 1998).

Singing for All

Teleri Bevan

The winter of 1946/47 was long, dark and cold and months of prolonged deep frost and snow took their toll. There were food shortages and a fuel crisis, and for much of the time I was hospitalized as I waited for a severely broken leg to heal. Books and the wireless were my constant companions, but it is the sound of one cheery voice and one song which brings to mind those inactive and frustrating months. Donald Peers, the boy from Ammanford, with his light baritone voice and effervescent personality had captured the mood and tempo of post-war Britain with the song 'By a Babbling Brook, in a Sunny Nook'. Innocuous and banal it may have been, but judging from the number of times it received an airing on the daily record request programme *Housewives' Choice*, Donald Peers was a star. He had touched a chord.

In the autumn of 1946 BBC radio had redefined itself with the launch of the Third Programme as the high-minded cultural network, separating the arts from general programming. Director General William Haley likened the three networks, Home, Light and Third, to the strata of a pyramid. Third was the apex, Home was the middle and would concentrate on spoken-word programmes, and the broad base, the Light Programme, would be populist, measuring success in terms of audience size. Idealistically, Haley saw listeners to popular entertainment being enticed eventually to esoteric and challenging highbrow programmes. It was Reithian in concept: to educate, inform and entertain. The grand design failed. Listeners developed thir own loyalties and tended to stick with them. Meanwhile, the individual networks also developed a competitive edge. The popular Light with its safe middle-of-the-road programmes got the audience and the elitist, experimental Third got the money. Much has changed in the last fifty years with more stations, generic networks, and stiffer competition, but that basic tenet remains true.

Yet, it was a period when mass entertainment as determined by radio and television grew in importance and influence and created a new sort of show business. The recording industry, still in its infancy during the war years, now gathered momentum and new stars flowered in the 1950s. Carole Carr, Alma Cogan, Frankie Vaughan and Tommy Steele were singers and entertainers who were often supported and backed by the 'Big' bands and orchestras led by musicians such as Joe Loss, Billy Cotton and Cyril Stapleton. The swinging sixties was the era of rock and roll with young, modern and vibrant groups like the Beatles and the Rolling Stones becoming icons of a world-wide pop culture. Their songs and style interpreted with veracity and realism the ferment of the decade. Consequently, the broad base of the pyramid expanded ever wider and pressure grew for a network devoted to pop and rock.

Yet middle-of-the-road mass entertainment, with its yearning for nostalgia and the good old days, was by no means cast aside. In 1968, Mary Hopkin from Pontardawe caught that spirit superbly with her hit song 'Those were the days'. A picture of vulnerable innocence and purity, her voice clear as a bell evoked images and sounds of times gone by. She appealed to young and old, untouched, unsullied by the realities of modern Wales.

Ivor Novello would have approved. His music made people sing, and it has survived the generations. The haunting melody of 'Keep the home fires burning', composed during the First World War, became a national marching song alongside 'Tipperary' and 'Pack up your troubles'. But it was the appeal of his extravagant musicals, written and composed over a period of ten years or so, that won public acclaim. *Glamorous Night*, *Perchance to Dream*, *The Dancing Years* and *Careless Rapture* created a Ruritanian world of romance, goodness and colour. His music, simple and emotional, appealed unashamedly to the heart. It still does. 'Shine through my dreams', 'Fold your wings', 'We'll gather lilacs', 'Someday my heart will awake' and 'Fly home, little heart' still find a place in many a singer's repertoire. The summer seasons of the great variety shows at pierhead theatres have now almost come to an end. Yet, in those years soon after the end of the Second World War, the Arcadia at Llandudno, run by Clive Scott and his wife with the popular organist Robinson Cleaver, regularly drew full houses. I can clearly recall too Sunday night Grand Concerts at the King's Hall Aberystwyth when we heard international singers such as sopranos Isobelle Baillie and Joan Hammond, tenors Edgar Evans and

Richard Lewis, with Charles Clements at the piano. Their repertoire would always include popular songs by Ivor Novello as well as operatic arias and ballads. Two voices stand out in my mind. The rich baritone of Trevor Anthony singing 'The trumpet shall sound' from *Messiah* and the clarity of Joan Hammond, the Australian soprano, singing 'Dove sono' from *The Marriage of Figaro*.

Ivor Novello defined his philosophy as populist, his music designed for happiness. 'I am not a highbrow, I am an entertainer. Empty seats and good opinions mean nothing to me. I have no pretensions. More than anything I don't despise the public.' That sentiment was very much that of his mother. The awesome Madame Clara Novello Davies, a larger than life national celebrity, took her Royal Welsh Ladies Choir on several tours to the United States in the 1890s and her house Llwyn yr Eos (Grove of Nightingales) in Cowbridge Road, Cardiff was a veritable salon where she entertained so many musicians and singers, including Clara Butt and Adelina Patti. Her son often wrote roles with singers in mind. There was Mary Ellis, Zena Dare, Vanessa Lee and particularly Olive Gilbert, the contralto from Llanelli who starred in five shows and made songs like 'We'll gather lilacs' and 'Fly home little heart' all her own. 'No show of mine would be complete without her,' he once remarked. 'She appeals directly to the audience.' The appreciation was mutual. When I interviewed Olive Gilbert some years later for a radio series, no longer singing but living in contentment on her rich and colourful memories, she told me how she adored Ivor. 'We both came from the same Welsh eisteddfodic background, and I treasure the fact that he wrote so many songs for me.'

Ivor Novello's world of make-believe was high-class entertainment and breathtakingly theatrical. On the other hand, Mai Jones embraced the new mass medium of radio, and her work as a composer, arranger and producer was popular, respected and revered. She was a musician to her fingertips, an accomplished pianist who had experienced the ups and downs of performing in music halls, vaudeville and on concert platforms, but it is as the producer of the top variety show *Welsh Rarebit* and composer of 'We'll keep a welcome' that she will always be remembered. There was an inherent Welshness about her work. At times sentimental and appealing, Mai Jones knew how to combine good tunes with surreal humour and bawdiness, and she brought to radio her wide experience and skills of knowing what elements made a successful variety show. Basically it was a matter of 'Booking the right acts and working out the right order', and it was her consummate knack of getting the mix right which made *Welsh Rarebit* broadcasts, live from the great temperance building, the Cory Hall, the most popular variety programme of its time.

Those who knew Mai will recall her generosity and her enthusiasm in encouraging new talent. Among her 'finds' were Harry Secombe, Bruce Dargavel and the comedienne Gladys Morgan, and there is the continuing dispute of whether she spotted Shirley Bassey and gave her that first engagement. She certainly gave Geraint Evans his first professional opportunity in the spot 'Youth Takes a Bow'. With Idris Lewis she arranged countless melodies to suit singers and choirs, and another of her successes was the long-running series *Silver Chords*, a sequence of religious music for Sunday mornings.

When I joined the BBC in the mid-1950s Mai was close to retirement, and although the constant diet of late nights and regular liquid refreshment had blunted her powers she still radiated 'show biz' from every pore. Tall, blonde, heavily made up with her large lips thickly covered with pillarbox red lipstick, she would appear at occasional meetings dressed in pastel-coloured gowns and wide-brimmed hats as if waiting for the next performance. Her comments, when they came, were delivered with impeccable timing and courtesy, and she would leave early, swaying slightly, to her next engagement.

The UK-wide success of Ivor Novello and Mai Jones had been nurtured and refined in live theatre, but in the 1950s the entertainment industry went through a dynamic change with a constant need for new material making enormous demands on writers, composers and artists. Many failed to make the transition, unable to adapt their material or to connect with the audience through the microphone and the camera. Shows specifically designed and produced for television soon became vehicles for new talent and created new stars. *The Black and White Minstrels Show* with its mixture of close harmony, dance and verve gave singer and entertainer Dai Francis a regular opportunity to show both the range and timbre of his voice and his subtle humour. The blackened face hid his real persona but his personality shone through. He was an integral part of a successful and popular series over many years, until changing sensibilities buried the concept.

In the early 1960s TWW, the commercial television company which won the first franchise for Wales and the West, created a musical show around Ivor Emmanuel and girl singer Sian Hopkins. Ivor was steeped in the eisteddfodic tradition, but he had made a name for himself in London musicals as a light baritone who could sing and act and was nimble on his feet. *Gwlad y Gân / Land of Song*, the first bilingual musical show to be networked, soon found a new audience for Welsh music. It made an immediate impact with Norman Whitehead's appealing sequential arrangements of Welsh and English songs, the happiness and joy of children singing and dancing, colourful design, clever lighting and high production values. Chris Mercer gave the show added momentum with his skilful camera direction as did the fun and energy of Ivor, 'y bachgen o Bontrhydyfen'. As television techniques developed, it soon became apparent to stars of light entertainment shows that a sympathetic and skilful director could enhance a performance.

Productions of musical extravaganzas from America dominated London theatres in the 1950s and 1960s as the music and songs from the shows of Rodgers and Hammerstein became immediate hits. Every singer of light music included songs like 'Some Enchanted Evening', 'Oh What a Beautiful Morning', 'Almost Like Being in Love' in concert performances. Shows such as *South Pacific*, *Carousel* and *Brigadoon* were resounding successes but it was *Oklahoma!*, first produced in 1943, which was revolutionary. Here were modern realism, believable characters and songs that integrated into the plot. But there were British successes too. There was *Oliver!* and *Salad Days*, and 'If I Ruled the World', a song from *Pickwick* first produced in 1963, became one of Harry Secombe's most successful recordings.

In a career spanning fifty years Harry had concentrated mainly on comedy, although he took voice training sessions seriously from his youth as a church choir boy. In his inimitable manner he wrote, 'I am not exactly a romantic lead, and my voice is not a drawing-room tenor – it's more of an outside the veranda type – glass chandeliers being in short supply.' He had to subdue his Neddie Seagoon sense of the ridiculous in the new role, but Samuel Pickwick Esq. was larger than life, a bit of a clown in many respects. As a result Harry had a hit on his hands. He went on to scale the heights and 'If I Ruled the World' became more or less his signature tune. Later, he evolved into a broad family entertainer. A man who was proud to have sung exacting arias with leading operatic singers, he later worked as presenter of *Highway* and *Songs of Praise*. In addition, he maintained the ability to project, when necessary, a warm, spontaneous and boisterous humour. And he never forgot Swansea.

Tessie O'Shea never forgot Cardiff, but unlike Harry she rarely referred to her background or her Welshness on stage. There was a transatlantic vaudeville air about her, even a hint of an American accent, but no one questioned Two Ton Tessie's commitment to Wales or her integrity within show business. In many respects she was no different from many of her contemporaries, Petula Clark and Tommy Cooper, who, although having close affiliations with Wales, preferred to operate under the British banner. It was fashionable to do so in the pre-devolution age. Tessie's routines were a mixture of popular songs and dance – some written especially for her. She dominated the stage, moving lightly and sprightly, finger pointing, blonde hair bobbing and blue eyes sparkling. A picture of fun, constant movement and energy with her 'Come on darlings. Join in', she embraced her audiences with a forceful personality and a sense of the ridiculous – 'Nobody wants a fairy when she's Forty!' She would face the reality of that comment in her retirement in Florida, where she bought a house to share with her musical director and his young family. By then the glamorous gaiety could still be seen in her body movements and professionalism, but her eyes seemed to betray loneliness and sadness – a combination perhaps of old age, of being ignored or even of being 'past it', and maybe of a trust turned sour. It often happens to those who make us smile, entertain us and who are generous of spirit.

There was a feeling of pent-up anger when the colourful Dorothy Squires stepped into the spotlight. Here was a performer who lived through her music and the adulation of her audiences and was driven by a desperate desire to prove herself again and again, not really knowing how or when to make an exit. She will be remembered as an aggressive performer who could be tender too, especially with her hit 'Say it with flowers' and her version of Gloria Gaynor's camp classic 'I am what I am'. Unfortunately, many of her appearances became outrageous melodramas, perfectly encapsulated in the vocal message 'I'd be a legend in my time'.

Iris Williams does not need histrionics to involve her audiences. There is a quality of repose in her performances and an air of security even as she expresses a range of emotions. As a competitor in Urdd Eisteddfodau her musicianship and talent soon became obvious, and she went on to become a regular performer on the Welsh-language television show *Disc a Dawn*. It is often one song which marks a turning-point in a successful career, but for Iris it happened twice. First there was 'Pererin wyf', a version of 'Amazing Grace' adapted by her producer Ruth Price, which was hauntingly melodic with words touching all the emotions. Then came a recording of a John Williams song, 'He was beautiful', based on the melody 'Cavatina', which brought her to the attention of a wider public. As her experience widened, the voice deepened, and this, coupled with her natural artistry for phrasing, musicianship and 'getting inside a song', led to her becoming an international star. Since making her base in America she has specialized in the American classic repertoire of songs by Jerome Kern, George Gershwin and Harold Arlen and her individuality is much in demand.

When there is perfection in the marriage between a singer and a song, the performance is a memorable celebration. The majority of singers, vocalists and entertainers depend on others for new and suitable material, but a few performers write their own. Ryan Davies, Max Boyce, Frank Hennessy, Dafydd Iwan and Caryl Parry Jones are prime examples of humourists, musicians and entertainers who are also social commentators on aspects of Welsh life. These are the troubadours of our age. Their tunes are often catchy and hummable, and their words combine pathos, romance, humour and irony to express a view, or to capture a mood. A few are politically motivated, but they all possess a deep concern for Wales as they understand and portray it.

Ryan was a multi-talented, mercurial entertainer steeped in the poetic, musical and oral traditions of Wales. He was the first to receive a full-time contract as an entertainer from BBC Wales in the 1960s, and his professionalism and originality did much to forge a new level of television entertainment in Wales, with series such as *Stiwdio B*, *Fo a Fe* and *Ar ei Ben ei Hun*. Together with Rhydderch Jones he wrote and performed many romantic songs such as 'Gwen Llwyd', 'Anwen' and 'Isabella' but it was his interpretation of the mysterious complexities of *penillion* or *cerdd dant*, which he translated as 'tooth singing', which was a must in every performance. He and his partner Ronnie went on to set Tom Jones's hit number 'Green, Green Grass of Home' to the old Welsh melody 'Cainc y Datgeiniad' as another example of words and music 'being able to finish together, on time'. It was also a means of bridging the gap between Welsh and English humour. And who can forget the panache of performances of the original song 'Blodwen and Mary from Abertillery' or the moving and individual rendering of the old favourites 'Ar Hyd y Nos' and 'Myfanwy'. Ryan could reach out and encompass everyone, but his roots were firmly in Wales, and much of his material stemmed from his observations and experiences.

Max Boyce has the same quality. The LP *Live from Treorchy*, produced in 1976, caught the public mood exactly right. Wales was winning rugby internationals with ease, the victorious Lions of '71 led by Carwyn James and John Dawes had beaten the All Blacks at their own game, and the outside-half factory was in full production. 'Hymns and Arias' caught the imagination and the spirit, and the Arms Park crowds in full voice reflected a national feeling of celebration and well-being. It still does. There is an innocence and vulnerability about Max's songs and performances; he can attack and cajole his audiences into believing his philosophy that 'a good little 'un can beat a good big 'un' if not by force and skill, then by wit and cunning. There is a more serious side too and, for my money, his ballads to the past and to his experiences in the mining industry have a timeless truth. The haunting 'Rhondda Grey' will stand the test of time. It was a feeling that Frank Hennessy also caught with his 'Farewell to the Rhondda', a kind of anthem to the miners' strike, and his feelings for roots and background were inimically expressed in 'Cardiff Born, Cardiff Bred'. Dafydd Iwan, on the other hand, gave expression to the tensions within Wales at the time of the investiture in 1969 with 'Carlo', his dislike of the choices within the education system in 'Cân yr Ysgol' and his basic credo in 'Yma o Hyd'.

Dafydd Iwan came to prominence as a direct result of his weekly appearances singing topical songs on the HTV news programme Y Dydd. It was at this time that he honed his skills as a communicator in the more intimate medium of the microphone and the camera. He is a performer who has bridged the generations of Welsh-language singers and entertainers nutured in those community-based chapel, eisteddfod and Noson Lawen traditions which have never recognized the theatrical flamboyance of showbiz or the backing of agents and impresarios. The impetus for the growth of popular Welsh entertainment came first from radio and then from television. It was led by one man – the legendary Sam Jones. In 1937 Sam became the BBC's North Wales representative based at Bangor and it was there, almost singlehandedly, that he developed the concept of popular programming and introduced new talent to a wider audience. Y Noson Lawen was born. It consisted of catchy songs, monologues and witty verses, but it was not until the immediate post-war years that the series really took off. New voices, modern and refreshing were now taking part. Triawd y Coleg – the close harmony of Meredydd Evans, Robin Williams and Cledwyn Jones – became household names, and their songs such as 'Pictiwrs bach y Borth' and 'Triawd y Buarth' were on everyone's lips. It was the time of the glorious amateur, although in the 1960s Meredydd Evans carried the torch forward towards greater professionalism. During his tenure as BBC Wales Head of Light Entertainment, Mered, known in his singing days as the Bangor Bing, encouraged another generation of singers and entertainers. Radio series like Helo Sut Dach Chi? presented by Hywel Gwynfryn and television programmes such as Disc a Dawn were a platform for Meic Stevens, Geraint Jarman, Heather Jones, Sidan and Hogia'r Wyddfa. Thanks to them, young people much influenced by English pop realized that Wales too had contemporary popular music of inherent appeal to them.

Dafydd Iwan and Huw Jones, now chief executive of S4C, ventured into the recording business and established their company

177

Sain in Pen-y-groes in the heartland of north Wales. They provided much-needed employment and brought to Welsh pop music aggressive marketing, a modern outlook and another outlet. Until that time singers from a broad spectrum of Welsh music had relied on recording companies such as the Pontardawe-based Qualiton, and London companies, Decca and Delyse. In many respects Qualiton, run by the indefatigable John Edwards, pioneered a successful recording industry by combining familiar talent and new artists. Choirs, groups and soloists such as Pegi Edwards from Aberystwyth singing 'Wyt ti'n cofio'r lloer yn codi' were accompanied by the Ralph Davies Quartet. But for two decades the most requested record of all time would be that of the two former miners, Jac and Wil, singing 'Pwy fydd yma ymhen can mlynedd' (Who'll be here in a hundred years?). Its success paralleled the post-war recording by Decca of tenor David Lloyd singing the hymn 'Lausanne' and the ballad 'Elen Fwyn'.

The BBC in Wales was fortunate to have on its staff at the same time two remarkable programme makers in Sam Jones and Mai Jones. They were unashamedly populist, unafraid of emotion and they discovered and promoted new talent. In their different ways, they set the agenda for the future. They would have applauded the sentiment expressed by Cerys Matthews and Catatonia, 'I thank the Lord I'm Welsh'.

Today there are ever younger voices making an international impact. Charlotte Church has tended to rely on old favourites for success, and at the age of fifteen she has already ensured a lifetime of riches with her phenomenal voice and three CD albums. In three years she has become a superstar who has performed before royalty, American presidents and the Pope. She sings with the freshness of youth classical favourites such as 'Panis Angelicus', 'The Lord's Prayer' 'Danny Boy' and 'Suo Gân' and echoes the achievements of Aled Jones in the 1980s.

Superstars from the operatic world are often reproached for diminishing their talent when they record albums of the more popular and less taxing songs and ballads. Bryn Terfel derives obvious pleasure from his interpretation of songs from the great musicals as did the great lyric Mozartian tenor Stuart Burrows when he sang the old Victorian ballads 'Thora' and 'Come into the garden

Maud'. But few popular singers have crossed over into the high art of opera. David Hughes, who was much in demand as a charismatic lead tenor in musicals, decided to take the opportunity, but unfortunately he died tragically before that aspect of his career could develop and flower.

Television, radio and the recording industry now dominate the entertainment scene. Albums and programme series are themed and packaged to maximize their marketing potential, and opportunities for 'variety' shows are few and far between. After the Second World War theatres turned into cinemas and bingo halls, but in the 1960s and 1970s performers found themselves involved in another scene and on other stages. The entrepreneurs and promoters had found another way to make money. Combining entertainment with drinking, the era of huge clubs like the Double Diamond in Caerphilly and Savas in Usk had dawned. Unprepossessing and shed-like on the outside, the glitter and glamour of cheap velour and bright lighting only emphasized the hard fact that the true purpose of the exercise was drinking. Punters turned up in droves. Pints of Brains on long trestle-like tables seemed to stretch into infinity, and entertainers were forced to compete with noise and to make contact through clouds of cigarette smoke. Those who survived, mainly comics, made money, but too many singers found they could not compete.

Perhaps the entertainment centre to be built in Cardiff Bay will herald yet another new dawn. It will be a fitting home for Welsh National Opera, but I hope it will also provide an impetus not just for them and for touring musical extravaganzas from London, but for a new generation of entertainers to perform popular new material in Wales and for Wales.

Acknowlegements
R. Alun Evans, *Stand By* (Llandysul, 1998).
Rhydderch T. Jones, *Cofiant Ryan* (Swansea, 1979).
Peter Noble, *Ivor Novello* (London, 1951).
Harry Secombe, *Goon Abroad* (London, 1982).
and Mark Owen for research.

Tom Jones

Trevor Herbert

It is only in the last decade that residents in one of the plushest Cardiff suburbs have started to recall that Tom Jones once worked in their neighbourhood as a labourer on a building site. Some can point to bricks he carried – but I do not know whether they are telling the truth. An expatriate, Welsh-born academic has dined out for years on a story that the push-chair in which he was transported as a child was bought directly from a Mrs Woodward of Treforest after her son Tom grew too old and big for it. The seat, the academic claims, was still warm when he first occupied it.

The proliferation of Tom Jones stories says something about the celebrity of the great man, and the way the perceptions of him as a Welsh singer have developed and mellowed since he entered his fifties. For every true Tom Jones story there are a dozen fabrications. My Tom Jones story is not just true; it is, for the purpose that I tell it here, important. It stands as a neat, cameo illustration of that key moment in the process of musical and cultural change when Tom Jones began his ascent to stardom. It also shows how distant those days are and how far Tom Jones has travelled since.

In the early 1960s I was the youthful trombone player with Bryn Samuels and his Embassy Ballroom Orchestra. Our eponymous leader was a Treorchy milkman who had previously played saxophone on ocean liners. Bryn was a good and versatile musician, even though his tastes had been terminally formulated by about 1932. In some ways he was an inspirational figure: a really good player with an almost obsessive preoccupation with 'professionalism', accuracy and musical discipline. Despite his travels round the globe, he had maintained an uncompromising allegiance to Nonconformist religion. He was a chapel deacon, and this is probably why the other six members of the band urgently sucked peppermints before returning from our twenty-minute drinks breaks when we played the dance halls of the south Wales valleys: Bryn's black looks were withering, and none of us wished to invite them. I was too young to go to the pub, so I spent those breaks drinking Vimto with Bryn, and listening to incongruous sermons about the dangers of 'glitter' as he took his text from the revolving mirrored-mosaic spheres that dominated the ceilings of dance halls at that time.

The band was well organized and presented, and Bryn's defence of musical formality, social propriety and 'clean fun' was stoic. His thesis seemed very wise and uncomplicated to me, but, though I did not realize it at the time, I was about to be part of a change from the old order to the new. And, though I was yet to reach my sixteenth birthday, I was unambiguously part of the old order.

The Embassy Ballroom Orchestra was a really good band: Bryn and the other players could have got jobs anywhere. There were seven of us – two saxophones (doubling clarinets), trumpet, trombone, piano, bass and drums. There was also a man whose name I cannot remember who was our 'MC'. He was immaculate and smelled strongly of cologne. He would sprinkle the dance floor with white powder before the dancers arrived, and make announcements into the microphone: 'And now ladies and gentlemen, please take your partners for the quickstep', or 'In response to several requests Bryn Samuels and his Embassy Ballroom Orchestra will now play for your pleasure – "THE GAY GORDONS"!' I think he was the neatest man I have ever met, and certainly the only one who carried Brylcreem in his pocket in case of emergencies. He wore a broad and seemingly permanent grin, but he was solemn-faced when he announced one night that our terms at the dance halls were to be 'adjusted'. Our breaks were to be extended to more than an hour and the hiatus was to be filled by 'rock-and-roll groups': the spot next week would be filled by Tommy Scott and the Senators. There was to be an appropriate and drastic amendment to our fee. Tommy Scott was the name used by Tom Woodward, who was to be more famous as Tom Jones.

On the way home in the milk van, Bryn confided to me that he was worried about what my colleagues would get up to in a one-hour break: he was thinking of giving them a firm lecture about 'professionalism' to forestall any possibility of transgression. Bryn was missing the point, for as we were to soon realize, a greater and more permanent danger beckoned.

The following week we cleared the stage for Tommy Scott's group. As soon as they started to perform, the dancers went wild; Bryn went pale and apoplectic, and muttered bilingual prayers in which words like 'Sodom', 'Babylon' and 'Gomorrah' were emphasized and given structural importance. By the time we returned to the stand to play out the rest of the evening the world had changed. We threw everything we had at them: 'Whistling Rufus', the Conga, the 'Military Two-step' and 'The Gay-bloody-Gordons' (as one *female* dancer was heard to put it), but nothing salvaged our image, which had become acutely drab and anachronistic. We sat ostentatiously and bow-tied behind our neat little band stands and pressed on, but the blandness of our reception was as palpable as were the signals of our imminent demise. It had taken Tom little more than an hour to render us asunder. As we packed away our instruments, Bryn mouthed words that may have haunted him for years: 'Don't take this seriously boys,' he said. 'It's a fad: it isn't going to last – I can remember the Charleston.'

Bryn was not just talking about Tommy Scott; he was talking about the wider effect of modern pop music in the valleys, and its implications for performers as well as its impact on repertoire. We now know that it did last and that it was not 'a fad'; we also know that even in those days Tom was giving the new music eloquent expression. The Senators and their lead singer were a part of the decisively new era. On that portentous evening the Embassy Ballroom Orchestra had merely provided a point of contrast to show, in sharp relief, just how fresh, energetic and radical that era was to be. It was not just the modernity of the sound. Indeed, even though the backing-group line-up of electric guitars and rhythm was very much in vogue, the actual songs were firmly based in a familiar, even homely, musical language – even then he sang upbeat, rock-and-roll reworkings of existing songs. It was all to do with the performance idiom. He really could sing – I thought this as soon as I heard him – but formality and musical neatness, social and musical decorum were forfeited in favour of a vocal style that was almost entirely instinctive, subjective, animated and passionate. Narrative was also important; words were acted out and given bodily emphasis with what seemed to be an almost total abandon. He was also charismatic: like one of the great old orators who employed a manner and style that made each of their listeners feel they were being addressed personally. Even in those early days the ingredients that were to be the basis of Tom Jones's success were visible and abundant.

Thomas John Woodward was born at 57 Kingsland Terrace, Treforest, on 7 June 1940. His father, like other male members of the family, was a coal-miner. Radio and cinema must have been as influential on him as on most young people at that time. They provided the source from which his musical intelligence and instincts could assimilate key transatlantic influences. Even at primary school he drew attention to himself by unaccountably singing 'Hen Wlad fy Nhadau' in the style of a Negro soul song. At home, the little boy would indulge his show-business fantasy by standing on the window-sill behind closed curtains, through which he would only appear when his mother announced loudly and convincingly to the empty room, 'Ladies and Gentlemen! Tom Woodward!'

In the mid-1950s he combined a near-total lack of commitment to a string of dead-end jobs (factory and paper-mill worker, and general labourer) with evenings singing in workingmen's clubs. He was a member of a concert party called the Misfits, and became the lead singer with the Senators some time later, when their regular front man unwisely asked Tom to deputize for him. He was a teenage Teddy boy who enthusiastically joined in the scuffles that were a ritualistic feature of valley weekends. In March 1957 he had married the 15-years-old, eight-months pregnant Linda Trenchard. By the time he was sixteen he was married with a baby son. He described himself as a 'builder's labourer' on the marriage certificate, but, in truth, his career and pecuniary prospects were little short of hopeless.

His ambition to be a professional popular singer was insatiable and all-consuming. It was an ambition that was not based entirely on speculation. Concert parties were the staple entertainment in the workingmen's clubs of south Wales. The audiences were dauntingly frank in their appraisal of singers, but they were also shrewd judges of talent. Tom had a good, strong tenor voice, an ability to move effortlessly across a variety of styles, and a natural ease with audiences. He also had self-confidence in industrial proportions. Within the realms of small-time valley show business he was well established and appreciated, but this was not enough. His relationships with his early managers – who appear to have been obsequious and largely talentless – were faltering and disappointing. His move to the major league came in 1964, when he encountered another Welshman: Gordon Mills.

Mills, who died of cancer in 1986, was an interesting and apparently appealing character. He was born in India in 1935, the son of a Welsh soldier father and an Anglo-Indian mother. After the war the family had settled in Tonypandy. Mills was bright, ambitious, confident, articulate and talented. He was briefly in the army before becoming a bus conductor, but his self-confident belief that he would make it big in show business was well founded. His entrée into professional music came as a harmonica player. He joined the hugely successful Morton Frazer's Harmonica Gang, and then the Viscounts, whose famous hit was the appallingly trite adaptation of the Negro folk-song 'Mama's little baby loves shortening bread'. Mills was musically illiterate but intent on being a songwriter. He left the Viscounts, and on his own and with others wrote a chain of UK hits, including 'Hungry for Love' and 'I'll never get over you' (for Johnny Kidd and the Pirates), 'I'm the lonely one' (for Cliff Richard) and 'Three Little Words' (for the Applejacks).

By the time he was persuaded to listen to Tom Woodward (who by then was using the name Tommy Scott) in the Top Hat Club, Cwmtillery, in 1964, Mills was well established in the British pop music business and famous in south Wales. The crowd at Cwmtillery that evening was buoyant and expectant, because no less a personage that Mandy Rice Davies was booked to make a personal appearance there. In fact, she did not turn up, but Tommy Scott did. Mills was later to admit that he had thought the young singer from Treforest was 'sensational' the first time he heard him, and immediately whisked him and the Senators to London to pursue stardom.

A change of name for Tom and the group was necessary. There was already a Tommy Scott on the pop music circuit. 'Tom Jones' seemed like a good idea. It was credibly Welsh, but more importantly it took advantage of the current success of the film of Fielding's novel in which Albert Finney had played the eponymous and outrageously rakish hero to great effect. The group's name was changed to the Squires to harmonize with the same theme – a theme to which Tom Jones enthusiastically warmed.

This was not the group's first attempt to break into the London scene, and initially it produced no more success than previous efforts. The first record for Mills, 'Chills and Fever', released in August 1964, was well promoted and reached number five in the Pontypridd hit parade (whatever that was), but was otherwise a singular flop. The major breakthrough, when it came, was fortuitous but spectacular. Gordon Mills and the composer/arranger Les Reed had been working on what was originally conceived as a country song called 'It's not unusual' for Johnny Kidd and the Pirates. When the song was completed, the two men agreed that it was better suited to the lighter tones of Sandie Shaw, who was at the height of her success following the release of her cover version of Burt Bacharach's 'Always Something There To Remind Me'. Tom Jones and the Squires were booked, for a tiny fee, to record the demo version. Tom immediately and instinctively wanted it. He pleaded with Mills to let him have the song. Mills steadfastly refused – almost certainly because he saw greater prospects for it in the hands of an established star. But remarkably, when Shaw heard the song she instantly and thoroughly hated it, and refused to record it.

The song was given to Tom and recorded in Decca's West Hampstead studios on 11 November 1964. Mills decided to drop the Squires and use an experienced professional group, the Ivy League, as the backing band. Tom's strong, masculine tones suited the song well, but the spectacular success of the recording is probably due to the intervention of Les Reed. It was Reed who, following the initial sessions, and against vehement resistance from everyone (including Tom Jones), recognized that the backing textures were insipid. He insisted on adding a brass chorus that strengthened the structure and momentum of the piece. The backings were rerecorded and it is this extra layer of timbre that punctuates the song to make it really work for Tom Jones. It was released late in January 1965, entered the UK charts immediately and was number one within a fortnight. It topped the charts in thirteen countries and stayed in the US *Billboard* chart (where it reached number ten) for nine weeks. In just four weeks the record sold more than 800,000 copies (sales eventually topped three million). Tom Jones was suddenly and emphatically a global pop star.

Since 'It's not unusual', Tom Jones has released more than sixty singles and about fifty albums. He has always been a major presence in show business but his career has not followed a continuously upward or even horizontal trajectory. Some songs – even, for example, the high profile 'Thunderball', the opening title music for the James Bond movie – made little mark. On the other hand 'Delilah', 'Green, Green Grass of Home', 'I'll never fall in love again', and a dozen others have become standards that are inexorably linked to his performance of them. This is an interesting feature of his work that says much about the distinctiveness of his performance idiom. A good proportion of his most successful songs have been reworkings of pieces that have had only modest success in the hands of others, but the process seems not to have operated in reverse. In other words, it is hard to think of a Tom Jones hit song that has subsequently been successfully exploited by another singer. His influence on songs seems to be profound and indelible. Tom Jones's singing style and the mannerisms that accompany it are singular and overtly masculine. This much may seem patently obvious, but this characteristic flavour originates not in his physicality, but in his musical persona and in particular in his unquestionable musical authority. It is as if he is in control of each moment of every song. Like other great singers he is able to impose a distinctive meaning on the songs he sings which sticks to them like mortar. This is one of two musical factors that have characterized the major hits that have appeared at almost equal distances throughout his career. Tom Jones is, in his way, a virtuoso singer. His singing voice is strong, clear, articulate and distinctive, and the Welsh accent can be caught in it. He senses the shape of songs and appears to have an innate ability to weld phrases together, or, alternatively, to segregate them, for maximum effect. The other factor is that when his arrangers and producers have applied his voice to different musical soundscapes he has always responded confidently, naturally and convincingly – as if the new style was just waiting for him to visit it.

A case in point is 'Green, Green Grass of Home', which was top of the UK hit parade for seven weeks from the end of 1966. This release followed a string of essentially loud rock-and-roll hits that started with 'It's not unusual' and included 'What's new pussycat?' and 'Thunderball'. 'Green, Green Grass of Home' had been most famously used by Jerry Lee Lewis, who included it in his album *Country Songs for City Folk*, from which Tom Jones personally chose it. But it was again Les Reed who reset what is essentially a simple, strophic, country song in a much more expansive ambience. In so doing, he created a distinctively new sound-world for Jones's voice, into which it fitted as if it were a bespoke garment. Some have suggested that the phenomenal success of 'Green, Green Grass of Home' is attributable to the generic appeal it had at the end of 1966. Indeed some have linked it specifically to the evocations it raised among US forces in Vietnam, and even to the deeply reflective sentiments that were universally shared in the aftermath of the Aberfan tragedy. It is likely that such matters did account, at least in part, for the song's reception. But these types of appeal do not appear to have been part of a conscious strategy. 'Green, Green Grass of Home' was top of the hit parade over the much-contested Christmas period that year, beating the Supremes' 'You keep me hanging on', and Elvis Presley's 'If every day was like Christmas'. It was to stay in the hit lists for almost six months. But for Tom Jones its significance was that it was the first of the many subtle re-versionings of him that have taken place in his career.

Just as 'Green, Green Grass of Home' provided a new type of vehicle for the Jones voice, there have also been commensurate amendments to his image. Between 1969 and 1971 the TV series *This is Tom Jones* provided a major opportunity for his refashioning. The shows were networked simultaneously in the UK and the US, and greatly acclaimed on both sides of the Atlantic. The persona he projected responded to the generation of his audience. 'I don't think *adults* will take rock from people with long, unkempt hair wearing jeans,' he said. He donned the tuxedo and open-necked shirt, and sang rock-and-roll and ballads to a post-teenage (particularly female) audience. The sets in which he was placed were glossy and luxurious, and projected images that would appeal to more mature tastes.

This imaging took its cue from the Las Vegas dimension of show business. His performances there, since he first appeared at Caesar's Palace in 1966, were phenomenal successes, and were particularly important to his career through the 1970s. It is said that he is singlehandedly responsible for reviving the fortunes of Bugsie Siegel's Flamingo Club, which was on the edge of terminal decline when he first sang there. His solo act came to maturity in Las Vegas and his persistent success as a live performer legitimized him (along with others like Andy Williams, Sinatra and Presley) as a member of an élite glitterati: someone with musical substance – who was considerably more than a transitory rock-and-roll singer.

The Las Vegas performances are also historically significant, because it was at one such performance that an item of female lingerie was, for the first time, accurately projected at him. No one knows whose knickers they were, but the incident seemed natural, even organic, and it soon became a ritual feature of his live shows. Even in his days in the valleys his act had been sexually provocative. But when criticisms of the sexually explicit nature of his performances have appeared, they have only served as a cue for him to increase the voltage. Implied or explicit lasciviousness is a hallmark of his performance style. It was encouraged and even manicured by his managers, and he seems to have put up little resistance to such encouragement. The eye-watering tightness of his trousers and his use of perspiration as a stage prop seemed to act as a drug on the women who squabbled for ringside seats at his shows. This may have all been light-hearted, but it was also premeditated, and while it is hard to see any of this as being bad for business, its resonances spilled over into his social and private life.

This raises the single enigmatic question about the Jones persona: his domestic arrangements. This sixty-year-old grandfather is still married to the girl he wed forty-five years ago in a Pontypridd registry office. Their son Mark manages Tom Jones Enterprises Inc., and his wife is her father-in-law's publicist. Mark and Donna Woodward seem to be extraordinarily good at their jobs, and must take much of the credit for sustaining the singer's career at such stellar heights. Family relationships appear to be robust, healthy, productive and relaxed. But, to outsiders at least, the place of Linda Woodward is difficult to understand.

From the start Linda was reportedly uncomfortable in the world that Tom Jones came to inhabit. Indeed, immediately after the success of 'It's not unusual', Gordon Mills audaciously marketed

Tom Jones as a single man, even though he was married with a child. It must have been something of a strain to sustain a marriage in a career in which implications of moral laxity were regarded as a bonus. But the two have never divorced. Jones's testimonials to family loyalty and married life suggest that either he has an over-developed sense of irony, or that his understanding of such matters is seriously idiosyncratic. I suspect that the latter is true. Certainly the stabilizing function of family life is a recurrent theme in his interviews with the media, and his utterances in this regard – against all odds – have the ring of truth about them.

Perhaps the present chapter of the Jones saga, as he moves yet further into his maturity, will shed more light on these things. Mark Woodward's most recent reversioning of his father has been one of the most impressive. The sideboards have gone and the zealously exhibitionist trousers have been replaced by garb of a more dignified tone. This was followed by the release of *Reload*, the immensely successful and in many ways iconoclastic album that featured Jones in partnership with a variety of other major artistes and groups, including the Stereophonics and, perhaps most famously, Cerys Matthews, with whom he gave an evocative performance of the classic 'Baby it's cold outside'.

How do we assess Tom Jones? It is too easy to allow the physicality of his image to obscure his musical importance. Elvis Presley regarded him as the only singer who could match his own vocal style, and he would repeatedly ring Memphis radio stations to request playings of Tom Jones's hits – it is said that he once insisted on hearing four consecutive playings of 'Green, Green Grass of Home'. The sound of his voice reached the US long before his image, and – as Dionne Warwick has famously pointed out – most Americans assumed him to be black, because no one had heard a white man sing that way.

I often wonder whether Tom Jones's significance as an expression of Welshness is adequately grasped within Wales. No one doubts the scale of his fame, but he still seems somewhat unembraced by whatever the forces are that rank our ambassadors. Why is this? Bryn Samuels's judgement of him included the proclamation that it was a 'criminal waste of a good voice'. Is it possible that those other terrible concerns that flooded Bryn's consciousness with such acidity all those years ago – lasciviousness, informality, delinquency and an indecent thirst for 'glitter' – have a residual presence in our collective national psyche? Do the gloss, the airborne underwear and the oscillating hips obscure the true potency of his talent, so as to render him intellectually and musically slight and inconsequential? Or is it to do with a more dubious product of our self-reflection? Is it possible that in assimilating the transatlantic influence so utterly convincingly, he has gone further from what we think we are than we want him to? If such is the case, we are deceiving ourselves, for in many ways his eclecticism reflects the cultural landscape that we truly inhabit. Tom Jones is a great Welsh singer, and his capacity to absorb disparate stylistic elements and then project them in a distinctly fresh light has always been the basis of his unique singing idiom and, to my mind, the classiest part of his Welshness. There can be little doubt that his celebrity and global fame eclipses that of any other singer that Wales has ever produced – and it is not without good cause.

Acknowledgements
L. Ellis and B. Sutherland, *Tom Jones: Close Up* (London, 2000).
S. Hildred and D. Gritten, *Tom Jones – The Biography* (Sidgwick & Jackson, 1990).
C. Macfarlane, *The Boy from Nowhere* (W. H. Allen, 1988).
Don't Fight It: the original versions of the songs that inspired Tom Jones. Various artists. 2000 Compact disc. Connoisseur Collection. VSOP CD 300.

Shirley Bassey

Dai Smith

Nothing Like a Dame.
First, the story line.

An implausible story at best, something scripted on speed and sieved through a crazed publicity machine. Rags, in the beginning, for sure. And even less. As a kid legend has it that she had to borrow spare knickers from a friend to go sliding down heaps of coal slag on a tin tray. The riches to come would then have been beyond belief. Even more so, maybe, the fame that would surround her in an aura of stardom right across the world for over forty years. And then there will be the accolade of recognition at the very pinnacle of society's Establishment. But recognition of what precisely . . . of raw, natural talent being relentlessly crafted into the sustained achievement of a Voice? . . . Of the uplifting model of a lifetime of financial success in a crushing, fickle on-stage Business? Of sheer dogged survival through training and diet and willpower? Of an atavistic popularity akin to and perhaps now beyond that of Royalty? Or just of a woman who always behaved as if she was more than just a dame, and so finally became one with a capital 'D'.

Then, the plot.

A woman, not blandly beautiful but touching in her startled-into-loveliness look, returns, suddenly and briefly, to her home town in the last year of the twentieth century. She seems, both up close and from afar, to be in her forties though she is, in fact, in her early sixties. Everything about her, from clothes to hair to make-up, has a bespoke elegance. When she left home, aged sixteen and for the first time, in 1953, it was as a big-eyed, crop-haired and gauche teenager in the decade that was busy inventing the term and her provincial town, already far removed from its bonanza times of half-a-century earlier, was a drab, workaday place. Yet now, in 1999, it too had had a make-over and was a-buzz with activity again. It had become, at long last, worthy of the title of capital city which it had borne, somewhat taken sheepishly, since 1956. The change is such that she claims not to be able to recognize it anymore. And, in truth, most of the flattening and rebuilding had been, since 1957 and with increasing pace, of the very area in which she had been born. Here, this late *fin de siècle* spate of modernizing reconstruction, even regeneration some said, transformed a city waterfront that was once a working docks into a newly urbane Bay in order to house the new democratic Assembly of her own country. Here, in her own, actual and mythical backyard.

It is, in fact, why she has come back on a cool July night to the space that has been cleared near the Gothic Pierhead Building, grandiose reminder of her youth, and one that will soon site the grand design of the Assembly. She waits, a slim, supple, honey-coloured woman with liquorice brown eyes that can glitter or glaze as the mood requires, to step centre stage before a shell-like canopy of electric stars, and into the open air, once more, before a huge and expectant audience; yet this one also, in its diverse mix, very much her own. She appears. Instantly recognizable; and, for these people, symbolically endearing. She is wearing their flag.

The applause crashes on and on, ricocheting off the memories of once Stygian pubs like The Packet and The Ship and Pilot, where once she sang, and down that fragment of Wall Street at the bottom of Bute Street where the palazzos of merchants and the pillared halls of coal millionaires conspired at a greatness that never came, until it swirls back through the unreal real estate of the boutiques-that-will-be and over a smorgasbord of international restaurants. Surely, she does not forget the over-crowded apartments into which grander Victorian mansions had been turned to make rent affordable or the allure of illicit gambling and after-hours drinking that enticed men to come below the Bridge to go a-whoring in Tiger Bay. For sure, she will remember the dismal grind to survive and the lively fun that accompanied it as a true salvation. So, she is wearing what is her flag, too. This most glamorous of fashion-orchestrated women is draped, and loosely so, from head to foot in green and white with the red heraldic Dragon of Wales emblazoned all over her. No wonder they clap on and on until her arms, sinuous and beckoning, still them. She begins to sing, in a voice so resonant that, if the building still stood, it could be heard in the rooms of 182 Bute Street where she was born in 1937. Shirley Veronica Bassey, here on this very spot, her back to the sea, facing all Wales and singing outwards from this transformed location into Wales, is At Home. Her voice is unique. Yet it is, in and by its individuality, redolent of twentieth-century Wales. Now, on this silent air, south of the city that had prospered and of those valleys that had foundered as both made Wales modern, it weaves itself, via television and radio, into the night, right across the nation and into the new century that is waiting, more pregnant with hope here in the Bay than anywhere else. Shirley, in particular, has earned the right to be part of this. If she had stayed, just kept working as a packer of enamel pots and pans in Curran's factory, waitressed in Frederick Street, married, sang solo in The Baltimore, then it would have been Veronica's by right anyway. The joy of it, for those with filled memories as well as those with blank expectations, was that La Bassey was choosing to exercise the right. She was definitely doing it Her Way. Kitsch couture met Cymru and post-modern irony kissed national solipsism. All in all, not a bad start for Welshness in the next century.

The last time Shirley Bassey had sung in the Bay was in 1957 on her first triumphant homecoming, by way of London and Las Vegas, when she topped the bill for the first time at Cardiff's New Theatre where, just three years before, she had been a scene-filling bit singer in a tawdry, touring revue *Hot from Harlem*. The intervening years had seen her solo act and her self-presentation shaped, sometimes rather savagely, by the first of a number of would-be Svengalis who thought they had seen beyond her raw vocal appeal. The journey back to Cardiff had been via one of the circuits of variety theatres which still connected the provincial towns of 1950s Britain like a necklace of lacklustre Venusbergs. Now a very stage-managed return to her own city saw this still fresh *ingénue*, floating rather than swimming on a floodtide of local fame, entertain the kids of the Rainbow Club, a social and youth club which had once helped to give her room to grow the talent which, from thirteen years onward, she had let rip, in versions of 'Stormy Weather' and 'Bye, Bye Blackbird' and 'Somewhere over the Rainbow', in the dingy male drinking dens of post-war Wales. Already the switch to diamanté sheath dresses or fish-tailed frocks like the ones Jane Russell or even Monroe were modelling on the new cinemascope screens had taken this twenty-year-old torch singer into a new plush world – even if the plushness of it, so far, was confined to crushed velvet tip-up seats in the make-believe cabaret of Variety 'turns.'

By the end of the next decade the cabaret would have become for real as she filled the Empire Room of New York's Plaza Hotel, made Hollywood's Coconut Grove shudder at her power and crossed the world over and over, from the 'Pigalle' of Paris to Las Vegas, Sydney and any London venue she chose. By then, too, the plot of her improbable life had twisted and turned – sometimes it would almost corkscrew out of control – as lurid headlines captured her life in tabloid flash-bulb mode. Shirley was kidnapped at gunpoint by an estranged lover; near murder ensued; affairs, casual and profound, and Pygmalionesque in the case of the actor Peter Finch, who was then heartbroken over her, would punctuate the years of her pomp; marriages would offer stability and yet founder, once on the rocks of suicide; and sudden death would haunt her again when her daughter, Samantha, drowned in 1985; and throughout, there was the incessant work-driven ethic that took her, in material things, further and further away from the time, when at seventeen and an unmarried mother, she was stuck, after her first doleful board-treading, back with her mother in Portmanmoor Road, Splott.

The family had moved there, Shirley, her brother and her five sisters, when she was just three. The upheaval was only a bus ride away from the Bay to the vicinity of the Dowlais Steel Works (moved down from Merthyr in 1911 and a vital aspect of Cardiff's economy until its closure in the 1970s), but Shirley never, ever, quite left Tiger Bay itself. Her first baby would be named Sharon, the name her own father had given her as an affectionate tribute, he said, to the queen of Sheba. His name was Henry Bassey, a Nigerian seaman who had jumped ship in Cardiff after the Great War and found there a Tyneside woman, Eliza Jane Metcalfe, whose last and seventh child would be Shirley Veronica.

As the Second World War began in earnest in 1940, Henry Bassey, his claim on British citizenship tenuous since his region of Nigeria was only a protectorate, was summarily deported. He had, as officialese would have it, 'fallen foul of the authorities'. His life, as party-giver, bed-provider, dice-thrower and occasional ship's stoker, had come to an end before his last daughter could come to know him. As she grew up – her mother in a new long-standing partnership with another Nigerian seaman, the smart and serious Mr Mendi who became her 'Dad' – the workaday world of Splott and Moorlands School cradled her, but it was the enticing pulse of her father's Tiger Bay that pulled her in.

The early memories are of a shy, almost fearful child, crouched under a chenille tablecloth in their two-storey terraced house, listening to the beat of music at one of Henry's impromptu parties, and singing. The place in which she was singing was perhaps the strangest Wales had yet created. Accents all around her, and way into the 1950s as she kept her friends and youthful forays into life on its particular streets and byways, were, as Gwyn Thomas wrote, formed by 'the high soft speech of a hundred tongues from Africa and the East, or perhaps from the lips of a child born in to the docks, an enchanting mixture of Somerset, Madagascar and Pontllanfraith'.

Even more miraculous was the manner in which the built environment had been given a domestic bedrock, a commercial purpose and a mercantile splendour that made it, uniquely in Wales, a world in cameo. In 1922, before Henry Bassey rented it, 182 Bute Street was the premises for Julius Bregartner, clothier and outfitter, whilst at 216 Bute Street, H. Berman and Co., self-styled as 'The Boston Tailors' held their own sartorial tea party, and at 165 Bute Street there was the fashion-conscious soirée of 'Latner and Redhouse (late L. Blanchard) . . . noted French house'. By the end of the 1930s only echoes remained of the consulate presence that represented the nations of the world on Bute Street, but the scent of their once having been there was still intense – up and down and around that square mile, for a moment in Wales, were the consulates of the Argentine Republic, of Belgium and Bolivia and Brazil, of Chile and Colombia, of Denmark and the Dominican Republic, of Ecuador, France, Greece, Italy, Norway – pause to register it was Edward Dahl, father of the more famous Roald – of young Soviet Russia and Spain and Sweden, and all the way down the alphabet to the United States of America, Uruguay and Venezuela. As she wandered, to a welcome from all over that populated globe, she would reflect that she inherited her love of the sea from her father. Maybe. And certainly she would have imbibed it, here, from birth.

There were, of course, plenty of mean streets where the working and the non-working poor of Butetown, that city-within-a-city 'below the bridge', lived. In those streets, still, as she matured would be the boarding houses, specialists all, for the various nationalities of this special place. A Trades Directory reads like an international roll call:

Boarding-House Keepers
Ahmed, Said, 38 Maria Street; Arabian boarding house
Arapis, Manouel, 50 Bute Street; Greek boarding house
Attard, F., 156 Bute Street; Maltese boarding house
Avoth, Mahomet, 19 Angelina Street; Arab boarding house and
    coffee shop
Campos, Mrs, 166 Bute Street; Spanish boarding house
Guerdiaga, Fidel, 150 Bute Street; Scandinavian boarding house
Lang, Hassan Ben, 8 Bute Terrace; licensed keeper, Malay, Singapore;
    British subject
Low, Hing, 22 Patrick Street; Chinese boarding house
Magri, Catherine, 214 Bute Street; Maltese boarding house
Oxley, John, 41 Peel Street, Butetown; West Indian boarding house
Risman, A., 1 Sophia Street; Latvian boarding house
Rodrigues J., 18 Maria Street; Portuguese boarding house
Zamith, Manuel, 161 Bute Street; licensed Maltese boarding house

Shirley Bassey would not be the only one to find fame in the world of popular culture from these origins. The great rugby league star, Gus Risman, would tantalizingly play the amateur Union game in the 1920s before heading for professional and legendary status in the North in 1929, and the wondrous Billy Boston, son of an Irish mother and West Indian father, hit the heights before his near contemporary, Shirley, did so when, in 1953, he signed for Wigan for £3,000 and a dazzling career as an all-time great. And already, in boxing, the most cultured fighter of his generation through the 1950s would be the (almost) heavyweight and immensely popular, Joe Erskine. J. Lee Thompson's 1958 movie now seems to provide a last-documented glimpse of this mixed race and tolerant society but, at that time, was just unblushingly able to use the name *Tiger Bay* as its title and know, unhesitatingly, that across the globe it would be as familiar and as instantly of Wales as, say, Rhondda. The personal names would reverberate on for a while yet, as boxing boasted Eddie Avoth in the 1960s and Peter Rodrigues became the first Welshman to lift the FA Cup since 1927 when he did it, not for his home-town club of Cardiff, but as captain of Southampton in 1976.

Tiger Bay, and perhaps the last real remnants of the culture and community it had created, was a lesser place then than the area had once promised. The pedimented and porticoed grandeur around the Pierhead and the beckoning elegance of the town houses of Loudon Square had been bulldozed by obtuse planners – the Philistines were the only ethnic group not welcome in the Bay – or fell silent about their dream of destiny. Only in the voice of Shirley Bassey and to the acute ear in her accented vowel sounds, can we still detect that dream and, maybe, its eventual destiny.

Not that it wasn't always strictly personal with Shirley. She knew that the myth of racial tolerance in Wales was rapidly deflated once you stepped outside Butetown – and, of course, the 1919 race riots in the aftermath of the Great War almost defined the geography of race in the city – and both she and her mother stood up against the name-calling whenever it came to the young girl. Later, on her transatlantic tour of 1960, the admired and admirable Sammy Davis Jr would protect her from the casual abuse of American racial slurs. Much later, when her perform-ances at South Africa's Sun City drew down anti-apartheid criticism, she would insist that she would never appear before racially segregated audiences. Yet her determination, at the same time, to affirm her own humanity came through in the accurate, but disingenuous, remark: 'My mother was white so I never thought I was anything else.' No one would label the individual Shirley Bassey unless it was Shirley herself. But Shirley Bassey the singer, at the beginning, had to succumb to the paraphernalia of exoticism that surrounded her early career, as singer and dancer, on stage. Even her first hit, in 1956, was 'The Banana Boat Song', and welcome though the break would be, she was, decidedly, no calypso singer (the closest she would ever have been to a banana boat was at Barry Docks). Nor was she quite in the mould of other British songbirds of the glutinous 1950s – not the sibilant Ruby Murray, the Clooneyish Joan Regan, the husky catch-in-the-voice Alma Cogan rooted in a froth of tulle, or the winsome Lita Rosa. Long before this, she had ruefully concluded, in duets of practice with her brother Henry, that she wanted to sound like Sarah Vaughan but came over more like Billy Eckstine.

Imitation fell away when, now being bruised by life's events, she stumbled on her distinctive singing persona and infused her voice with the secret: her captivating sexuality and its attendant vulnerability. Sometimes this would figure as a come-hither, over-the-top playfulness – as in her lubricious rendering of 'Kiss Me, Honey, Honey' – where she snaps out the words 'Honey-Honey' more like an impatient dismissal than a term of endearment – and, later, meld into the draggy jokiness of 'Hey Big Spender' for whom, alone and smilingly for everyone watching, she will 'pop her cork'. Mostly, though, it is an urgent, snarling sexual predatoriness – the elongated phrasing of 'Goaal-Fingaah' matching the voraciousness of the lyrics – and, most affectingly, squeezed out, reluctantly, in her first, and dearly prized by her, mammoth hit song of 1961, 'As Long As He Needs Me'.

Her judgement about her own songs in her own career became infallible. The gut instinct came first when the spine shivered and she knew 'that is my song'; the cerebral bit was, always, 'that the story line is something that has happened to me along the way'. Then the identification became complete and the innocuous originals, picked up like 'Grande Grande Grande' when listening to Italian radio as she sojourned in and around her favoured Monte Carlo, became transmuted via new arrangements and English lyrics, as did the resounding 'Never, Never, Never' and the heartstopping 'This is my life' whose bravura defiance makes Sinatra's 'My Way' sound like a small boy's petulance.

Since the mid-1960s her experience and her range have come together with consummate ease in her professional packaging of Shirley Bassey. She has garnered endless recording awards and kept her new and re-trod albums constantly in the upper reaches of chart sales. The concert tours continue to give the audiences the essence of what they require – technically adept, superbly staged and sprinkled with that peculiar baggage of evanescent pop starriness: instant nostalgia (a million Dansettes spin a myriad number of vinyl 45s and LPs every time she mouths her past on stage). None the less, this is not what will ensure Shirley Bassey's memory as a singer. Sure, she, as well as anyone, can deliver classic standards, from Bacharach or the Beatles or reaching back to the jazz-pop American basis of her youth; and the Cold War spy-fest that laminated our eyeballs with the techno-cool social snobbisme of Bond movies handed Shirley a video backdrop, an audience of zillions and a niche in film history via *Goldfinger*, and *Diamonds Are Forever*. But what will resonate will be the songs she delivered as if they were the personal arias of her own life.

This connection between Shirley and singing which is beyond the technical is at the heart of her appeal. When she does this the base metal which she has sometimes polished too thin melts away and we are left with no impurities. The phrasing is unmistakable. She skeeters, word by word, almost in a recitative manner as the song's tale begins. She roars in ferocity ('Love me – Hate me – Love me – Hate me') and trembles tearfully into submission only ('I am what I am') to spit reaffirmation of a life back in the face of fate. It is bravura singing. The names to conjure with then are those of Judy Garland, of Edith Piaf and Maria Callas. The latter is not over-fanciful. Her voice coach – for she works out on all parts of her body daily – Helena Shenel observed that her voice, one that is 'naturally very big', 'doesn't need a mike to fill the Albert Hall'. And the powerfully-voxed opera star, Jesse Norman, rapt with admiration, asked Shirley after one riveting show 'How do you do it? *I* don't do the same – *I* couldn't sustain the power for an hour.' What Shirley Bassey actually projects though, is not power, but love.

At the start of her career in the mid-1950s, escaping from the Carmen Miranda head-dresses of the Al Read show where another northern English despot masquerading as a comic wished to pin her down, she sought the effective disguise of low-cut simple black dresses and a doe-eyed, transfixed look to distract attention from the dreadful messages of 'Jezebel' and 'Ebb Tide'. At midpoint in her career, she exposed one silvery leg from toes to thigh in a slashed sequinned dress and allowed Morecambe and Wise to pinion her high-heeled foot on a stage set's step in a wonderfully comic downplaying of her act ('I'm a stripper at heart' she has said more than once). No one is really fooled. The voice tells of trust and betrayal, of passion and despair, of triumph and adversity. The body is inseparable from it. Its beauty is the cause of her misery and joy. It is undeniable and it is, as the voice reveals, at risk. She is still, said the lyric writer Norman Newell, 'a volcano on the stage'. When most dormant, in her presence, she is least extinct, in the force she is about to unleash: 'On the stage I become another person. I am not Shirley Bassey the wife or mother.'

Watch recordings of the 1992 Royal Albert Hall. Her hair is like a purple cloud framing her mobile, expressive face. She wears a flesh-toned spangled top and a skirt, revealingly cut in the back, of a beaten copper colour that glints with a dull, then suddenly incandescent sheen beneath the lights as she moves and swirls. Or stands stock still as she does for 'I Who Have Nothing'. The music swoops and soars, familiar, almost banal in its abrupt endings. The lyrics plonk as you rehearse them in your mind. It does not matter. This is all now transformed.

She stands before us. Her hands are extended slowly, modestly beseeching, put before us as a supplicant, then clutched to her breast as she tells us quietly of the bereftness of her life. Then, as the music and narrative drive upwards, her arms are thrown out, out, wider and wider, not to envelop us, but to take us in. The hands speak to us, fluttering like deranged butterflies beating hopelessly against the glass of their captivity. Finally they suggest her open-palmed stigmata.

When she sings 'As Long As He Needs Me' the body language is heavily transferred to her face. She is not afraid, as she searches for the soulfulness of the song, letting her emotion, even her tears, well up from within her, to make a pout which other singers seek to avoid. Her nose twitches, pulls down, down to the left as her mouth, now the size it seems of a third of her face, now a curved slice, lets out the tremolo sound she has mastered as much as the full-throated yowl of her be-damned-to-it-all ballads. As the meaning of her words and of her public presentation of them dawn on her afresh her eyes open wide as if she is making love. And perhaps she is.

Certainly, at moments like this in her act, the non-threatening bump and grind of 'Big Spender' are left far behind and 'As I love you, more and more and more' reaches out reminding us of how young and determined she was in 1959, we just wait, for the ups and downs of 'This is my life' to end with those expressive arms pulled down, inevitably, and against her will, only to be raised in a spiritual conquering of all closures and all pettiness.

'There's something of my past in every song' is what Dame Shirley Bassey knows. She does not need to spell it out further. It is there in her voice. And her voice has used the makings of a universal popular culture of song to invest it with an ineradicable and distinctive Welsh identity. She is what we are.

Acknowledgements
Muriel Burgess, *Shirley: An Appreciation of the Life of Shirley Bassey* (London, 1988).
Gwyn Thomas, *A Welsh Eye* (London, 1964 and 1984).
The Slate, BBC Wales: Shirley Bassey.

Kelly, Cerys and James Dean Bradfield

Dai Griffiths

At the very end of the twentieth century three Welsh rock bands, the Manic Street Preachers, Catatonia, and the Stereophonics were popular enough to play large-scale venues, and it fell to the voices of their lead singers, James Dean Bradfield, Cerys Matthews, and Kelly Jones, to fill the space of the various arenas, fields and stadiums. The story of how Welsh pop music reached this stage is interesting and complicated and involves two strands, each aware and largely respectful of the other. First, in the mid 1980s, with Geraint Jarman as key influence, Welsh-language pop music underwent something of a change in attitude. Post-punk bands like Anrhefn and Datblygu attempted to reach beyond the specifically Welsh-language media, for instance by performing and getting played on the John Peel radio programme in England. In music-industry terms, Welsh-language pop music was already independent in a sense that the British genre 'indie' was incapable of conceiving, and the Welsh record label Ankst, set up in 1988, reflected that condition. Secondly, at about the same time, with John Cale arguably the great precedent, something also happened in English-language Welsh pop music. In the late 1980s, the Manic Street Preachers started to put together a conception of pop music which contained elements of a traditional art-school approach, but was now more fiercely given to historical and political awareness which, if not incapable of appearing elsewhere, carried considerable baggage from its origin in south Wales. The Manics began on English independent labels, Damaged Goods and Heavenly, but, in another sign of things to come, soon signed to a major label, Columbia. During the 1990s these two strands interacted, proliferated, and eventually became popular, both in the situation of live performance and eventually in album sales. Thus, Welsh pop music by the end of the century helped fill not only venues like the big festivals at Glastonbury and Reading but also, quite unpredictably, locations such as Margam Park, Morfa Stadium near Swansea, and the Millennium Stadium in Cardiff which opened just as the year 2000 seemed to bring these developments to a punctuation point.

A further historical point worth making is the distinction between the Welsh popular voice as stylist, such as Tom Jones and Shirley

Bassey, interpreting songs written and sometimes originally recorded by others, and the more immediate pressures attendant upon self-conscious originality which we encounter here. These three lead singers all have more than a stake in the writing of the songs themselves, not least in earning a publishing royalty in addition to the funds accrued from records sold or through live performance. They enter the ongoing battle over the condition of the pop song, where the perceived necessity of engaging with pop song as form was arguably again stronger as a tradition in Welsh-language pop music. Indeed, the relation between these voices and how they perceive Wales and being Welsh is a recurring theme: all of them developed a prickly relation to what was marketed in the 1990s as Britpop, while all had some demonstrable affinity with Wales, albeit in different and healthily problematic ways.

I want to travel backwards and start with the most recent band, the Stereophonics, and their lead singer Kelly Jones. All three band members were born at Aberdare General Hospital: Stuart Cable the drummer in 1970, Kelly Jones and bass player Richard Jones four years later, and they grew up in the village of Cwmaman, to the people of which their first album was dedicated. They had all played in local bands, mostly doing sets comprising cover versions for local gigs, but when they formed as Stereophonics in 1996 things started to move very quickly indeed. Signed to V2, a Richard Branson label, there was more than an element of brand design about this, as though marketing departments had collectively learned through the success of Britpop, groups like Suede, Blur, Pulp, and Oasis, exactly how to translate the excitement and identity claims of British rock music based in live performance, through albums, videos, and logo-branded merchandise. To a sceptic, it seemed as though by 1997 Britpop was running out of steam and then, suddenly, there were Travis and the Stereophonics to push the thing through to the millennium and beyond. Stereophonics belonged more to the 'dadrock' (Oasis and Ocean Colour Scene) than the 'art-school' (Suede, Blur and Pulp) ends of Britpop, but they also had a heavier edge too, consistent with the blurring of rock, hard rock and heavy metal popular in industrial towns and areas of Britain, south Wales included, and an important constituency for the band. From the start, sound, appearance and career trajectory were carefully constructed and controlled, and by the time of the second Stereophonics album *Performance and Cocktails* in 1999 the sleeve would include, U2-style, website references for Amnesty, Greenpeace and the Free Tibet Campaign.

Kelly Jones was at the heart of the trio, as prime songwriter, controller of words, singer and guitarist. The songs are derived, more so on their first album, *Word Gets Around* of 1997, from realist and detailed observation of local life. If this makes the songs sound like the poetry of Idris Davies, then the music adds a further dimension, much as form or rhyme can to the valley poet. With 'Local Boy in the Photograph', 'More Life in a Tramp's Vest' or 'Too Many Sandwiches' you can sing along a good few times before realizing the lurid or pointed nature of the detail. Their tone is conversational, an element of the words as well as the music, and Jones often employs first and second person as though talking to a friend in the pub: these are singer-songwriter songs projected on to the power trio. As ever with realism's chief device, metonym, what matters is the way that the small detail can project itself on to the general situation, so that for a heavy drinker to have his name printed on a glass, as in 'Last of the Big Time Drinkers', supplies both a familiar detail and commodity fetish while projecting outwards into the fate of the imagination in village life.

The voice of Kelly Jones combines pitch precision with sedimented dirt, in a mixture and trio context sure to recall Kurt Cobain of Nirvana. Indeed, the heavy metal constituency must have heard something in Jones's guitar style and voice, the convention of which was established thirty years earlier by Ian Gillan of Deep Purple and Robert Plant of Led Zeppelin, building on roots in rhythm and blues. So there's plenty of 'strangulated' expression, and a big vocal range: 'Looks Like Chaplin' demonstrates Jones's control and the character of his three registers, a low and understated area for rumination, a second and higher, more expressive layer, and a pitch-certain falsetto. With a song like 'The Bartender and the Thief' on the second album, Jones's central range supplies the detail of the chorus, against overdubbed vocal riffs, while the verse is characterized by more Cobain-like grain. The band inhabits established rock territory, and one suspects that the Stereophonics' success had something to do with the coming-of-age of some of their listening audience for whom such 'rifftastic' music was new to their own lives. If many of Jones's guitar riffs are prefigured in American 1990s slacker rock (Eddie Vedder, J. Mascis, Perry Farrell) this is due not to imitation so much as shared roots. That said, to me, 'A Thousand Trees' sounds curiously similar to 'Insomniac' by mid-1990s indie band Echobelly, and there's something in Jones's voice which recalls that of Sonya Madan, their lead singer, an ability to be bang on the note within a strong central vocal range.

It is probably fair to say that the Stereophonics represent a traditional nationalism on the part of the south Wales valleys, only vaguely aware of the Welsh language, fiercely aware of local identity, and defined at its strongest negatively, through a clear definition of England. The England of the Stereophonics is as much an imagined community as their Wales, and it was this ambivalence which led to disquiet on the part of a section of their English audience at the Morfa Stadium concert in 1999. The band's attempt to reflect national sentiment – although entertained as 'tradition' at international rugby matches between Wales and England – seemed to sections of the English audience who had travelled to Morfa close to biting the hand which fed it. In sport the other team is there on the field, of course, with a sporting chance of success, whereas musical performance is a projection on to a singular audience. Jones's solo song 'As Long as We Beat the English', recorded to be shown before a rugby match in 1999, nicely reflects the accepted folk wisdom of the rugby international, but would need to be kept under wraps if the Welsh Development Agency were attempting to secure 'inward investment' across the border. Pop music had an established tradition of at least harbouring the conceit that the concert or festival represented albeit briefly an idealized or utopian coming-together with differences of identity dissolved. On the other hand, there was always the more politicized tradition of Detroit's MC5, or London's Clash, where the idea was to enrage the audience sufficiently to get things changed, and in Cymdeithas yr Iaith (Welsh-language society) gigs, at least in the 1970s, the idea was that we would leave these rural gatherings refreshed and all the more certain of the need for national independence or at least a television channel. The Stereophonics remain, to date at least, more the realist reflection of attitude rather than a programme of political action. Catatonia dipped in these waters too, although their pique seemed directed more specifically towards London as metropolitan dominant. As devolution arrived in Wales, however, curiously the place where these negotiations of national identity were made with most determination, where flags flew like question marks, was not so much at sporting events as at the rock gig or festival, and gradually over larger and more inclusive crowds.

In fact, Catatonia had emerged from an apprenticeship longer and very different from that of the Stereophonics, with most of the band having put in hard years of graft in the Welsh-language pop world. As Y Cyrff, Mark Roberts and Paul Jones had issued several records on the Ankst label, the early career of Catatonia was guided by Rhys Mwyn of Anrhefn, and the earliest Catatonia releases in 1993 and 1994 were on Welsh-language label Crai, a subsidiary of Sain. Dafydd Ieuan, drummer on Catatonia's first recordings and now with Super Furry Animals, is almost a one-man potted-history of Welsh pop during the period. One single followed on English independent Nursery, before the band was signed to the Blanco y Negro subsidiary of Warner. As David Owens's excellent book makes clear, the core of Catatonia was the northern Roberts, born in 1968 in Llanrwst, and the southern Cerys Matthews, born in Cardiff in 1969, and the band has since been based on a combination of solid musicianship (Roberts and Owen Powell guitars, Paul Jones bass, and Aled Richards drums), songwriting shared between Roberts, Matthews and Powell, and Matthews's voice. Many of the early Catatonia releases were collected in 1996 on their first album, *Way Beyond Blue*, a solid debut for all its nature as compilation.

Everything came together for Catatonia with their second album, *International Velvet*, in 1998. Over a well-balanced sequence of tracks, Catatonia cracked a songwriting style with words which made slightly skewed reference to issues and concerns of the day, and a slight touch of fantasy, all kept within strong song forms. Matthews and Roberts's song 'Road Rage' is a great example of the latter: basically employing the musical trick of going 'up the tone' twice across the song, something which can be done tremendously badly (try Stevie Wonder's 'I just called to say I love you'), here little but subtle and telling changes of phrasing ensure that the gradual build-up is achieved beautifully and unpredictably. The production style carefully placed Cerys's voice in the foreground: where the first album presented the songs more as the band might have performed them live, *International Velvet* has a more produced sound designed as support to Matthews's voice. Her voice is superb here, packed with character and body. It is Owen Powell's song 'Strange Glue', to my mind, which really defined Cerys Matthews's vocal character. Within a fairly simple song she takes on the fateful air of the great popular diva, and there is the queasy sense even in ordinary listening that the song might be alluding to direct experience. Even though Catatonia is a collective operation, Matthews blurs real life and the songs in a manner recalling both the strength and the burden of female singer-songwriters such as Joni Mitchell or Rickie Lee Jones. In truth, however, she imbues more or less any phrase with the same heartfelt quality, a big part of which is her enduring accent, touchingly enough the Welsh accent of a Welsh speaker speaking in English. Matthews also has a particular kind of voice, one located neither largely in the head, like Neil Young or Liam Gallagher, nor largely in the body, like Elvis Presley or Tom Jones. There is simply something going on in the tubes which gives the voice that gravelly trace, that bodily presence – a comparison could usefully be made with Rod Stewart. The gravel in both voices brings a range of emotional contradiction: sass, heartache, vulnerability, assertion. Put bluntly, as with Marilyn Monroe's renditon of 'Happy Birthday' for President Kennedy, Cerys could be singing 'Postman Pat' or 'Blwyddyn Newydd Dda', and you would still be thinking of sex and alcohol (and, funnily enough, with both Rod and Cerys it's alcohol and not drugs). In this respect, Everett True's inspired depiction of Cerys as 'a Shirley Bassey for the Nike generation', is hard to beat.

With the track 'International Velvet' itself – and what an obscure title for a song with such a strong and straightforward hook! – Catatonia also entered the vexed area of Welsh pop's relation to England and the English language. The chorus adapts a line from a traditional Jewish prayer into a terrific singalong chorus, 'Everyday that I wake up I thank the Lord I'm Welsh', but in a context made more complicated, not to say impossible for most listeners, by having the chorus follow verses in Welsh, these too delivered to a weird synthesized sound evoking some Celtic or Eastern resonance. Cerys in Welsh does sound slightly differently from her voice in English, and the idea of putting both languages to use was something shared with two other prominent bands of the 1990s, Gorky's Zygotic Mynci and Super Furry Animals. At the concert held to celebrate devolution in Cardiff in 1999, this song in a way said it all, used as it was as culmination even in Catatonia's absence, as the luminaries of popular music in Wales clapped away to verses they could not all understand. Indeed, one of the great achievements of the reinvented Welsh-language bands (Y Cyrff as Catatonia, Ffa Coffi Pawb as Super Furry Animals, Gorky's Zygotic Mynci, Beganifs as Big Leaves) was to use the Welsh language as question mark concerning the nature of language and national identity, not only and most obviously for Welsh speakers but also for English speakers in Wales and even beyond.

The third Catatonia album, *Equally Cursed and Blessed*, followed with what even at the time seemed like risky haste in 1999. Their established verbal trick, to drop in references to the popular culture of the day, now became mannered and more often than not misfired. The words arguably always stuck out in Catatonia and may have something to do with English as learned language. Consider as an example the dreadful run, 'my selfish gene it fills my spleen with bile', which closes *International Velvet*, especially when set next to the ease with English cliché of a Damon Albarn for Blur at the time: 'streets like a jungle/so call the police' ('Girls and Boys'), 'when I feel heavy metal/and I'm pins and I'm needles' ('Song 2'). All this, as we will see, would be anathema to the Manic Street Preachers, where maintaining the dissonance and awkwardness of word-music correspondence was surely the band's purpose.

The Manics appeared in the late 1980s. The four members all come from a pair of towns along the Sirhowy river in Gwent, Blackwood and Pontllanfraith. Richey Edwards was oldest, born in 1967, James Dean (*sic*) Bradfield the singer and Nicky Wire the bass player two years later, and drummer Sean Moore in 1970. The story of the Manics is complicated and profoundly tragic, and turns on the disappearance in 1995 of Edwards, now presumed dead although still, at the time of writing, with no conclusive evidence. From a band history far more than most worth attending to in its detail (Simon Jones's fine book one suspects will be the first of many), I want to emphasize two things as background for Bradfield as singer and part-songwriter. First, the respect for education which underlay the band as a whole but Wire and Edwards in particular and secondly, arising from this, their particular approach to songwriting which saw Wire and Edwards control absolutely the words to the songs while Moore and Bradfield supplied the music, a division of labour maintained with closed-shop consistency. Their songwriting technique meant that what was delivered rarely aspired to the condition of lyric poetry, the basic model for popular song, but appears more as prose statement, often reflecting upon learning in a manner positively academic when compared to most pop bands. It also gave the relation between words and music a peculiar edge, since quite frankly the musical setting very often did not scan properly, or at least properly according to the lyric principle, but this technique or fault-line, allied with subject matter, helped define the Manics' collective world-view, which often sets such prosaic observation within a variety of musical style. This, in turn, varies with seeming ambivalence between a punk-metal edge and a lush romanticism: while the former reached its apogee on *The Holy Bible* in 1994, the latter remained ascendant through the last two albums.

Musically, the Manics were driven powerfully by Moore and Wire on drums and bass, and further characterized by Bradfield's guitar. Bradfield as guitarist is able to shift with impressive speed from rhythm chords to rhythm licks to lead lines, and the combination of this with singing, and his particular style of singing, makes his a singular musical talent. His is a big tenor with a wide range, able to soar and plunge. His range is well illustrated, oddly enough, when he performs the Bacharach and David song 'Raindrops keep falling on my head' (at least on a live recording taped from Radio One of a concert in Manchester in 1997): he keeps the verse in his low register but leaps an octave for the chorus ('But there's one thing I know . . .'), and that high register often gives the Manics their sense of uncompromising expression. 'We don't talk about love. We only want to get drunk.' Bradfield is able to swoop with the ease if not quite the pitch perfection of a Freddie Mercury or George Michael, and there is more than a trace of the big heavy metal voice there too, perhaps more so on the early singles and first album. For *The Holy Bible* in particular, Bradfield has to pack tremendous energy and anger into the spiky litanies of Wire and Edwards. This was also the great feature of early tracks like 'New Art Riot', 'Motown Junk' or 'You love us', some of which were gathered in 1992 on the debut album *Generation Terrorists*. 'Motorcycle Emptiness' is beautiful recording and a manifesto for the bringing-together of rock cliché with determined statement, although it is a song unlikely to get covered in anything other than tribute, so distinctive is the song's phraseology. More romantic, operatic qualities come through on softer-sounding records like 'From Despair to Where' or 'La Tristessa Durera' on *Gold Against the Soul* (1993) or 'Design for Life' and the title track on *Everything Must Go* (1996). A feature of *Everything Must Go* was its experimentation with texture, on tracks like 'Kevin Carter' and, especially, 'Small Black Flowers that Grow in the Sky', where Bradfield's voice occupied a different position in relation to a harp accompaniment. If there was a certain disappointment in the last Manics album, *This is My Truth Tell Me Yours* (1998), to my mind it lay in the return to a very solid and predictable textural setting for Bradfield's voice. In fact, all three bands suffer from having to fill too much time on compact disc and end up padding out material, though one suspects that their imaginations were formed and inspired by classic vinyl albums by the Beatles, Stones and Led Zeppelin, albums which rarely outstayed their welcome.

Bradfield is perhaps the least overtly Welsh of the three voices, in that he simply does not go on about it as much, especially so since much of the public persona of the Manics on this as on most other affairs is left to Nicky Wire. That said, the Manics are conceptually the most Welsh of the three bands, albeit in ways which need to be interpreted (educational background, historical inheritance, musical proficiency) rather than heard immediately. Why basic features of the Manics both mattered and had something to do with south Wales – features such as having literary references accompanying each track on the sleeve of *Generation Terrorists*, little quotations at the start of each track on *The Holy Bible*, the claim of hard rock and metal, the art-school inheritance, the idea of starting a song with a line like 'libraries gave us power' – is not easy to explain but not untrue either. The Manics were the most important single element of Welsh pop across this crucial decade, but their origin in Gwent looked two ways, west to the great range of music which was being produced in Wales as well as capping a local scene centred specifically on Newport.

Record charts can be deceptive, but in under one remarkable year all three bands reached number one in the British album listings: Catatonia, *International Velvet* on 11 May 1998, Manic Street Preachers, *This is My Truth Tell Me Yours* on 20 September, and Stereophonics, *Performance and Cocktails* on 20 March 1999. Yet at the time of writing there were signs of change, with talk of the Manics calling it a day and Kelly Jones touring as a solo singer-songwriter. The disappearance, at the very end of 2000, of a consistent supporter of rock authenticity in Britain, the weekly paper *Melody Maker* (founded in 1926), hinted at the serious possibility for the bands that the age of the big rock gig was drawing to a close, at least the particular bloom which they along with other Britpop groups had enjoyed. While all of this was going on, what began around 1985 simply as dance music in discos had not only grown in popularity but also diversified to the point of being a leisure and lifestyle option, encompassing merchandise and travel. In this the DJ remained the pivotal figure, and both the Manics and Catatonia were able to adapt to the principles of remix as musical activity. What then of the bands, their transits and lorries lumbering along another motorway? On their great and self-reflexive song, 'Sorted for E's and Wizz', on *Different Class* of 1995, Pulp's Jarvis Cocker began by posing the question, 'Is this the way they say the future's meant to feel or just 20,000 people standing in a field?' and the question would haunt the very success of Welsh pop as stadiums served to broaden the audience and make money, for sure, but, arguably, diluted the unique and unprecedented vision of the Manics, Catatonia's roots in the privilege of being born bilingual, or the Stereophonics' defence of a community under threat. That the stakes seem so high is tribute enough to what these voices had achieved.

Acknowledgements
Simon Jones, *Everything* (a book about Manic Street Preachers) (London, 1999).
David Owens, *Cerys, Catatonia and the Rise of Welsh Pop* (London, 2000).
I am also grateful to Chris Porter for his help with material on the Stereophonics.

Postlude

Peter Stead

On 26 May 1999, at the end of a millennium, Wales entered a new era. On that day Queen Elizabeth II travelled to Cardiff to sanction the new constitutional status of a nation which, after centuries of romantic assertion, could now point to a democratically elected National Assembly for Wales as confirmation of its identity. During a busy day involving a religious service, banquets and a procession, nothing was more appropriate than the open-air concert at Cardiff Bay that brought the ceremonies to a close. In the long decades that preceded devolution Wales had always sought to explain its identity by reference to its 'wealth of talent', whether in politics, education, sport or the arts. Necessarily, on this special night in the Bay it was the 'Voices of a Nation' which were showcased and everyone thought it entirely proper that Wales should mark the most important change in its constitutional status for 500 years with what was, notwithstanding all the glamour, essentially a good old-fashioned celebrity concert.

Together with many of those standing around me that evening I wanted to cheer the performers, all of whom appeared before us as if magically summoned from the Bay itself. It was pleasing to see the great actors, but of course it was the singers who brought lumps to the throat and tears to the eyes. Above all it was Shirley Bassey in her Red Dragon dress, Tom Jones, Max Boyce, Charlotte Church and John Cale with his 'Rage, rage against the dying of the light' who had me punching the air with pleasure. But in terms of my sense of Wales it was the operatic performances which occasioned the most pride and which seemed to hold out the promise of the country making its mark in the new century. The WNO Chorus appeared and were introduced by Vincent Kane as 'the Welsh team that won all its fixtures'. Then came world-class entertainment in the form of Anne Evans, Della Jones, Robert Tear, Rebecca Evans, Jason Howard and Dennis O'Neill, all of whom evoked memories of past triumphs and made us all wish that we could hear them regularly in productions in Cardiff and throughout Wales. In recent years I had seen them all perform in costume in various international opera houses but, as they appeared in turn that evening in the Bay, I came to see the event as the grand culmination of all those concerts and recitals that had been a hallmark of Wales for the past 150 years and in which our own choirs and soloists had come before us essentially as entertainers. We had lived in a culture defined by musical performances and in which the vital element had been singing. It was a tradition in which there had been no room for affectation and little for formality and solemnity. Certainly there had been standards; excellence was treasured but only just ahead of pure enjoyment. Our singing was performed and listened to in a spirit of natural enthusiasm. It was on those terms that singing, whether by choirs or soloists, had become indigenous.

Fighting back my tears on that May evening many memories came flooding back. I found myself thinking in particular of Maesteg, the Llynfi Valley town where my mother had grown up and where I had spent many of the happiest holidays of my childhood and adolescence. It was in Maesteg that I really discovered rugby, pubs, girls and dancing (more or less in that order) and first became aware of the extent to which the rhythms of life in a coal-mining town were determined by a musical calendar in which hymn-singing, gymanfas, quarterly meetings, oratorios, celebrity concerts and locally produced musicals (always referred to as 'operas') played a part. The Maesteg image that the Cardiff Bay concert had brought back to me was my mother's story of how she had once queued to hear her favourite tenor, David Lloyd, sing in Maesteg Town Hall and of how she and her friends had almost swooned when he had appeared in his Guard's uniform. This story had been repeated whenever we heard David Lloyd on the radio and it had always come to mind whenever I had felt privileged to be at a great recital. I had thought of it as I once listened to Sir Geraint Evans and Margaret Price sing duets in Barry and even more when I saw Bryn Terfel at Tabernacle, Morriston, when his overpowering presence had threatened a religious revival.

Even as a non-performer I became caught up in the irresistible and ubiquitous musical culture of the Valleys which in the 1950s struck me as being as lively as any place in the western world. Pretending that I had mastered the intricacies of tonic sol-fa and attempting desperately and probably dangerously to lower my voice, I became a gymanfa groupie and joined the basses in the gallery, if only to get a better view of the girls in their stunning Easter fashions on the opposite side of the chapel. I was a total fraud and was duly exposed when I lost my place during a particularly challenging anthem. However, I was carried along vicariously in this all-important musical world entirely by family connections. Clearly, in the Valleys one was judged solely by the quality of the voices in your particular family. The hierarchy was entirely vocal; social class had nothing to do with it for obviously we were all in the same boat in that respect. Sopranos were valued but it was known that they were not easy to live with; they were temperamental, highly strung like pedigree pets, and in every concert one worried that there would be a disaster either vocally or in the décolletage. Contraltos were more respected for they sang to the soul. In Maesteg the great Kathleen Ferrier was spoken of as a spiritual leader, not least because she had some local connections. Tenors were the great entertainers; they were always meant to be the stars of the show. An evening could be ruined by a 'dodgy' tenor, whilst the term 'lovely' was always the highest accolade. Tenors were certainly a breed apart, and perhaps in that sense they were thought to be a bit 'show-biz', a little unnatural. We were more comfortable with the lower male voices. In Maesteg I was associated with relatives who worked underground, played rugby and who sang as bass soloists in *Showboat*, *White Horse Inn*, *Messiah*, *Elijah* or whatever show was on that week. They were local aristocrats and I loved the fullness and effortlessness of their multi-dimensioned culture.

What strikes me most about those days was how neatly rugby and singing coexisted. We would argue as to who were the best tenors or outside-halves in exactly the same terms, and just as we always wanted the Old Parish to beat Bridgend we would go to the National Eisteddfod to cheer on favourite choirs. The Saturday of the Male Voice battles was as special as any rugby international day, and the passions were stirred even as Alun Williams announced 'Côr Meibion Mynydd Mawr' or whoever. On one such Saturday, when the Eisteddfod was in north Wales, I had been unable to get to the Maes and, as it happened, that evening I was walking from Caerau to

Maesteg. I exchanged a greeting with an elderly gent with a stick who was sitting on the window ledge of a terraced house. At this point a woman emerged from the house and said, 'Dad, you'd better come in now, Treorchy are coming on.' The old-timer had pre-empted the judges and had merely been waiting for the class act to be broadcast.

That musical culture which had seemed so intense and vital in the 1950s was to be greatly diminished in subsequent decades as the age of the chapel was replaced by the electronic media. The musical agenda was now determined by the radio and the record companies, and the format of the celebrity concert was taken up by television in what I thought of as 'the Ivor Emmanuel era'. Meanwhile from front-room windows there came the as yet unpromising sound of drums as our more eccentric mates tentatively prepared for fame. Inevitably at that stage we began to wonder whether Wales could and should have done more with its musical heritage. The essays in this volume celebrate a tradition of musical excellence, and Hywel Teifi Edwards and Kenneth Bowen have reminded us that, long before the eras of Sir Geraint and Bryn Terfel, Wales was thought of as the breeding ground of great singers. But clearly the very nature of our working-class culture, bereft as it was of middle-class patronage, meant that our finest soloists had to go to London to sustain a professional career whilst at home, except for guest or returning celebrities, all our performances were amateur. In later years, when one came across professional opera companies and orchestras operating in small continental (especially German) towns, one appreciated how tragically Wales had missed the musical boat. Occasionally at performances of the Neath Operatic Society at Craig-y-nos or at touring productions of Music Theatre Wales or Opera Box, one has some sense of what Wales could have achieved if the patronage had been there. Perhaps it is too idealistic to think that we could have staged *Nabucco* or *La traviata* in every village, but surely some kind of 'pro-am' structure as employed at Craig-y-nos and very commonly in the United States could have been possible. In 2001 Rodney Milnes welcomed the return of D'Oyly Carte to the West End and wondered why England 'did not have a national company for light opera'. The Wales of the twentieth century had cried out for such a body; it would have naturally rounded off our national culture.

And yet we revelled in our amateur world, loving all the drama that homespun productions guaranteed. It was this willing acceptance of the home-grown that led one historian to talk of 'the myth of Welsh musicality'. The sheer informality of our music was beautifully conveyed in two famous feature films. We have made little effort to record our heritage and we should be grateful for these delightful reminders of what once was commonplace. In *The Proud Valley*, made in 1939, a choir of Welsh miners find themselves rehearsing Mendelssohn's *Elijah* without a bass soloist. The conductor volunteers to mark out the solo part, but then at the crucial moment the part is sung, better than ever before, by an unseen singer who had been listening to the rehearsal in the street below. Only at the end of 'Lord God of Abraham' can the choir rush to the window to learn what we already know. The mystery bass is an itinerant black sailor, played of course by Paul Robeson, a singer who was subsequently to become a folk hero in Wales. I love the enthusiasm and excitement of this magical scene and take it to be typical of a whole age. Similarly the 1953 Ealing Comedy *Valley of Song* gloriously exposed the implications of the Welsh phrase *Cythraul y Canu* as it told the story of the amateur musician who comes home to his village from London and is invited to conduct that year's *Messiah*. Surveying the available talent he opts for new soloists and the result is a family walk-out and subsequent chapel and choral breakaways. In Welsh villages the unjustly promoted soloists tend to be recalled as readily as blacklegs. This highly amusing story always reminds me of the Swansea Borough organist who described the annual *Messiah* which he conducted at Siloh Newydd, Landore, as being 'like the pantomime; we have to do it every Christmas'. In 2001 Sarah Sugarman's film *Very Annie Mary* is another comedy in which musical talent is treated as just one strand in the rich and zany pattern that constitutes Valleys' life. On this occasion one of our greatest actors, Jonathan Pryce, plays a baker who loves to sing opera and dresses as Pavarotti to make his deliveries, but who is determined nevertheless to prevent his daughter's career from taking off. One would like to think that Wales is now ready for something more than farce as it attempts to understand how musical talent emerges. In *Beautiful Mistake* (2000) director

Marc Evans charted nine days of musical collaboration between John Cale and other Welsh musical stars. The time is certainly ripe for our film-makers and musicians to light a bonfire of the stereotypes and aim for greatness.

Meanwhile, there are thankfully still vestiges of the old tradition and Wales is still a good place to hear singing. If one travels to Morriston, Landore and Dunvant a little less often to hear Verdi, Handel and Mozart, the Brangwyn Hall still plays host to the local male choirs and to the marvellous Swansea Philarmonic, whilst at St Mary's or Oystermouth one can hear the Swansea Bach Choir. Why is it that Swansea did not shape its musical festival along the lines of the Three Choirs Festival and become recognized as one of the great centres of choral singing? Above all, these days one associates the thrill of great singing with the WNO. One's memory now is packed with recollections of great evenings spent in the company of Stuart Burrows, Arthur Davies, Helen Field, Suzanne Murphy, Dennis O'Neill and many other favourites. The Company's finest moment came in 1986 when it staged a complete *Ring* cycle and Anne Evans, Phillip Joll and Jeffrey Lawton gave world-class performances in Göran Järvefelt's production conducted by Richard Armstrong. Those four days constituted one of the finest experiences in my life. I vividly recall, however, that on my way to *Siegfried* I met the then leader of South Glamorgan who, on realizing my destination, asked me to consider how much his voters were subsidizing my seat. It remains the case that essential elements in our society are unhappy with high culture and throughout this volume there are references to Cardiff's failure to build an opera house. In Swansea, attendances at WNO productions can be anticipated in advance. The scale varies from the full house for the combination of O'Neill and Verdi to a small gathering of the faithful for Janáček. Our national opera company has thrilled the critics and won itself a hard core of devotees but it has not succeeded in making Wales an opera-loving country. We boast of our stars, but remain ambivalent about the art form.

There is nothing ambivalent, however, about our response to popular contemporary music. There is 'live' music everywhere, in every bar, café, conference hall, college and park. Ours is an age of 'gigs' and in particular of mass rallies of the faithful in which sensational groups draw crowds that earlier generations of preachers and politicians let alone choirs and soloists would have died for. Undoubtedly our new musicians are good, witness the critical acclaim for successive albums and the national press's total fascination with every development in Charlotte Church's career and with every utterance of Cerys Matthews, who, on the face of it, would seem to be the most interesting Welsh woman and musician ever.

As was testified by that night in Cardiff Bay in 1999 (and confirmed by the shape of this volume), in Wales we love our singers as heroes. Clearly we look to entertain and be entertained, but over and above that we want our great singers to confirm our identity. All too often we rely on this cult of personality and crude boosting as a substitute for real social thinking and artistic planning. In the past our music grew out of a distinctive and attractive society. Today we still have great voices a plenty but our new 'hymns and arias' are a product of a yet unshaped post-industrial society in which most cultural patterns have yet to be determined.

Index